PANTON EDUCATION ADVISORS:

English	: RICHARD BEMBRIDGE
French	: MARIE FRANCE FIESCHI
Spanish	: VICENTE E. COZZARELLI SANDOVAL
German	: NORBERT BRAUN / HANNA WÜST
Italian	: DORA BILISCO

Cover design by : SAMSA

The
PANTON
BOOK
of IDIOMS
FOR POLYGLOTS

PANTON EDUCATION MILAN

ABBREVIATIONS:

PROV. for proverbs and proverbial sayings
COMP. for idiomatic comparisons
(♦) for illustrated expressions
(p.) for page of illustration

ABACK

To be taken aback.
Etre pris au dépourvu / Etre décontenancé.
Ser cogido de sorpresa.
Bestürzt (verblüfft, überrascht) sein.
Essere colto di sorpresa (alla sprovvista) / Essere sconcertato.

A.B.C.

He doesn't know the A.B.C. of good manners.
Il ne connaît pas l'A.B.C. des bonnes manières.
No sabe ní jota de buenas crianzas.
Er kennt das Einmaleins des guten Benehmens nicht.
Non conosce l'A.B.C. dell'educazione.

ABIDE

I cannot abide his rudeness.
Je ne peux supporter son impolitesse.
No puedo soportar su descortesia.
Ich kann seine Unverschämtheit (Grobheit, Frechheit) nicht ertragen.
Non posso sopportare la sua scortesia.

A good citizen abides by the law.
Un bon citoyen respecte les lois.
Un ciudadano que merece tal nombre, respecta las leyes.
Ein guter Bürger befolgt das Gesetz.
Il buon cittadino rispetta le leggi.

ABOUT

To be out and about.
Lever à peine de maladie / Etre rétabli.
Sentirse restablecido.
Wieder auf den Beinen sein.
Essere ristabilito.

ABSENCE

Absence of mind.
Distracción.
Distracción.

1

Geistesabwesenheit / Zerstreutheit.
Distrazione.

ABSENT

Absent minded.
Distrait.
Distraido / Absorto.
Geistesabwesend / Zerstreut.
Distratto.

ABSTAINER

A total abstainer.
Une personne tout à fait sobre.
Una persona abstemia.
Ein völliger Abstinenzler / Ein totaler Abstinenzler.
Una persona assolutamente astemia.

ACCIDENT

By accident.
Par inadvertance / Par hasard.
Por casualidad.
Zufällig.
Per sbaglio / Per caso.

A chapter of accidents.
Une série d'ennuis.
Una serie de dificultades.
Eine Serie (Reihe) von Unglücksfällen.
Una serie di guai.

I opened the letter by accident.
J'ai ouvert cette lettre par inadvertance.
Abrí la carta por pura casualidad.
Ich öffnete den Brief versehentlich.
Ho aperto la lettera senza intenzione (per caso).

ACCORD

Of one's own accord.
Spontanément.

2

Espontáneamente / Voluntariamente.
Aus eigenem Antrieb / Freiwillig.
Spontaneamente.

ACCORDING

According to them.
Selon eux.
Según ellos / Conforme a ellos.
Gemäss Ihnen / Nach Ihnen.
Secondo loro.

ACCOUNT

To give a good account of oneself.
Se distinguer / Donner une bonne impression de soi.
Lucirse.
Sich bewähren.
Farsi onore.

People of no account.

Personnes qui ne sont pas dignes d'intérêt.
Gentuza.
Menschen ohne Bedeutung.
Gente da poco (di nessun conto).

ACCOUNTING

There is no accounting for tastes.
Tous les goûts ne sont pas identiques.
No todos los gustos son iguales.
Geschmäcker sind verschieden.
Geschmack ist Ansichtssache.
Non tutti i gusti sono uguali.

ACCOUNTS

By all accounts.
Selon l'avis général / Selon ce qu'en dit tout le monde.
Por lo que dicen todos.
Nach allem, was man hört.
A quanto dicono tutti.

3

That accounts for her strange behaviour.
Voilà qui explique son étange conduite.
Ésto explíca su comportamiento tan extraño.
Das erklärt ihr sonderbares Benehmen.
Ciò spiega la sua strana condotta.

ACROSS

To come across.
Rencontrer par hasard / Tomber sur ...
Encontrarse con ... / Tropezarse con ...
Zufällig treffen (begegnen).
Imbattersi in / Incontrare per caso ...

ACT

Caught in the act.
Pris sur le fait.
Ser cogido con las manos en la masa.
Auf frischer Tat ertappt / Dabei erwischt.
Colto sul fatto; con le mani nel sacco.

ACTION

To bring an action against someone.
Intenter un procès contre quelqu'un.
Demandar a alguien.
Jemanden verklagen.
Intentare una causa a qualcuno.

ADAM

I don't know him from Adam.
Je ne le connais ni d'Eve, ni d'Adam.
No tengo ní idea de quien es.
Ich kenne ihn überhaupt (absolut) nicht.
Ich habe nicht die entfernteste (geringste) Idee, woher er sein könnte.
Non ho la più lontana idea di chi sia.

ADD

To add insult to injury.
Aggraver l'offense / Aggraver son cas.

Añadir el insulto a la injuria.
Das Unrecht vergrössern / Wer den Schaden hat, braucht für
den Spott nicht zu sorgen.
Oltre al danno, la beffa.

ADMISSION

Free admission.
Entrée libre.
Admisión gratuita.
Eintritt frei.
Ingresso libero.

ADMITTANCE

No admittance.
Entrée interdite.
Entrada prohibida.
Zutritt verboten.
E' vietato l'ingresso.

ADO

Much ado about nothing.
Beaucoup de bruit pour rien.
Mucha bulla por nada.
Viel Lärm um nichts.
Un gran chiasso per niente.

Without more ado.
Sans autres difficultés.
Sin otras dificultades.
Ohne weitere Umstände.
Senza ulteriori difficoltà.

ADVANCE

To pay in advance.
Payer d'avance.
Pagar por adelantado.
Im voraus zahlen.
Pagare in anticipo.

ADVANTAGE

May I take advantage of your kindness?
Puis-je abuser de votre gentillesse?
No quisiera aprovecharme de su amabilidad, pero . . .
Darf ich Ihre Freundlichkeit in Anspruch nehmen?
Posso approfittare della vostra cortesia?

AFFECT

To affect ignorance.
Feindre d'ignorer / Faire le niais.
Hacerse uno el sueco.
Unwissenheit vortäuschen / Sich dumm stellen.
Fare lo gnorri.

To affect indifference.
Feindre l'indifférence.
Fingir indiferencia.
Gleichgültigkeit vortäuschen.
Fingere indifferenza.

AFFLUENT

In affluent circumstances.
Très riche / Cousu d'or.
En una posición muy acomodada.
In wohlhabenden Verhältnissen / Sehr gut situiert.
Molto ricco.

AFFORD

I cannot afford . . .
Je ne peux pas m'offrir le luxe de . . .
No puedo permitirme el lujo de . . .
Ich kann es mir nicht leisten zu . . .
Non posso permettermi il lusso di . . .

AFFIRMATIVE

To answer in the affirmative.
Répondre par l'affirmative.
Decir qué sí / Responder afirmativamente.

Bejahen / Positiv beantworten / Zusagen.
Dir di sì / Rispondere affermativamente.

AFIELD

I shall not go far afield.
Je n'irai pas bien loin.
No iré muy lejos.
Ich werde mich nicht weit entfernen.
Non andrò molto lontano.

AFOOT

There is some plan afoot.
Il y a anguille sous roche.
Algo se está preparando.
Es ist etwas im Anzug (im Kommen) / Es ist etwas im Gange.
C'è qualcosa che bolle in pentola.

AFTER

After the French fashion.
A la française.
A la francesa.
Nach (gemäss) der französischen Mode.
Alla francese.

That man is after your money.
Cet homme en a après votre argent.
Ese hombre persigue únicamente su dinero.
Dieser Mann ist hinter Ihrem Geld her.
Quell'uomo corre dietro al vostro denaro.

AGAIN

Again and again.
Encore et encore.
Una y otra véz.
Immer wieder / Wiederholt.
Ripetutamente.

AGAINST

Against the grain.
A contrecœur.

Con pesar.
Gegen den Strich.
A malincuore.

To put money against a rainy day.
Prévoir en cas de besoin.
Ahorrar para los tiempos duros / Ahorrar por aquello de las malas.
Geld für schlechte Zeiten zurücklegen / Geld für schlechte Zeiten auf die hohe Kante legen.
Risparmiare per previdenza.

AGE

To be of age.
Etre majeur.
Ser mayor de edad.
Volljährig sein.
Essere maggiorenne.

To be under age.
Etre mineur.
Ser menor de edad.
Minderjährig sein.
Essere minorenne.

AGES

I haven't seen you for ages.
Ça fait une éternité que je ne te vois plus.
Desde hace tiempo que no te veo.
Ich habe dich seit einer Ewigkeit nicht gesehen.
E' un secolo che non ti vedo.

AGENT

I am a free agent.
Je suis libre de ma personne / Je suis libre de faire ce que je veux.
Puedo hacer lo que quiero / Soy bala al áire.
Ich bin mein eigener Herr.
Sono libero di fare ciò che voglio.

AGREE

I agree to your conditions.
J'accepte vos conditions.
Acepto Vuestras condiciones.
Ich bin mit Ihren Bedingungen einverstanden.
Accetto le vostre condizioni.

I agree with you.
Je suis d'accord avec vous / Je suis de votre avis.
Estoy de acuerdo con Usted.
Ich stimme Ihnen zu / Ich bin mit Ihnen einverstanden.
Sono d'accordo con voi.

Cheese does not agree with me.
Je ne supporte pas le fromage / Le fromage me fait mal.
El queso me hace daño.
Käse bekommt mir nicht.
Il formaggio mi fa male.

Mountain air agrees with me.
L'air de la montagne me convient.
El áire de la montaña me sienta bien.
Gebirgsluft bekommt mir gut.
L'aria di montagna mi fa bene.

AGREED

Agreed!
D'accord!
¡Está bien! / ¡De acuerdo! / ¡Claro!
Abgemacht / Einverstanden!
Sta bene! / D'accordo!

AGREEMENT

By mutual agreement.
D'un commun accord.
De común acuerdo.
In gegenseitigem Einvernehmen.
Di comune accordo.

AHEAD

Go ahead!
Entrez! / Allez-y!
¡Siga Usted por favor!
Vorwärts! / Fahr fort! / Weiter!
Andate avanti!

AIR

To air one's opinion.
Exprimer son opinion.
Expresar las propias ideas.
Seine eigene Meinung kundturn (sagen).
Esprimere la propria opinione.

To air one's grievances.
Se plaindre.
Lamentarse / Quejarse.
Seine Beschwerden vortragen.
Lamentarsi.

AIRS

To put on airs.
Se donner des airs.
Jactarse.
Sich wichtig machen.
Darsi delle arie.

AIRING

To take an airing.
Prendre l'air.
Tomar un poco de áire.
Frische Luft schöpfen.
Prendere l'aria.

ALIKE

We are alike.
Nous nous ressemblons.
Nos parecemos / Somos iguales.
Wir sind uns ähnlich.
Ci assomigliamo.

10

ALIVE

Look alive!
Réveillez-vous! / Dépêchez-vous!
¡Despierta! / ¡Date prisa!
Mach schnell! / Schlaf nicht!
Svegliati! / Fate presto!

ALL (♦)

She is not all there.
Il lui manque une case.
Le falta una tuerca / Es un poco chiflada.
Sie ist nicht ganz da / Sie ist nicht ganz bei Trost.
Le manca un venerdì.

Come by all means!
Venez sans tarder!
¡Vengan con seguridad! / ¡Vengan sea como sea!
Kommt unbedingt / Kommt auf alle Fälle!
Venite di sicuro!

All day long.
Toute la journée / Toute la sainte journée.
Por todo el día.
Den ganzen Tag lang.
Tutto il giorno.

All important.
De première importance.
De toda importancia.
Von grösster Bedeutung (Wichtigkeit).
Di prima importanza.

On all fours.
A quatre pattes.
En cuclillas.
Auf allen Vieren.
Carponi.

One and all.
Tous sans exception.
Todos, sin ninguna excepción.
Einer wie der Andere / Ohne Ausnahme.
Tutti senza eccezione.

To go for good and all.
S'en aller pour toujours.
Irse para siempre.
Für immer fortgehen.
Andarsene per sempre.

All at once.
Tout à coup.
De repente.
Auf einmal / Plötzlich.
Tutto ad un tratto.

She is not at all kind.
Elle n'a pas un brin de gentillesse.
No es muy amable.
Sie ist überhaupt nicht freundlich.
Non è per niente gentile.

All the better.
Tant mieux!
Mucho mejor.
Um so besser.
Tanto meglio!

(♦) All the rage. (p. 13)
Le dernier cri.
El último grito de la moda.
Der letzte Schrei / Die grosse Mode.
L'ultimo grido.

She all but died.
Elle était sur le point de mourir.
Estaba a punto de morir.
Sie wäre beinahe gestorben.
Era lì lì per morire.

ALLOW

To allow for . . .
Etre indulgent / Tenir compte de . . .
Tener en cuenta.
In Betracht ziehen / Berücksichtigen.
Tener conto di . . .

13

ALLOWANCE

To make allowance for . . .
Faire preuve d'indulgence envers quelqu'un / Faire preuve d'indulgence pour quelque chose.
Tener en cuenta que . . .
Anrechnen.
Tener conto di . . .

ALLURING

Not very alluring.
Pas très attrayant.
Poco atrayente.
Nicht sehr verlockend (verführerisch).
Non molto attraente.

ALONE

Let her alone!
Laissez-la tranquille!
¡Déjala sola!
Lass sie allein! / Lass sie in Ruhe!
Lasciatela stare!

Let well alone.
Le mieux est l'ennemi du bien.
Lo mejor es enemigo de lo bueno.
Lass es gut sein / Lass die Finger davon.
Il meglio è nemico del bene.

ALONG

Come along!
Venez!
¡Vengan!
Kommt mit! / Kommt doch schon!
Venite!

She is difficult to get along with.
Il est difficile de s'entendre avec elle.
Es muy difícil llevarse bien con ella.
Es ist schwierig, mit ihr auszukommen.
E' difficile andare d'accordo con lei.

14

She knew it all along.
Elle le savait dès le début.
Lo sabía desde el principio.
Sie wusste alles von Anfang an.
Lo sapeva fin da principio.

ALOOF

To stand aloof.
Rester de côté.
Mantenerse aparte.
Für sich bleiben.
Starsene in disparte.

ALTERNATIVE

There is no alternative.
Il n'y a pas d'autre alternative.
No hay otra / No hay más remedio.
Es gibt keine Alternative / Es gibt keine andere Möglichkeit.
Non c'è alternativa.

ALTOGETHER

He was in the altogether.
Il était comme l'avait fait sa mère.
Estaba en pelota.
Er war splitternackt.
Era come mamma l'ha fatto.

In the alternative.
Dans l'éventualité.
En el caso que . . .
Für den Fall, dass . . .
Nell'eventualità che . . .

AMATEUR

An amateur actor.
Un acteur amateur / Un dilettant.
Un actor aficionado.
Ein Laienschauspieler / Ein Amateurschauspieler.
Un attore dilettante.

AMENDS

To make amends for . . .
Réparer une erreur.
Resarcir / Dar satisfacción por . . .
Schadenersatz leisten für . . . / Es wiedergutmachen.
Riparare (ad un fallo commesso).

AMISS

Do not take my frankness amiss.
Que ma franchise ne vous offense pas!
No lleven·a mal mi sinceridad.
Nehmen Sie mir meine Offenheit nicht übel.
Non offendetevi per la mia franchezza.

ANSWER

To answer back.
Riposter à . . .
Rebatir.
Freche Antworten geben / Schlagfertig erwidern.
Rimbeccare / Ribattere.

APPEAL

It does not appeal to me.
Ça ne m'attire pas / Ça ne me dit rien.
No me atrae para nada.
Es interessiert mich nicht / Es zieht micht nicht an.
Non mi attira.

APPEARANCE

To put in an appearance.
Faire un saut chez quelqu'un.
Dar un vistazo rápido.
Persönlich erscheinen.
Fare una capatina.

Of good appearance.
Une chose belle à l'apparence.
De buen semblante.
Von guter Erscheinung / Gut aussehen.
Di bell'aspetto.

16

For appearance sake.
Pour sauver les apparences.
Para salvar las apariencias.
Um den Schein zu wahren.
Per salvare le apparenze.

APPLE

He is the apple of his mother's eye.
C'est la prunelle des yeux de sa mère.
Es la niña de los ojos de su madre.
Er ist der Augapfel seiner Mutter.
Sua madre non ha occhi che per lui / E' il pupillo di sua madre.

To upset a person's apple cart.
Faire tout tomber à l'eau.
Romperle a uno los cascos.
Jemandes Pläne über den Haufen werfen.
Rompere le uova nel paniere ad uno.

Apple pie order.
Ordre parfait.
Orden absoluto.
Schönste Ordnung / Perfekt.
Ordine perfetto.

APRIL

April fools' Day.
Le premier avril.
El día de los inocentes / El primero de Abril.
Der erste April.
Il primo di Aprile.

April fool.
Poisson d'avril.
Primo di aprile.
¡Por inocente!
Aprilnarr.
Pesce d'aprile.

APRON (♦)

(♦) He is tied to his mother's apron strings. (p. 580).
Il est toujours pendu aux jupes de sa mère.

Está colgado de las naguas de su madre.
Er hängt an seiner Mutter Rockzipfel.
E' attaccato alle sottane di sua madre.

APT

Sleeping too much is apt to make one feel sleepy all the time.
De trop dormir fait qu'on se sent toujours endormi.
El dormir demasiado puede volverle a uno somnoliento todo
el día.
Zuviel Schlaf macht müde.
Il dormire troppo può far sì che ci si senta sempre assonnati.

ARM

To walk arm in arm.
Aller bras dessus-bras dessous.
Caminar de bracete.
Arm in Arm gehen.
Andare a braccetto (sottobraccio).

To keep at arm's length.
Tenir à distance.
Mantener la distancia.
Sich vom Leibe halten.
Tenere a distanza.

ARRANGE

I'll arrange to be there.
Je ferai en sorte d'y être.
Haré lo posible para estar allí.
Ich werde es einrichten, da zu sein.
Farò in modo di esserci.

ARTICLE

A leading article.
Article de fond.
Editorial.
Ein Leitartikel.
Articolo di fondo.

AS

As to you.
Quant à vous.
En cuanto a Ustedes.
Was Sie anbetriff (anbelangt / angeht).
Quanto a voi.

ASK

To ask to dinner.
Inviter à déjeuner.
Invitar a almorzar.
Zum Essen einladen.
Invitare a pranzo.

Ask her in.
Priez-la d'entrer.
Pídale que entre.
Bittet sie einzutreten / Bittet sie herein!
Pregatela di entrare.

She asked after you.
Elle vous demanda.
Pidió por Usted.
Sie fragte nach Ihnen.
Chiese di voi.

ASS

To make an ass of oneself.
Se couvrir de ridicule.
Hacer el ridículo.
Sich lächerlich machen / Sich selbst zum Narr machen.
Rendersi ridicolo.

ASTRAY

To go astray.
Se perdre / Sortir du droit chemin.
Extraviarse / Perder el camino.
Vom rechten Wege abkommen / Sich verirren.
Smarrirsi / Andar fuori strada.

ATTACHED

To be attached to . . .
Etre attaché à . . .
Tenerle cariño a . . .
Hängen an . . .
Essere affezionato a . . .

AVAIL

It was all to no avail.
Tout fut inutile.
Todo fue inútil / Todo fue de balde.
Es war alles nutzlos (umsonst).
Tutto fu inutile.

AVERAGE

On an average.
En moyenne.
Por término medio / En promedio.
Im Durchschnitt.
In media.

AWARE

I was not aware of the fact.
Je n'avais pas connaissance du fait.
No estaba enterado del hecho.
Ich war mir der Sache (Tatsache) nicht bewusst / Ich wusste nichts davon.
Non ero al corrente del fatto.

AWE

To stand in awe.
Etre intimidé.
Estar pasmado / Quedarse pasmado.
Eine Scheu besitzen vor . . . / Sich fürchten vor . . .
Essere in soggezione.

AWFULLY

I'm awfully sorry.
Je suis vraiment désolé.

Lo siento muchísimo.
Es tut mir schrecklich leid.
Mi dispiace tanto.

AXE

To have an axe to grind.
Faire venir l'eau à son moulin.
Tener un interés personal.
Eigennützige Zwecke verfolgen.
Avere un interesse personale.

BABY (♦)

(♦) To be left holding the baby. (p. 22)
Etre dans le pétrin / Etre dans de beaux draps.
Ser dejado en dificultades.
Die Sache am Hals haben.
Essere lasciato nei pasticci.

BACK (♦)

He is back in New York.
Il est de retour à New York.
Está de regreso a Nueva York.
Er ist wieder in New York.
E' di ritorno a Nuova York.

To back a horse.
Miser sur un cheval.
Apostar sobre un caballo.
Auf ein Pferd setzen.
Puntare su un cavallo.

To back up an opinion.
Appuyer une opinion.
Respaldar una opinión.
Für eine Meinung eintreten.
Appoggiare un'opinione.

He backed out at the last minute.
Il se retira au dernier moment.
En último momento se retiró / Se retractó en último momento.

Er zog sich im letzten Moment zurück / Er gab im letzten Moment auf / « Er zog im letzten Moment den Schwanz ein ».
Si ritirò all'ultimo momento.

(♦) **To put one's back into something.** (p. 24)
Y mettre tout son cœur.
Hacer todo lo que esté al alcance de uno.
Alles daransetzen.
Mettercela tutta.

BACKBONE

He has no backbone.
C'est un ramolli / C'est une chiffe molle.
Tiene horchata en las venas / No tiene fibra.
Er hat kein Rückgrat.
E' uno smidollato / E' senza coraggio.

English to the backbone.
Anglais jusqu'à la pointe des ongles.
Inglés hasta lo último.
Englisch bis auf das Mark.
Inglese fino alle midolla.

BAD

To use bad language.
Dire des gros mots.
Decir palabras soéces.
Schimpfworte benutzen.
Dire parolacce.

We are on bad terms.
Nous sommes brouillés / Nous sommes en froid.
No nos llevamos bien.
Wir stehen auf schlechtem Fuss.
Siamo in rotta.

That's too bad!
C'est le comble!
¡Esto es el colmo!
Das ist doch zu dumm / Das ist der Gipfel.
E' il colmo!

BADLY

He is badly off.
Il est dans de beaux draps!
Se encuentra en una situación económica difícil.
Er ist nicht gut dran / Es geht ihm finanziell schlecht.
Si trova in cattive acque / Sta male finanziariamente.

BAG (♦)

Left holding the bag.
Se retrouver dans de beaux draps.
Ser dejado en dificultades.
Im Unglück gelassen werden.
Essere lasciato nei guai.

(♦) To let the cat out of the bag. (p. 89)
Laisser échapper un secret.
Dejarse escapar un secréto.
Die Katze aus dem Sack lassen / Ein Geheimnis preisgeben.
Rivelare involontariamente un segreto.

She is a bag of bones.
C'est un squelette ambulant.
Es esquelética.
Ein lebendes Skelett sein.
E' ridotta pelle e ossa.

BALANCE

To be off one's balance.
Avoir perdu la boussole.
Haber perdido el propio equilibrio (psíquico).
Sein Gleichgewicht verloren haben / Seinen Kopf verloren
haben.
Aver perso la bussola.

BALD

To be as bald as a coot. (comp.)
Tondu comme un œuf / Chauve.
Tener la cabeza como una bola de billar / Ser calvo por com-
pleto.
Völlig kahl sein.
Pelato come un uovo / Essere molto calvo.

BALL (♦)

(♦) To be on the ball. (p. 27)
Etre en forme.
Ser arrecho.
Auf Draht sein.
Essere in gamba.

Fancy dress ball.
Bal masqué.
Báile de máscaras.
Kostümfest / Maskenball.
Ballo in costume.

To keep the ball rolling.
Entretenir la conversation.
Mantener viva la conversación / Animar la conversación.
Das Gespräch in Gang halten.
Tenere viva la conversazione / Sostenere la propria parte in una conversazione.

BAND

To be on the band wagon.
Avoir de l'influence / Avoir le bras long.
Ser influyente / Ser uno de los mandamases.
Die Hand im Spiel haben / Einflussreich sein.
Essere influente / Avere le mani in pasta.

BANDY

To bandy words with ...
Trouver à redire à ...
Tener algo que redecir con ...
(Böse) Worte wechseln mit ...
Avere a che dire con ...

BANG

To bang the door.
Claquer la porte.
Dar un portazo.
Die Tür zuschlagen (zuknallen).
Sbattere la porta.

26

BANKRUPT

The firm went bankrupt.
L'entreprise a fait faillite.
La sociedad ha quebrado / La sociedad ha entrado en bancarota.
Die Firma ging bankrott.
La ditta fallì.

A mental bankrupt.
Un idiot.
Un imbécil.
Ein Schwachsinniger.
Un deficiente.

BARE

He is a bare faced liar.
C'est un fieffé menteur.
Es un mentiroso descarado.
Er ist ein skrupelloser (unverschämter) Lügner.
E' uno sfacciato bugiardo.

BARGAIN

To make a capital bargain.
Faire une bonne affaire.
Hacer un buen negocio.
Ein blendendes Geschäft machen.
Fare un affare d'oro.

To make the best of a bad bargain.
Faire de nécessité vertu.
Hacer de tripas, corazón.
Sich so gut wie möglich aus der Affäre ziehen / Aus der Not eine Jugend machen.
Fare di necessità virtù / Fare buon viso a cattivo gioco.

I didn't bargain for this!
Je ne m'attendais pas à ça!
¡No me lo esperaba!
Darauf war ich nicht gefasst (vorbereitet)!
Non me l'aspettavo!

BARGEE

To swear like a bargee.
Jurer comme un païen / Jurer comme un charretier.
Jurar como turco.
Fluchen wie ein Landsknecht.
Bestemmiare come un turco.

BARK (♦)

(♦) His bark is worse than his bite. (prov.) (p. 676)
Chien qui aboit ne mord pas.
El perro que ladra no muerde.
Hunde, die bellen, beissen nicht.
Can che abbaia non morde.

BARKING

You are barking up the wrong tree.
Vous accusez à tort / Vous vous trompez de personne.
Ustedes acusan sin fundamento / Se han equivocado de persona.
Sie sind auf dem Holzweg.
Voi accusate ingiustamente / State sbagliando persona.

BASK

To bask in the sun.
Se chauffer au soleil / Lézarder.
Calentarse al sol.
Sich in der Sonne suhlen.
Crogiolarsi al sole.

BAY

To keep at bay.
Surveiller / Tenir quelqu'un en respect.
Tener a raya.
Jemanden in Schach halten / Jemanden hinhalten.
Tenere a bada.

BE

A would-be friend.
Une personne qui voudrait être amie d'une autre.
Alguien que quisiera ser amigo.
Jemand, der gern Freund sein würde.
Uno che vorrebbe essere amico.

BEAN

I haven't a bean.
Je suis fauché (comme les blés) / J'ai les poches plates.
Estoy sin blanca.
Ich habe keinen roten Heller / Ich habe keinen Pfennig.
Sono in bolletta / Sono al verde.

BEANS (♦)

(♦) Full of beans. (p. 31)
Du vif-argent.
Lleno de vida / Con salero.
Übermütig / Aufgedreht.
Vivacissimo / Su di giri.

BEAR

To bear up under strain.
Avoir du cœur à l'ouvrage.
Aguantar, sin cejar, una tarea muy dura.
Mit Geduld (Kraft) tapfer standhalten.
Sopportare con animo una grande fatica.

I can't bear that person.
Je ne peux souffrir cette personne.
No puedo aguantar ese tipo.
Ich kann diese Person nicht ausstehen (leiden /riechen).
Non posso sopportare quella persona.

Please bear in mind.
Veuillez tenir compte de . . .
Por favor, tenganlo en cuenta.
Bitte behalten Sie im Gedächtnis!
Vogliate tener presente.

Grin and bear it!
Serre les dents et tiens bon!
¡Apriétate el cincho y aguanta!
Mach gute Miene zum bösen Spiel! / Beiss auf die Zähne!
Stringi i denti e tieni duro!

Don't bear me a grudge.
Ne m'en veuillez pas.
No me guarden rencor.
Hegen Sie keinen Groll gegen mich.
Non serbatemi rancore.

BEARING

Past all bearing.
Vraiment insupportable / Passer les limites.
Verdaderamente inaguantable.
Wirklich unerträglich.
Veramente insopportabile.

BEARINGS

To lose one's bearings.
Etre désorienté.
Estar desorientado.
Sich verlieren / Im Ungewissen sein / Im Dunkeln tappen.
Essere disorientato.

BEAT (♦)

(♦) To beat about the bush. (p. 33)
Tourner autour du pot.
Dar largas / Irse por las ramas.
Wie die Katze um den heissen Brei herumgehen / Um die Sache herumreden.
Menare il can per l'aia.

To beat up somebody.
Frapper quelqu'un.
Darle una paliza a alguien.
Jemanden schlagen / Jemanden verprügeln.
Pestare qualcuno.

32

To beat somebody black and blue.
Tanner le cuir à quelqu'un / Battre comme plâtre.
Poner morada, de golpes, a una persona / Vestir de cucurucho
a una persona.
Jemanden blau und grün schlagen.
Coprire qualcuno di lividi.

Beat generation.
Jeunesse brûlée.
Juventud perdída.
Beat Generation.
Gioventù bruciata.

BEATEN

To be off the beaten track.
S'éloigner des chemins battus.
Alejarse de los viejos caminos / Estar fuera de ruta.
Abseits liegen / Weg sein von . . .
Allontanarsi dalle vie battute / Essere fuori strada.

BEAUTY

That's the beauty of it!
Ça c'est le beau de l'affaire! / Ça c'est le clou de l'affaire!
¡Esto es lo bueno!
Das ist das Schöne daran.
Questo è il bello!

Beauty is but skin deep.
Tout ce qui brille n'est pas or / Il ne faut pas se fier aux ap-
parences / L'habit ne fait pas le moine.
No es oro todo lo que reluce.
Es ist nicht alles Gold, was glänzt / Der Schein trügt.
Non è tutto oro quel che luccica / Non si deve giudicare dalle
apparenze.

BECK

To be at the beck and call of somebody.
Etre toujours aux ordres de quelqu'un.
Estar a las ordenes de alguien.

Jemandem auf den (leisesten) Wink gehorchen / Nach jemandes Musik tanzen.
Essere sempre pronto a scattare agli ordini di qualcuno / Stare ai cenni di qualcuno.

BECOMING

Your dress is very becoming.
Votre robe vous va à ravir.
Este vestido le sienta a Usted muy bien.
Ihr Kleid steht Ihnen gut.
Il vostro vestito vi dona molto.

BED (♦)

To take to one's bed with 'flu.
Etre au lit avec la grippe.
Meterse en la cama por la gripe.
Sich mit Grippe ins Bett legen.
Mettersi a letto con l'influenza.

(♦) He who makes his bed must lie on it. (p. 36)
Vous devez assumer la responsabilité de vos actes / Faire son lit comme on se couche.
¡Ustedes han hecho la canción, ahora bailenla! / ¡A lo hecho, pecho!
Wie man sich bettet, so liegt man.
Assumersi la responsabilità delle proprie azioni.

To get out of bed on the wrong side. (p. 37)
Se lever du pied gauche.
Levantarse de la cama de mal humor / Levantarse con el pié Izquierdo.
Mit schlechter Laune erwachen (aufstehen) / Mit dem verkehrten (linken) Fuss zuerst aufstehen.
Alzarsi di malumore / Alzarsi con la gamba sinistra.

Between you and me and the bedpost.
Ceci dit entre nous.
Dicho entre nos / Dicho en confianza.
Unter uns (gesagt) / Im Vertrauen (gesagt).
Detto fra noi / Vi dico in confidenza.

37

BEE (♦)

(♦) To have a bee in one's bonnet. (p. 39)
Avoir une idée fixe, une manie.
Tener una idea metida en la cabeza.
Einen Vogel haben / Übergeschnappt sein / Spinnen.
Avere un'idea fissa, una mania / Essere fissato.

BEGGARS (♦)

(♦) Beggars cannot be choosers. (p. 40)
Il n'y a pas le choix / C'est ça ou rien.
Herrar el banco.
Arme Leute dürfen nicht wählerisch sein.
O mangiar questa minestra o saltar dalla finestra.

BEGUN

Well begun is half done. (prov.)
A moitié fait qui bien commence.
Lo que comienza bien, termína bien.
Gut begonnen ist halb gewonnen.
Chi ben comincia è a metà dell'opera.

BEHALF

I'm going on behalf of a friend.
Je vais de la part d'un ami.
Voy de parte de un amigo.
Ich gehe im Namen (im Auftrag) eines Freundes.
Vado per conto di un amico.

BEHIND

To be behind the times.
Etre arriéré.
Ser anticuado / No estar a la zaga de los tiempos.
Hinter der Zeit zurück sein / Rückständig sein / Altmodisch sein.
Essere antiquato.

BEING

For the time being.
Pour le moment.

38

Por ahora / Por el momento.
Für den Augenblick.
Per il momento.

BELIEF

To the best of my belief.
Que je sache!
Por lo que me consta.
Nach bestem Wissen und Gewissen.
Per quanto mi consta.

BELIEVE

To make believe.
Faire semblant.
Simular.
Glauben machen / Vorgeben / Vortäuschen / Tun als ob ...
Far finta.

BELFRY

(♦) To have bats in the belfry. (p. 42)
Etre un peu fou.
Estar un poco chiflado.
Verrückt sein / Einen Vogel haben / Spinnen.
Essere un po' matto.

BELONGINGS

All my belongings.
Tout ce que je possède.
Todo lo que poseo / Todas mis pertenencias.
All mein Besitz / Mein ganzer Besitz.
Tutto ciò che posseggo / Tutti i miei averi.

BELT (♦)

To tighten one's belt.
Serrer la ceinture.
Apretarse el cincho.
Den Gürtel enger schnallen.
Stringere la cinghia.

(♦) To belt up. (p. 44)
Se taire.
Estar callado.
Still sein / Schweigen / Den Mund halten.
Stare zitto / Chiudere il becco.

BENEFIT

To give somebody the benefit of the doubt.
Accorder à quelqu'un le bénéfice du doute.
Darle a alguien el beneficio de la duda.
Den vorhandenen Zweifel zu jemandes Gunsten auslegen.
Dare a qualcuno il beneficio del dubbio.

BESIDE

To be beside oneself.
Etre hors de soi.
Estar fuera de sí.
Ausser sich sein / Wütend sein.
Essere fuori di sè.

Beside the point.
Non pertinent.
No hace al caso / No es pertinente.
Nicht zur Sache gehörig.
Non pertinente / Incongruo.

That is beside the question.
Ça n'a rien à voir.
No se trata de eso / No hace al caso.
Das gehört nicht zur Frage / Das ist nicht massgebend.
Questo non c'entra.

BEST (♦)

Best seller.
« Best seller » / Le livre le plus vendu.
El libro más vendido / El libro de más venta / « Best seller ».
Bestseller / Verkaufsschlager.
Il libro più venduto / « Best seller ».

44

I'll do my best.
Je ferai de mon mieux.
Haré todo lo que esté a mi alcance.
Ich werde mein Bestes tun.
Farò del mio meglio.

To be in one's Sunday best.
Mettre l'habit du dimanche.
Ponerse el traje de domingos.
Sein Sonntagskleid anhaben.
Indossare l'abito della festa.

(♦) To put one's best foot forward. (p. 46)
Se dépêcher / Hâter le pas.
Darse prisa.
Sich beeilen / So schnell wie möglich laufen.
Affrettarsi / Camminare il più rapidamente possibile.

The best is enemy of the good. (prov.)
Le mieux est l'ennemi du bien.
Lo mejor es enemigo de lo bueno.
Das Bessere ist der Feind des Guten.
Il meglio è nemico del bene.

BET

You bet I'm going!
Vous pouvez être certain que j'y vais de ce pas!
¡Pueden apostar que yo iré!
Aber sicher, ich gehe / Sie können sicher sein, dass ich gehe!
Potete giurare (scommettere) che ci vado!

BETTER

All the better!
Tant mieux!
¡Mucho mejor!
Um so besser.
Tanto meglio!

You look better.
Vous avez meilleure mine.
Tienes mejor semblante.
Sie sehen besser aus.
Avete un aspetto migliore.

I thought better of it.
Je suis revenu sur mon opinion.
Me retracto.
Ich habe meine Meinung geändert.
Mi sono ricreduto.

He has been better than his word.
Il a fait plus qu'il ne l'avait laissé entendre.
Ha hecho más de lo prometido.
Er hat mehr getan als er versprách.
Ha fatto più di quanto avesse promesso.

BETWEEN

Between the devil and the deep blue sea.
Se trouver entre l'enclume et le marteau.
Entre la espada y la paréd.
Zwischen zwei Feuern / Zwischen zwei Übeln.
Fra l'incudine e il martello.

BID

To make a bid for something.
Essayer d'obtenir quelque chose / Faire des pieds et des mains
pour . . .
Tratar de obtener algo / Hacer la cacha.
Sich um etwas bemühen.
Cercare di ottenere qualcosa.

BIG (♦)

(♦) Big shot. (p. 48)
Un gros bonnet / Une grosse légume.
Pájaro gordo.
Grosses Tier / Bonze.
Pezzo grosso.

To talk big.
Parler avec des mots ronflants.
Darse bombo.
Grosse Worte gebrauchen (machen).
Usare parole roboanti / Usare paroloni.

(♦) To be too big for one's boots. (p. 63)
Se monter la tête / Se donner des airs.
Presumir / Darse infulas.
Sich wichtig machen / Angeben.
Montarsi la testa / Darsi delle arie.

BIRD (♦)

Bird of ill omen.
Oiseau de mauvais augure.
Pájaro de mal agüero.
Unglücksvogel.
Uccello del malaugurio.

Better a bird in the hand than two in the bush. (prov.)
Un tiens vaut mieux que deux tu l'auras.
Mejor un pájaro en mano que cien volando.
Ein Sperling in der Hand ist besser als eine Taube auf dem Dach.
Meglio un uovo oggi che una gallina domani.

(♦) The early bird catches the worm. (prov.) (p. 164)
L'avenir appartient à ceux qui se lèvent tôt.
A quien madruga Dios le ayuda.
Morgenstund hat Gold im Mund.
Le ore del mattino hanno l'oro in bocca.

BIRDS

Birds of a feather flock together. (prov.)
Qui s'assemble se ressemble.
Cada oveja con su pareja.
Gleich und gleich gesellt sich gern.
Ognuno ama il suo simile.

Bird's eye view.
Vue à vol d'oiseau.
A vista de pájaro.
Vogelperspektive.
Vista a volo d'uccello.

To kill two birds with one stone.
Faire d'une pierre deux coups.
Matar dos pájaros con un tiro.

Zwei Fliegen mit einer Klappe schlagen.
Prendere due piccioni con una fava.

BIT

He is a bit of a bore!
C'est un raseur / C'est un casse-pieds.
Es un pelmazo / Es fastidioso / Es un engorroso.
Er ist ein lästiger Mensch / Er ist eine Nervensäge.
E' un seccatore!

I gave him a bit of my mind.
Je lui ai parlé en toute franchise.
Le he hablado con franqueza.
Ich sagte ihm (gehörig) die Meinung.
Gli parlai molto francamente.

BITE (♦)

To bite the dust.
Mordre la poussière.
Morder el polvo.
Ins Gras beissen.
Mordere la polvere.

(♦) To bite off more than one can chew. (p. 52)
Faire le pas plus long que la jambe.
Meterse en camisa de once varas.
Die Augen grösser haben als den Magen / Sich zuviel zumuten.
Fare il passo più lungo della gamba.

BITTEN (♦)

Once bitten, twice shy.
Chat échaudé craint l'eau froide.
Gato escaldado, del agua fría huye.
Gebranntes Kind scheut das Feuer.
Il gatto scottato teme l'acqua fredda.

He was bitten with a real mania for tennis.
Il était pris d'une véritable passion pour le tennis.
Le había agarrado el vicio del ténis.
Er war von einer Manie (Sucht, Leidenschaft) für das Tennisspiel befallen / Er hatte einen Fimmel für Tennis.

Era tutto preso da una vera e propria mania per il tennis.

(♦) **You've bitten off more than you can chew!** (p. 52)
Tu as fait le pas plus long que la jambe!
¡Te has metido en camisa de once varas!
Sich zuviel zumuten / Den Mund zu voll nehmen.
Hai fatto il passo più lungo della gamba!

BITTER

To the bitter end.
Jusqu'au bout.
Hasta el fondo del cáliz amargo.
Bis zum bitteren Ende / Bis zur bitteren Neige.
Fino in fondo.

BLACK

To have something down in black and white.
Ecrire quelque chose noir sur blanc.
Poner una cosa por escrito.
Etwas schwarz auf weiss haben.
Mettere nero su bianco.

I'm in her black books.
Je suis mal vu d'elle / Je ne suis pas dans ses papiers.
Estoy en su libro negro.
Ich stehe auf ihrer schwarzen Liste.
Sono mal visto da Lei.

As black as pitch. (comp.)
Noir comme le charbon.
Negro como la noche.
Schwarz wie Pech / Schwarz wie die Nacht.
Nero come il carbone (come la pece).

BLACKMAIL

To blackmail somebody.
Faire chanter quelqu'un / Faire du chantage.
Chantajear a una persona / Hacer un chantaje.
Jemanden erpressen.
Ricattare qualcuno.

53

BLANK (♦)

(♦) A blank look. (p. 53)
L'air absent / Le regard vague.
Un áire distraido.
Ein verdutzter (verblüffter, verlegener) Blick.
Uno sguardo assente.

He told me point blank.
Il me l'a dit clair et net.
Me lo dijo claro y tendido.
Er erzählte es mir klipp und klar.
Me lo disse chiaro e tondo.

BLANKET

A wet blanket.
Un trouble-fête.
Un aguafiestas.
Ein Spielverderber.
Un guastafeste.

BLAZES (♦)

(♦) To go to blazes. (p. 55)
Aller au diable.
Irse al diablo.
Sich zum Teufel scheren.
Andare all'inferno.

To run like blazes.
Courir comme l'éclair / Courir à perdre haleine.
Correr hecho pistola.
Wie verrückt laufen / Um sein Leben rennen.
Correre come se ne andasse della vita.

BLEED

To bleed white.
Saigner à blanc / Epuiser / Réduire à l'extrême.
Desangrar / Extorsionar.
Bis zum Weissbluten auspressen.
Dissanguare / Ridurre allo stremo.

54

BLESSED

Well, I'm blessed!
Mon Dieu, j'ai peine à y croire! / Mon Dieu, est-ce possible!
¡Dios bendito!
Na, so was!
Dio mio, è mai possibile!

BLIND

To turn a blind eye.
Faire semblant de ne rien voir.
Cerrar un ojo.
Ein Auge zudrücken.
Fingere di non vedere / Chiudere un occhio.

As blind as a bat. (comp.)
Etre aveugle comme une taupe.
Cegatón.
Stockblind.
Completamente cieco / Orbo come una talpa.

BLOCK (♦)

(♦) A chip off the old block. (p. 57)
Quelqu'un qui ne fait pas mentir ses origines / Tel père tel fils.
De tal palo, tal astilla.
Ganz wie der Vater.
Chi rivela le caratteristiche del ceppo da cui deriva / Figlio
che assomiglia al padre per carattere.

BLOOD

You cannot get blood out of a stone. (prov.)
C'est comme tirer l'huile d'un mur / C'est demander l'impossible.
No se puede sacar agua de una piedra.
Unmögliches von jemandem verlangen.
Non si può cavar sangue da una rapa.

Blood is thicker than water. (prov.)
Le sang, ce n'est pas l'eau.
La sangre no es agua.
Blut ist ein ganz besonderer Saft.
Il sangue non è acqua.

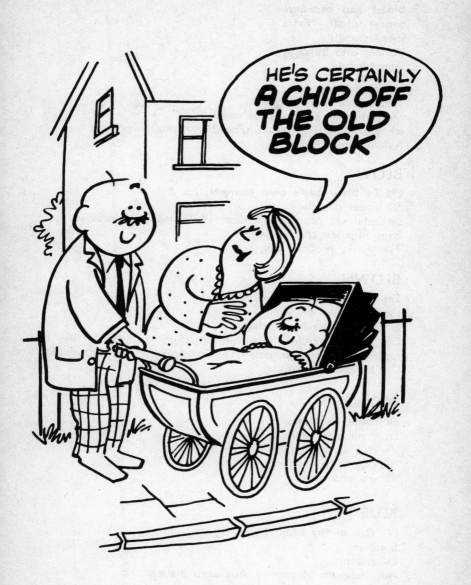

Blood and thunder!
Sensationnel! / Extra.
¡Sensacional!
Donner und Blitz!
Sensazionale!

My blood was up.
J'étais sorti de mes gonds.
Me hirvió la sangre de las venas.
Ich war ausser mir / Ich habe die Kontrolle verloren.
Avevo perso le staffe.

BLOW

(♦) To blow one's own trumpet. (p. 59)
Se lancer des fleurs.
Decantar las propias virtudes / Alabarse / Jactarse.
Sein eigenes Lob singen.
Tessere le proprie lodi.

BLOWN

The trouble has blown over.
L'agitation est passée.
El problema se ha disipado.
Die Schwierigkeiten haben sich in Dunst aufgelöst / Die Aufregungen sind vergangen / Die Sorgen sind wie weggeweht.
L'agitazione è sfumata.

BLOWS

To come to blows.
En venir aux mains.
Venir a las manos.
Handgemein werden.
Venire alle mani.

BLUE (♦)

(♦) Out of the blue. (p. 678)
Soudain.
De repente.
Aus heiterem Himmel / Aus dem Blauen.
Improvvisamente.

59

To feel blue.
Avoir l'âme en peine / Etre mélancolique.
Sentirse triste.
Niedergeschlagen sein.
Sentirsi triste / Essere malinconico.

Once in a blue moon.
Tous les trente-six du mois.
Una véz en cada muerte de Papa.
Alle heiligen Zeiten / Höchst selten / Ab und zu.
Una volta ogni morte di papa (vescovo).

BOO
She wouldn't say boo to a goose.
Il ne ferait pas de mal à une mouche.
No le haría mal a una mosca.
Sie würde keiner Fliege etwas zuleide tun.
Non farebbe male a una mosca.

BOAT (♦)
(♦) To be in the same boat. (p. 61)
Nous faisons tous partie du même lot / Etre dans le même
bateau.
Estar todos en el mismo baile.
In der gleichen (misslichen) Lage sein / Im selben Boot sitzen.
Essere nella stessa barca.

BOB
To bob up like a cork.
Revenir à la surface / Faire surface / Se reprendre.
Volver en auge.
Immer wieder hochkommen / Sich nicht unterkriegen lassen
Tornare a galla (in auge) / Riprendersi subito dopo una disfatta.

BODY
To keep body and soul together.
Sauver sa peau.
Mantenerse en vida / Salvar el cuero.

Leib und Seele zusammenhalten.
Salvare la pelle / Mantenersi in vita.

BOLD

As bold as brass. (comp.)
Effronté.
Descarado.
Unverschämt / Frech wie Oskar.
Sfacciato / Sfrontato.

BOLTED

He bolted out.
Il prit ses jambes à son cou.
Puso piés en polvorosa.
Er brannte durch / Er machte sich aus dem Staube.
Se l'è data a gambe / Si lanciò fuori.

BOOT

To get the boot.
Etre licencié.
Ser despedido del trabajo.
(Plötzlich) entlassen (gefeuert) werden.
Essere licenziato in tronco.

BOOTS (♦)

My heart was in my boots.
J'avais la tremblote.
Tuve mucho miedo / Se me aguadó.
Das Herz fiel mir in die Hose.
Avevo la tremarella / Avevo molta paura.

To lick somebody's boots.
Lécher les bottes de quelqu'un.
Sobarle la leva a alguien.
Jemandem in den Hintern kriechen / Jemandem schmeicheln.
Leccare i piedi a qualcuno.

(♦) To be too big for one's boots. (p. 63)
Se faire remarquer / Se donner des airs.

Darse ínfulas.
Sich wichtig machen / Grössenwahnsinnig sein.
Darsi delle arie / Mettersi in mostra.

BONE

To have a bone to pick.
Se fourrer dans un drôle de guêpier.
Estar en un buen apuro.
Ein Hühnchen zu rupfen haben.
Avere una brutta gatta da pelare.

I have a bone to pick with you.
J'ai de bonnes raisons de me plaindre de vous.
Tengo motivo de queja contígo.
Ich habe ein Hühnchen mit Ihnen zu rupfen.
Ho motivo di querela con voi.

BONES

He made no bones about it.
Il n'a pas eu de scrupule à le dire.
No ha tenido ningun problema para decirlo.
Er machte nicht viel Federlesen.
Non si è fatto scrupolo di dirlo.

BORED

To be bored to tears.
S'ennuyer à mourir.
Estar muerto de aburrimiento.
Zum Sterben langweilig sein.
Essere annoiato a morte.

BORE

He is such a bore!
Il est tellement embêtant!
¡Es una persona tan aburrida!
Er ist solch eine Nervensäge!
E' così noioso!

BORN (♦)

(♦) To be born with a silver spoon in one's mouth. (p. 66)
Etre né coiffé.
Haber nacido con la camisa puesta.
Ein Glücksind sein / Ein Sonntagskind sein.
Essere nato con la camicia.

BOTTLED

He bottled up his grief.
Elle contint sa douleur.
Mantuvo el pesar para sus adentros.
Er verbarg seinen Gram / Er behielt seinen Kummer für sich.
Tenne il suo dolore dentro di sè.

BOTTOM

What's at the bottom of all this?
Qu'y-a-t-il derrière tout ça?
¿Que hay escondido debajo de todo ésto?
Was ist der Grund von alledem? / Was steckt dahinter?
Che c'è all'origine di tutto questo?

BOUNDS

To keep within bounds.
Ne pas dépasser les limites.
Mantenerse dentro de ciertos límites.
In vernünftigen Grenzen halten.
Non uscire dai limiti.

BOW

To bow low.
Se prosterner.
Inclinarse.
Sich zu Füssen werfen.
Prosternarsi.

BRACING

Bracing air.
Air fortifiant.

66

67

Aire estimulante.
Eine erfrischende Brise / Ein erfrischender Luftzug.
Aria corroborante.

BRAIN

To brain somebody.
Casser les reins à quelqu'un.
Romperle a alguien la cabeza.
Jemandem den Schädel einschlagen.
Spaccare la testa a qualcuno.

He has women on the brain.
Il ne pense qu'aux femmes.
Piensa solo en mujeres.
Er hat nur (die) Frauen im Kopf.
Non pensa che alle donne.

BRAND

Brand new.
Flambant neuf.
Nuevecito / Flamante.
Brandneu.
Nuovo di zecca.

BRAVE

To put on a brave face.
Faire contre mauvaise fortune bon cœur.
Ponerle buena cara a las dificultades.
Gute Miene zum bösen Spiel machen.
Far buon viso a cattivo gioco.

BREAD (♦)

To quarrel with one's bread and butter.
Se plaindre de son état.
Quejarse de la propia situación.
Mit seinem Los unzufrieden sein.
Lamentarsi del proprio stato.

(♦) To take the bread out of somebody's mouth. (p. 67)
Oter le pain de la bouche à quelqu'un.

68

69

Quitarle el pan de la boca a una persona.
Jemandem sein Brot nehmen.
Levare il pane di bocca a qualcuno.

BREADWINNER

The breadwinner.
Le chef de famille.
El cabeza de familia.
Das Familienoberhaupt / Der Ernährer / Der Geldverdiener.
Il capofamiglia.

BREAK (♦)

A lucky break.
Un coup chanceux.
Un golpe de suerte.
Glück / Ein glücklicher Umstand.
Un colpo fortunato.

To break down into tears.
Eclater en sanglots.
Estallar en llanto.
In Tränen ausbrechen.
Scoppiare in pianto.

(♦) To break the ice. (p. 69)
Briser la glace.
Romper el hielo.
Das Eis brechen.
Rompere il ghiaccio.

To break the news.
Faire part d'une nouvelle / Annoncer une nouvelle.
Dar una noticia.
Eine Neuigkeit mitteilen (verbreiten).
Comunicare una notizia.

BREAKDOWN

A nervous breakdown.
Une dépression nerveuse.
Agotamiento nervioso.
Ein Nervenzusammenbruch.
Un esaurimento nervoso.

BREAKNECK

At breakneck speed.
Courir comme un dératé.
A topa tolondro / Malamente.
In halsbrecherischer Geschwindigkeit.
A rotta di collo.

BREAST

To make a clean breast of something.
Se délivrer d'un grand poids / Avouer.
Confesarlo todo / Librarse la conciencia.
Offen gestehen.
Confessare tutto / Togliersi un peso dallo stomaco.

BREATH

To be short of breath.
Avoir le souffle court.
Estar jadeando / Estar sin aliento.
Kurzatmig sein / Von kurzem Atem sein / Ohne Ausdauer sein.
Avere il fiato grosso.

BREATHER

To take a breather.
Prendre un bol d'air.
Tomar una bocanada de áire.
Luft schnappen.
Prendere una boccata d'aria.

BREATHLESS

Breathless silence.
Un silence plein de mystère.
Un silencio embarazante.
Atemberaubende Stille / Totenstille.
Un silenzio pieno di aspettativa.

BREWING

Something is brewing.
Il y a anguille sous roche.

Hay algo en el áire.
Es braut sich etwas zusammen / Es liegt etwas in der Luft.
Qualcosa bolle in pentola.

BRIBE

To take a bribe.
Se laisser corrompre / Accepter un pot-de-vin.
Dejarse sobornar.
Sich bestechen (verführen) lassen.
Lasciarsi corrompere.

BRIGHT

As bright as a new pin. (comp.)
Brillant comme un sou neuf.
Radiante.
Blank wie Silber (Gold) / Glänzend / Leuchtend / Strahlend.
Lucentissimo.

BRING (♦)

To bring up a child..
Elever un enfant.
Criar un niño.
Ein Kind erziehen (aufziehen).
Educare un bambino / Allevare un bambino.

I couldn't bring myself to do it.
Je ne pus me décider à le faire.
No me resolví a hacerlo.
Ich könnte mich nicht dazu aufschwingen, es zu tun.
Non potei decidermi a farlo.

(♦) To bring down the house. (p. 289)
Faire s'écrouler le théâtre sous les applaudissements.
Hacer venir abajo el teatro por los aplausos.
Stürmischen Beifall auslösen.
Fare crollare il teatro per gli applausi.

To bring up to date.
Ajourner.
Ponerse al día.
Auf den neuesten Stand bringen.
Aggiornare.

72

To bring off.
Réussir.
Lograr / Llevar a cabo una cosa.
Zustande (fertig) bringen.
Riuscire / Condurre in porto qualcosa.

BROUGHT

I was brought to do this.
Je fus poussé à agir ainsi.
Fui obligado a hacer tal cosa.
Ich wurde dazu gebracht, das zu tun.
Fui spinto a fare questo.

I brought it upon myself.
Je l'ai bien cherché.
Me lo merezco.
Ich habe es selbst verschuldet.
Me lo sono cercato io.

BROAD

To give a broad hint.
Faire une allusion explicite / Faire comprendre clairement.
Hacer una insinuación clara.
Einen Wink mit dem Zaunpfahl geben.
Fare un'allusione esplicita / Fare capire molto chiaramente.

BROADLY

Broadly speaking.
En général.
A lo máximo.
Grundsätzlich gesprochen / Allgemein gesagt.
In linea di massima.

BROKE

I'm stone broke.
Je suis fauché.
Estoy pelado (sin un cinco).
Ich bin pleite / Ich bin abgebrannt / Ich bin bankrott.
Sono al verde / Sono in bolletta.

To go broke.
Courir à la ruine.
Arruinarse.
Bankrott gehen.
Andare in rovina.

BROKEN

Broken English.
Anglais incorrect / Anglais estropié.
Inglés incorrecto.
Gebrochenes Englisch / Fehlerhaftes Englisch.
Inglese scorretto.

To speak broken French.
Baragouiner le français.
Farfullar el Francés.
Französisch gebrochen sprechen.
Balbettare il francese.

BROWN

As brown as a berry. (comp.)
Bronzé.
Muy bronceado.
Braun wie ein Neger.
Molto abbronzato.

BRUNT

I bore the brunt of the expense.
J'ai soutenu la majeure partie des frais.
Yo pagué la mayor parte de los gastos.
Ich trage die Hauptlast der Ausgaben.
Io sostenni la maggior parte della spesa.

To bear the brunt of an attack.
Résister au coup d'une attaque.
Sobrellevar la fuerza de un ataque.
Die volle Wucht des Angriffs auf sich nehmen.
Sostenere l'urto d'un attacco.

74

BRUSH (♦)

(♦) To give someone the brush off. (p. 76)
Se débarrasser de quelqu'un.
Sacudirse de alguien.
Jemanden abwimmeln (loswerden).
Liberarsi di qualcuno / Scaricare qualcuno.

To brush up one's German.
Repasser son allemand.
Ponerse al día con el alemán.
Sein Deutsch auffrischen.
Rispolverare il proprio tedesco.

BUBBLE

To bubble over with joy.
Semer la bonne humeur.
Rebosar de gozo.
Aus Freude übersprudeln.
Scoppiare di gioia.

To bubble over with anger.
Etre noir de colère.
Hervir de cólera.
Aus Wut (Zorn) überschäumen (Kochen).
Bollire d'ira.

BUCK

Buck up!
Dépêchez-vous! / Courage!
¡Cobren ánimo!
Kopf hoch! / Los!
Sbrigatevi! / Coraggio!

BUD

Nipped in the bud.
Tué dans l'œuf.
Cortado en gérmen / Destruido al nacer.
Im Keim erstickt.
Soffocato sul nascere.

BULL

To take the bull by the horns.
Prendre le taureau par les cornes.
Tomar el toro por los cuernos.
Den Stier bei den Hörnern fassen (nehmen).
Prendere il toro per le corna.

BUNDLE

To bundle off.
Plier bagage.
Liar los bártulos.
Sich davonmachen / Aus dem Staub machen / Abhauen.
Far fagotto.

BURN

To burn one's boats.
Couper les ponts.
No tener lazos con el pasado / Hacer borrón y cuenta nueva.
Alle Brücken hinter sich abbrechen.
Tagliarsi i ponti dietro le spalle.

To burn the candle at both ends.
Brûler la chandelle par les deux bouts.
Desvelarse y luego madrugar.
Raubbau mit seiner Gesundheit treiben.
Vegliare fino a tardi e alzarsi presto.

BURY (♦)

(♦) To bury the hatchet. (p. 78)
Faire la paix.
Hacer las paces.
Das Kriegsbeil begraben.
Fare la pace.

(♦) To bury one's head in the sand. (p. 79)
Refuser de voir les choses en face / Fermer les yeux.
Cerrar los ojos a la realidad.
Seinen Kopf in den Sand stecken.
Chiudere gli occhi alla realtà / Nascondere la testa nella sabbia.

BUSY

As busy as a bee. (comp.)
Assidu au travail.
Muy atareado.
Fleissig wie eine Ameise (Biene).
Laborioso come un'ape (una formica).

BUTTER

She looks as if butter wouldn't melt in her mouth.
On dirait une sainte nitouche.
Parece una mosquita muerta.
Sie sieht aus, als könnte sie nicht bis drei zählen.
Sembra una santarellina.

BUTTONHOLE

To buttonhole someone.
Tenir la jambe à quelqu'un.
Ser parlanchín con alguien.
Anbändeln mit jemandem.
Attaccare bottone con qualcuno.

BYGONES

Let bygones be bygones.
La page est tournée / Oubliez et pardonnez.
Borrón y cuenta nueva.
Lass das Vergangene vergangen sein.
Acqua passata non macina più / Dimenticate e perdonate.

CAKE

You can't have your cake and eat it. (prov.)
On ne fait pas d'omelettes sans casser les œufs.
No se puede obtenerlo todo.
Du kannst nur eines von beiden tun oder haben / Entweder
oder! / Man kann nicht auf zwei Bällen tanzen.
Non si può avere la botte piena e la moglie ubriaca.

A piece of cake.
Une chose simple comme bonjour.
Una cosa de nada.

Eine leichte Sache / Eine Kleinigkeit.
Una cosa facile.

He takes the cake for rudeness.
C'est lui qui a le pompon pour ce qui est de l'impolitesse.
Es un campeón de descortesía.
Den Rekord an Unhöflichkeit schlagen / Er schlägt den Rekord an Grobheit.
Detiene il primato della scortesia.

CALL (♦)

I shall call for you.
Je passerai vous prendre.
Iré por Ustedes.
Ich werde Sie abholen.
Passerò a prendervi.

To call at the Smiths.
Passer chez les Smith.
Pasar por la casa de los Smith.
Die Smith besuchen / Bei Smith vorsprechen.
Passare dagli Smith.

To call a strike.
Proclamer une grève.
Declarar huelga.
Einen Streik ausrufen.
Proclamare uno sciopero.

To call someone names.
Injurier quelqu'un / Traiter une personne de noms d'oiseaux.
Injuriar una persona.
Eine Person beschimpfen.
Ingiuriare una persona.

(♦) Let's call it a day! (p. 82)
Ça suffit pour aujourd'hui!
¡Suficiente por hoy!
Es reicht für heute!
Basta per oggi!

CAME

I don't know how it came about.
Je ne sais pas comment cela est arrivé.

No sé como pasó.
Ich weiss nicht, wie es geschah.
Non so come avvenne.

He came into a lot of money.
Il hérita d'une grosse fortune.
Ha heredado un montón de dinero.
Er erbte viel Geld.
Ereditò molto denaro.

CANDIDATE

To be a candidate for . . .
Etre candidat à . . . / Aspirer à . . .
Ser aspirante a . . .
Ein Kandidat sein für . . . / Kandidieren für . . .
Aspirare a . . .

CANDLE

Not worth the candle.
Le jeu n'en vaut pas la chandelle.
No merece la pena.
Es ist nicht der Mühe wert.
Il gioco non vale la candela.

He can't hold a candle to his brother.
Il n'arrive pas à la cheville de son frère.
No es digno ni de lustrarle los zapatos a su hermano.
Er kann seinem Bruder nicht das Wasser reichen.
Non è degno di lustrare le scarpe a suo fratello.

CAP

She has set her cap at him.
Elle a posé les yeux sur lui.
Le ha puesto los ojos encima.
Sie hat ein Auge auf ihn geworfen.
Gli ha messo gli occhi addosso.

A feather in one's cap.
Une chose dont on peut se vanter.
Algo de que sentirse orgulloso.

Darauf kann man stolz sein.
Una cosa di cui vantarsi.

The cap fits.
Observation pertinente / Faire mouche.
La observación es pertinente.
Die Beobachtung stimmt.
L'osservazione è giusta.

CAPITAL

A capital dinner.
Un excellent déjeuner.
Un almuerzo mágnifico.
Ein ausgezeichnetes Essen.
Un ottimo pranzo.

CARD

A knowing card.
Un malin de première grandeur.
Un hombre astuto / Un buen pícaro.
Jemand, der die Karten kennt / Ein Erzschlauer / Ein Fuchs.
Un furbo matricolato.

To throw up one's card.
S'avouer vaincu.
Darse por vencido / Tirar la toalla.
Eine Karte hinwerfen / Sich als besiegt geben.
Darsi per vinto.

CARDS

It's on the cards.
C'est possible.
Es muy posible.
Es ist (durchaus) möglich.
E' possibile.

CARE

I don't care a hang (damn, cent).
Je m'en fiche éperdument / Je m'en fiche royalement / Je m'en
fiche comme de l'an quarante.

No me importa un comino.
Das ist mir völlig gleich / Das kümmert mich einen Dreck.
Non me ne importa un fico secco.

CARRY

To carry out a plan.
Mettre à exécution un plan / Réaliser un plan.
Llevar a cabo un plan.
Einen Plan ausführen.
Realizzare un piano.

To carry the day.
Remporter une victoire.
Salirse con la suya.
Siegen / Sieger bleiben.
Riportare una vittoria / Spuntarla.

CART (♦)

(♦) To put the cart before the horse. (p. 86)
Mettre la charrue avant les bœufs.
Enganchar los bueyes detrás de la carreta.
Das Pferd beim Schwanz aufzäumen.
Mettere il carro innanzi ai buoi.

CASH

Cash in hand.
Payer rubis sur l'ongle / Payer comptant / Payer « cash ».
Con dinero en efectivo.
Barbestand / Kassenbestand.
Soldi alla mano.

CAST

To cast lots.
Tirer au sort.
Echar suertes / Sortear.
Auslosen / Das Los ziehen.
Tirare a sorte.

CAT (♦)

A cat may look at a king. (prov.)
Nous sommes tous égaux.
Somos todos iguales.
Wir sind alle gleich.
Siamo tutti uguali.

(♦) There isn't room to swing a cat! (p. 88)
L'espace est très restreint.
¡No hay lugar ni para un alfilér!
Dort ist kaum Platz zum Umdrehen.
Lo spazio è ristrettissimo!

(♦) To let the cat out of the bag. (p. 89)
Laisser échapper un secret.
Dejarse escapar un secréto.
Die Katze aus dem Sack lassen.
Lasciarsi scappare un segreto.

A cat and dog life.
Une vie faite de querelles continuelles / Etre comme chien et chat.
Vivir como perro y gato.
Wie Hund und Katze leben.
Una vita di continui litigi.

Care killed the cat.
Il n'y pas de quoi fouetter un chat / Il ne faut pas s'en faire.
No hay que preocuparse demasiado.
Es lohnt sich nicht, sich Sorgen zu machen.
Non conviene preoccuparsi.

CATCH

It wasn't a great catch.
Il n'a pas tellement fait prise.
No hizo gancho.
Es war kein grosser Fang.
Non fece molta presa.

To catch it.
Recevoir une râclée / Se faire rosser.
Meterse en líos.

Strafe (Tadel) bekommen.
Buscarne delle belle / Prenderle.

Catch me going there!
Je ne risque pas d'y aller!
¡No correré el riesgo de ir!
Es besteht keine Gefahr, dass ich gehe!
Non c'è pericolo che ci vada!

To catch cold.
Prendre froid / Attraper un rhume.
Coger un resfriado / Resfriarse.
Sich erkälten.
Raffreddarsi / Prendere un raffreddore.

CATS
To rain cats and dogs.
Il pleut des cordes / Il pleut à verse.
Llover a cántaros.
Es giesst (schüttet / regnet) in Strömen.
Piovere a dirotto (a catinelle).

CAUGHT
To be caught in the rain.
Etre surpris par la pluie.
Ser sorprendido por la lluvia.
Vom Regen überrascht werden.
Essere sorpreso dalla pioggia.

CENT
He hasn't got a cent.
Il n'a pas un sou / Il n'a pas un rond.
No tiene un centavo.
Er hat nicht einen roten Heller / Er besitzt keinen Pfennig.
Non ha il becco di un quattrino.

CEREMONY
Please don't stand on ceremony.
Ne fais pas tant de cérémonies!

Por favor, no hagas ceremonias.
Bitte sei nicht so förmlich.
Ti prego di non fare complimenti.

CHALK

As like as chalk and cheese. (comp.)
N'être semblables qu'en apparence.
Ser aparentemente iguales.
Sich dem Anschein nach ähnlich sein.
Essere simili solo in apparenza.

Not to know chalk from cheese.
Prendre des vessies pour des lanternes.
Tomar gato por liebre.
Ein X nicht vom U unterscheiden können.
Prendere lucciole per lanterne.

He is the best by a long chalk.
Il est de loin le meilleur.
A la larga es el mejor.
Er ist bei weitem der Beste.
E' di gran lunga il migliore.

CHANCE

If ever I get the chance.
Si j'en avais seulement l'occasion!
Si tendré la oportunidad.
Wenn ich jemals die Gelegenheit habe.
Se mai me ne capitasse l'occasione.

To stand a good chance of success.
Avoir de grandes chances de réussir.
Tener muchas posibilidaded de triunfar.
Gute Möglichkeiten haben zu gewinnen / Gute Aussichten
haben, erfolgreich zu sein.
Avere una buona probabilità di successo.

I'll take my chance.
Je courrai le risque.
Tomaré el riesgo.
Ich will mein Glück versuchen.
Correrò il rischio.

A chance acquaintance.
Une connaissance fortuite.
Un conocimiento fortuito.
Eine Zufallsbekanntschaft / Eine zufällige Bekanntschaft.
Una conoscenza fortuita.

CHANCES

The chances are against you.
Tu as peu de chances de... / Le sort est contre toi.
Tienes pocas probabilidades de triunfar.
Die Umstände sind gegen dich.
Hai poche probabilità.

CHANGE (♦)

Have you any change?
Avez-vous de la monnaie?
¿Tienen cambio?
Haben Sie etwas Kleingeld?
Avete spiccioli (moneta)?

Keep the change.
Gardez le reste.
Tenga Usted el vuelto.
Behalten Sie den Rest!
Tenete il resto.

Go away for a change.
Allez changer d'air!
Vayan a cambiar áire.
Zur Abwechslung fortgehen (verreisen) / Einen Tapetenwechsel brauchen.
Andate a cambiare aria.

(♦) To change one's mind. (p. 375)
Changer d'idée.
Cambiar de idéa.
Seine Meinung ändern.
Cambiare idea.

CHARGE

In the charge of...
Sous la surveillance de...

A cargo de . . .
Beauftragt mit . . . / Verantwortlich für . . .
Sotto la custodia di . . .

How much do you charge for . . . ?
Combien prenez-vous pour . . . ?
¿Cuanto se paga para . . . ?
Wieviel berechnen Sie für . . . ?
Quanto fate pagare per . . . ?

He is in charge of that office.
Il est à la tête de ce bureau.
Está a cargo de aquella oficina.
Er ist der Leiter dieses Büros.
Egli dirige quell'ufficio.

CHARITY

Charity begins at home. (prov.)
Charité bien ordonnée commence par soi-même.
La caridad comienza por uno mismo.
Jeder ist sich selbst der Nächste.
La prima carità è quella di casa (comincia in famiglia).

CHATTERED

His teeth chattered.
Il claquait des dents.
Sus dientes castañeaban.
Seine Zähne klapperten.
Gli battevano i denti.

CHEAP

Don't make yourself cheap!
Ne te vends pas pour une bouchée de pain!
¡No te vendas por nada!
Setz dich nicht selber herab! / Mach dich nicht billiger als
du bist!
Non degradarti!

CHECK

To hold oneself in check.
Se dominer / Se maîtriser.

Controlarse.
Sich in Schach halten / Sich beherrschen.
Dominarsi.

CHEEK

To have the cheek to ...
Avoir le toupet de ... / Avoir le culot de ...
Tener el descaro de ...
Die Frechheit besitzen zu ...
Avere la faccia tosta di ...

CHEER

Be of good cheer!
Prenez courage! / Courage!
¡Anímense!
Guter Dinge sein!
Fatevi coraggio!

CHEESE

A cheese paring spirit.
Parcimonie mesquine / Tas de choses sans valeur.
Tacañería / Un montón de cosas sin valor.
Ein knauseriger (geiziger / kleinlicher) Mann.
Avarizia gretta / Accozzaglia di cose senza valore.

CHEQUERED

A chequered career.
Une carrière mouvementée / Une carrière aventureuse.
Una carrera tortuosa / Una carrera muy movida.
Eine abwechslungsreiche Karriere.
Una carriera movimentata.

CHESHIRE

To laugh like a Cheshire cat.
Sourire de façon stéréotypée.
Sonreir melindrosamente.
Übers ganze Gesicht lachen.
Sorridere in maniera stereotipata.

CHICKEN

To be chicken.
Ne pas avoir de cran.
Ser cobarde.
Keinen Mut haben.
Non avere fegato.

CHICKENS

To count one's chickens before they hatch.
Vendre la peau de l'ours avant de l'avoir tué.
Echar la cuenta sin la huéspeda.
Das Fell des Bären verkaufen, ehe man ihn erlegt hat.
Vendere la pelle dell'orso prima di averlo preso.

CHINWAG

To have a chinwag.
Faire la causette.
Charlar.
Sich unterhalten / Plaudern.
Fare una chiacchierata.

CHIP (♦)

To have a chip on one's shoulder.
Avoir envie de se disputer / Chercher la petite bête.
Estar irritado / Tener ganas de reñir.
(Vor Zorn) geladen sein.
Aver voglia di litigare.

To chip in.
Interrompre une conversation.
Interrumpir una conversación / Entrometerse en una conversación.
Ins Wort fallen.
Mettere il becco / Interrompere una conversazione.

(♦) A chip off the old block. (p. 57)
Il est le digne fils de son père! / Tel père tel fils.
De tal palo, tal astilla.
Ganz wie der Vater.
Un figlio che assomiglia al padre per carattere.

CHOOSES

He is a man that picks and chooses.
C'est un homme difficile (à contenter).
Es un hombre muy difícil de contentar.
Er ist ein Mann, der an allem etwas auszusetzen hat / Er ist
ein Mann, der immer meckert.
E' un uomo difficile da accontentare (dai gusti difficili).

CHUMP

He is off his chump.
Il a perdu la raison.
Ha perdido la cabeza.
Er ist nicht ganz bei Trost.
E' fuori di senno.

CHURCH

As poor as a church mouse. (comp.)
Etre pauvre comme Job / Etre sur la paille.
Pobre como una rata.
Arm wie eine Kirchenmaus.
Povero in canna.

CLAMOUR

To clamour for something.
Réclamer quelque chose.
Pedir a gritos una cosa.
Wütend nach etwas verlangen / Nach etwas laut schreien.
Chiedere gridando una cosa.

CLASH

These colours clash.
Ces couleurs jurent / Ces couleurs sont criardes.
Estos colores no están entonados.
Diese Farben passen nicht zusammen / Diese Farben harmo-
nieren nicht miteinander.
Questi colori stonano (fanno a cazzotti).

96

CLEAN

To get clean off.
Avoir les mains propres / Etre réhabilité.
Salir con las manos limpias.
Sauber davonkommen.
Venirne fuori pulito.

CLEAR

Keep clear of him!
Evitez-le!
¡No se acerquen a él!
Vermeiden Sie ihn / Halten Sie sich fern von ihm!
Evitatelo!

To clear oneself.
Prouver son innocence / Se disculper.
Demostrar la propria inocencia.
Seine Unschuld beweisen.
Dimostrare la propria innocenza.

To clear out.
S'esquiver / Décamper / Jouer la fille de l'air.
Largarse / Salir pitando / Tomar soleta.
Sich aus dem Staube machen / Verschwinden / Sich verziehen /
Abhauen.
Svignarsela.

To clear up a misunderstanding.
Dissiper un malentendu.
Aclarar un malentendido.
Ein Missverständnis aufklären.
Chiarire un malinteso.

To clear up.
Faire le ménage.
Hacer limpieza.
Abräumen / Forträumen / Saubermachen / Rein machen /
Putzen.
Fare le pulizie.

CLEARING

The weather is clearing up.
Le temps se remet au beau.

97

El tiempo está mejorando.
Das Wetter klärt sich auf.
Il tempo si sta rasserenando.

CLEFT

In a cleft stick.
Ne pas pouvoir se remuer / Etre à l'étroit.
En un espacio muy limitado / Estar apretujado.
In einer schwierigen Lage / In der Klemme.
Non aver spazio neanche per girarsi / Essere in una situazione difficile.

CLIMB

To climb down.
Diminuer ses prétentions.
Bajar a gatas / Reducir lo que uno pretende.
Nachgeben / Klein beigeben.
Ridurre le proprie pretese.

CLOAK

Cloak and dagger story.
Roman de cape et d'épée.
Novéla de capa y espada.
Spionagegeschichte.
Romanzo di cappa e spada.

CLOCK (♦)

(♦) A clock watcher. (p. 99)
Un impatient.
Un tipo impaciente.
Ein Ungeduldiger.
Una persona impaziente.

CLOCKWORK

Like clockwork.
Avec la plus grande précision.
Con la máxima puntualidad.
Genauestens.
Con la massima esattezza.

CLOSE

It's close in here.
L'air est vicié là-dedans / On étouffe ici.
El áire es sofocante aquí adentro.
Die Luft ist schwül (dumpf) hier drinnen.
L'aria è soffocante qua dentro.

Close weather.
Temps lourd.
Un tiempo bochornoso.
Schwüles Wetter.
Tempo afoso.

To be close-fisted.
Etre avare / Etre radin.
Ser tacaño.
Geizig sein / Knauserig sein.
Essere avaro.

CLOTH

Cut your coat according to your cloth.
Menez le train de vie que vous permettent vos moyens / N'ayez
pas la folie des grandeurs.
Hay que vivir conforme a las proprias posibilidades.
Strecken Sie sich nach der Decke!
Non fare il passo più lungo della gamba.

CLOUD

Every cloud has a silver lining. (prov.)
Chaque chose a du bon.
Todo tiene su lado bueno.
Jedes Unglück hat auch sein Gutes.
Ogni cosa ha il suo lato buono.

To be under a cloud.
Etre mal vu.
Ser malquerido.
Ungern gesehen sein / Schlecht angesehen sein / Verdächtig
sein.
Essere malvisto / Essere sospettato.

CLOUT

Never cast a clout till May is out. (prov.)
En avril ne te découvre pas d'un fil, en mai fais ce qui te plaît.
No hay que desabrigarse en Abril.
Man soll den Tag nicht vor dem Abend loben.
Aprile non ti scoprire.

CLOVER

To be in clover.
Vivre dans le luxe / Etre comme un pacha.
Vivir como rey.
Im Wohlstand leben / Wie ein König leben.
Vivere nel lusso / Stare come un papa.

CLUB

Let's club together.
Partageons les frais.
Compartamos los gastos.
Lassen Sie uns zusammenlegen / Tun wir uns zusammen.
Dividiamo la spesa / Facciamo alla romana.

COAL

As black as coal. (comp.)
Noir comme le charbon.
Negro como el carbón.
Schwarz wie Kohle.
Nero come il carbone.

COALS

To carry coals to Newcastle.
Porter de l'eau à la rivière.
Llevar agua al río.
Eulen nach Athen tragen.
Portare vasi a Samo.

COBWEBS (♦)

(♦) To blow away the cobwebs. (p. 102)
Se rafraîchir les idées.

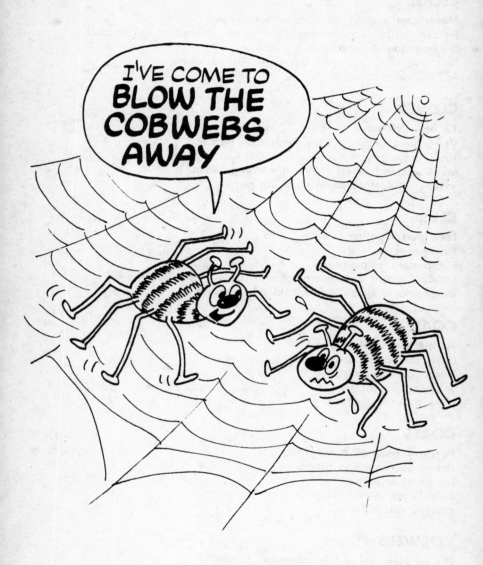

Renfrescarse las ideas.
Sich einen klaren Kopf schaffen.
Rinfrescarsi le idee.

COCK (♥)

The cock of the walk.
Le coq du village.
Hombre amado por las mujeres / Un picaflor.
Der Hahn im Korbe.
Il gallo della checca.

A cock and bull story.
Des sornettes / Des balivernes / Des blagues.
Una patraña.
Ein Ammenmärchen / Eine Lügengeschichte.
Una panzana / Una fandonia.

(♦) To cock a snook at someone. (p. 104)
Faire un pied-de-nez à quelqu'un.
Hacer muecas.
Jemandem eine lange Nase machen.
Fare marameo a qualcuno.

COD (♥)

(♦) Cods wallop. (p. 105)
Une gifle.
Un bofetón.
Eine Ohrfeige.
Una sberla / Pesci in faccia.

COIN

To coin a word.
Forger (créer) un mot.
Acuñar una palabra / Inventar una palabra.
Ein Wort prägen.
Coniare una parola.

To coin money.
Gagner de l'argent à la pelle.
Ganar montones de dinero.
Geld wie Heu verdienen.
Fare soldi a palate.

AND WHAT IF I **COCK A SNOOK** AT YOUR REQUEST FOR A RAISE IN SALARY, MISTER JONES ?

MANAGER

COLD (♦)

Stone cold.
Froid comme le marbre.
Frío como el hielo.
Eiskalt.
Freddissimo / Freddo come il marmo.

To throw cold water on a plan.
Décourager une entreprise.
Echarle agua fría a un proyecto.
Einen Plan verderben.
Scoraggiare un progetto.

To give the cold shoulder.
Traiter avec froideur.
Comportarse con frialdad.
Die kalte Schulter zeigen.
Trattare freddamente.

(♦) To get cold feet. (p. 107)
Avoir peur.
Tener miedo.
Kalte Füsse bekommen / Angst kriegen.
Avere paura.

(♦) To be left out in the cold. (p. 108)
Etre négligé / Etre négligent.
Ser abandonado.
Übergangen (ignoriert) werden.
Essere trascurato.

COLLAR

I collared him on the doorstep.
Je l'ai arrêté sur le seuil.
Lo detuve en el umbral.
Ich fasste (erwischte) ihn auf der Türschwelle.
Lo fermai sulla soglia.

COLLECT

Give me time to collect myself.
Donnez-moi le temps de me ressaisir.

107

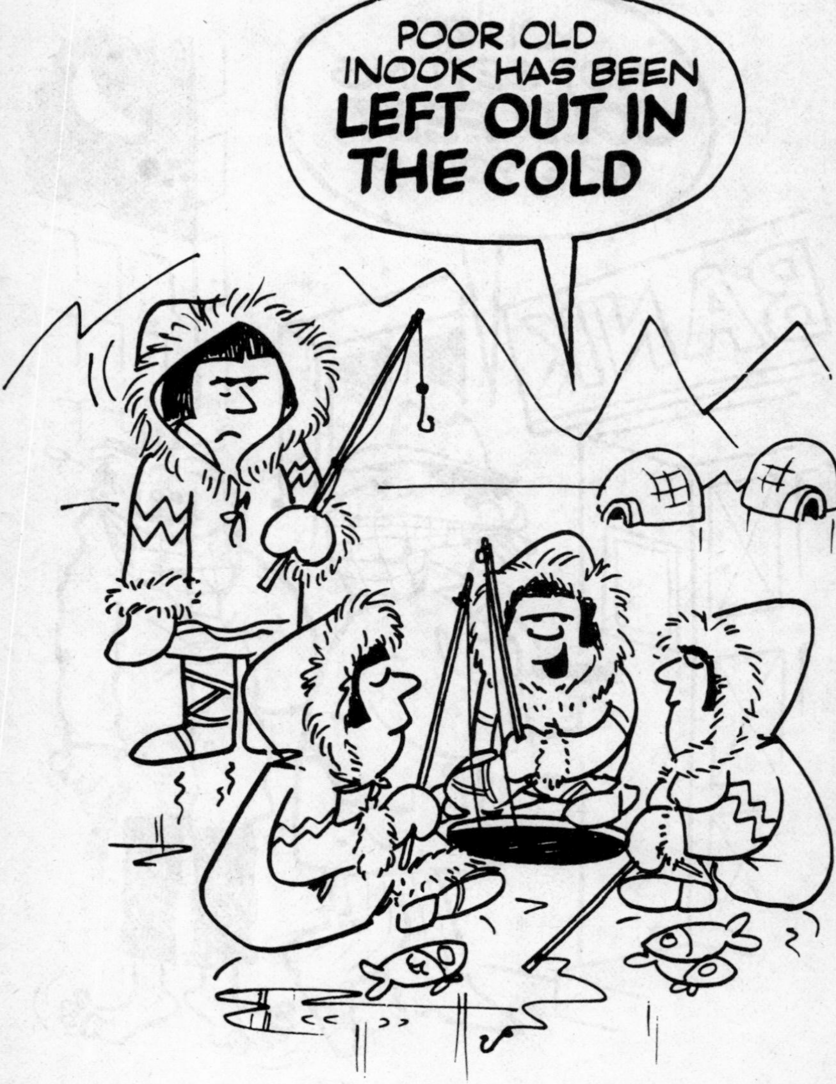
POOR OLD INOOK HAS BEEN LEFT OUT IN THE COLD

Dame tiempo para recobrarme.
Geben Sie mir Zeit, mich zu fassen.
Datemi il tempo di riprendermi.

COLLIDED

The two planes collided.
Les deux avions entrèrent en collision.
Los dos aviones chocaron.
Die zwei Flugzeuge stiessen zusammen.
I due aerei entrarono in collisione.

COLOUR

To be off colour.
Changer de couleur / Se sentir mal.
Estar chueco / No estar muy bien.
Sich nicht wohl fühlen.
Stare poco bene.

COLOURLESS

A colourless person.
Une personne insignifiante / Une personne fade.
Una persona descolorida.
Eine blasse Person / Eine farblose Person.
Una persona scialba.

COLOURS

To come out in one's true colours.
Montrer son vrai caractère.
Revelar el verdadero carácter de uno.
Sein wahres Gesicht zeigen / Sein wahres Wesen zeigen.
Mostrare il proprio vero carattere.

To come off with flying colours.
S'en tirer avec les honneurs.
Salir con honra de un asunto.
Mit fliegenden Fahnen siegen.
Uscire da un'impresa con tutti gli onori.

To stick to one's colours.
Ne pas retourner sa veste / Etre fidèle à ses principes.

No cambiar de bando / No ser como veleta al viento.
Einer Sache treu bleiben / Die Fahne nicht wechseln.
Non mutare bandiera / Restar fedele ai propri principi.

COME

Come out with it!
Décidez-vous à parler!
¡Resuélvase a hablar!
Sprechen Sie es aus! / Heraus mit der Sprache!
Decidetevi a parlare!

Look what I've come to!
Regardez à quoi je suis réduit!
¡Miren hasta donde he llegado!
Schauen Sie, wohin ich gelangt (gekommen) bin!
Guardate come sono ridotto.

To come out of it well.
Bien s'en tirer.
Salir bien parado de un asunto.
Gut abschneiden (gut wegkommen) bei einem Geschäft (einer Sache).
Venire fuori bene da un affare.

To come to no good.
Mal finir.
Acabar mal.
Es niemals zu etwas Gutem bringen / Schlecht enden.
Finir male.

To come in handy.
Convenir / Cela me convient.
Acomodar / Convenir.
Gelegen kommen / Sich gut treffen.
Far comodo.

Come to think of it.
Maintenant que j'y pense.
Ahora que lo pienso.
Wenn ich es bedenke.
Ora che ci penso.

To come down upon ...
Faire un lavage de cerveau à ...

110

Dar un rapapolvo a . . .
Sich stürzen auf . . . / Jemandem aufs Dach steigen / Jeman-
dem den Kopf waschen.
Dare una lavata di capo a . . .

To come in useful.
Etre utile.
Ser útil.
Nützlich sein.
Essere utile / Tornare utile.

COMING (♦)

(♦) I don't know if I'm coming or going! (p. 112)
Je ne sais plus si je monte ou si je descends!
¡No etiendo ni jota!
Nichts mehr verstehen / Durcheinander sein.
Non capisco un'acca! / Non capisco un tubo!

COMMIT

He wouldn't commit himself.
Il n'a pas voulu s'engager / Il n'a pas voulu se compromettre.
No quiso comprometerse.
Er wollte sich nicht verpflichten.
Non volle impegnarsi.

COMMON

As common as dirt. (comp.)
Très vulgaire.
Vulgarote.
Gewöhnlich / Ordinär.
Volgarissimo.

COMMONPLACE

He's very commonplace.
Il est très banal / Il est d'un commun!
Es muy banal.
Er ist sehr banal.
E' molto banale.

COMPANY

I sin in good company.
Des hommes mieux que moi en ont fait autant.
Hombres mejores que yo lo han hecho igual.
Bessere Menschen als ich haben das auch gemacht / Bessere
Leute tun das ebenfalls.
Uomini migliori di me hanno fatto altrettanto.

We parted company.
Nous prîmes congé / Nous nous séparâmes.
Nos separamos.
Wir trennten uns.
Ci separammo.

Two's company three's none. (prov.)
On est mieux quand on est peu nombreux.
Menos gente, mejor.
Viele Köche verderben den Brei.
Poca brigata, vita beata.

COMPARE

To compare notes.
Echanger des points de vue (des idées).
Tener un intercambio de puntos de vista.
Meinungen (Erfahrungen) austauschen / Sich beraten.
Scambiare vedute.

COMPLAINT

There is no reason for complaint.
Il n'y a pas de quoi se plaindre.
No hay porqué lamentarse.
Es gibt keinen Grund zur Klage.
Non c'è motivo di lamentarsi.

COMPLIMENTS

To pay one's compliments.
Faire ses hommages.
Saludar.
Seine Empfehlungen senden.
Fare i propri omaggi.

COMPOSURE

To recover one's composure.
Reprendre son sang-froid.
Recobrar ánimo.
Seine Fassung wiedergewinnen.
Riprendere il proprio sangue freddo.

CONCEITED

He is a conceited ass.
Il est plein de suffisance / Il est plein de morgue.
Es un presuntuoso.
Er ist voller Dünkel (Einbildung).
E' pieno di boria.

CONCERNED

I'm concerned about John.
Je suis inquiet pour John.
John me preocúpa.
Ich bin besorgt um John.
Sono preoccupato per John.

The parties concerned.
Les parties concernées.
Las partes interesadas.
Die Beteiligten.
Le parti interessate.

CONCOCTION

What a concoction!
Quel mélange!
¡Qué menjurje!
Welch komische Mischung!
Che strano miscuglio!

CONFESS

A fault confessed is half redressed. (prov.)
Faute avouée est à moitié pardonnée.
Una falta confesada está medio reparada.
Ein eingestandener Fehler ist halb behoben / Eine zugegebene

Schuld ist halb verziehen.
Peccato confessato è mezzo perdonato.

CONFOUND

Confound them!
Qu'ils aillent au diable!
¡Que vayan al diablo!
Zum Teufel mit ihnen!
Che il diavolo se li porti!

CONJURE

To conjure up a picture.
Evoquer une image.
Evocar una imágen.
Ein Bild heraufbeschwören.
Evocare un'immagine.

CONNECTIONS

To have good connections.
Avoir des connaissances / Etre connu / Avoir le bras long.
Estar bien conectado.
Gute Beziehungen haben / Vitamin B haben.
Avere conoscenze autorevoli / Essere ben introdotto.

CONS

The pros and the cons.
Le pour et le contre.
Los pros y contra.
Das Für und Wider / Pro und Kontra.
Il pro e il contro.

CONSENT

Silence gives consent. (prov.)
Qui ne dit mot consent.
Quien calla aconsiente.
Stillschweigen bedeutet Zustimmung.
Chi tace acconsente.

CONSIDERATE

A considerate man.
Un homme plein d'attentions.
Un hombre considerado.
Ein rücksichtsvoller Mann.
Un uomo pieno di riguardi.

CONSISTENTLY

To act consistently.
Agir en conséquence / Agir de façon cohérente.
Actuar con coherencia.
Konsequent (logisch) handeln.
Agire coerentemente.

CONSUMMATE

With consummate ease.
Avec la plus grande facilité.
Con gran facilidad.
Mit grösster Leichtigkeit.
Con la massima facilità.

A consummate liar.
Un fieffé menteur.
Un embustero.
Ein perfekter Lügner.
Un bugiardo matricolato.

CONVENIENCE

At your convenience.
A votre convenance.
Cuando le convenga a Usted.
Wann es Ihnen passt.
Con vostro comodo.

COOK

To cook somebody's goose.
Faire sa fête à quelqu'un / L'arranger!
Zurrar a alguien la badana.

116

Es jemandem besorgen / Jemanden fertigmachen / Jemanden
auf den Pelz rücken.
Conciare qualcuno per le feste.

COOKS

Too many cooks spoil the broth.
Trop de personnes, cela nuit à la tâche.
Demasiados medicos matan el paciente.
Viele Köche verderben den Brei.
Troppi medici ammazzano il malato.

COOL

As cool as a cucumber. (comp.)
Très frais / Ayant du sang-froid.
Fresquito / De sangre fría.
Kalt wie Eis / Eiskalt / Kaltblütig.
Freschissimo / Di sangue freddo.

To cool one's heels.
Poiroter / Attendre longtemps.
Esperar a alguien por mucho tiempo.
Warten müssen.
Stare ad aspettare a lungo.

COPE

We can't cope with him.
Nous ne pouvons lui tenir tête.
No podemos con él.
Wir sind ihm nicht gewachsen.
Non possiamo tenergli testa.

CORE

He is English to the core.
Il est Anglais jusqu'au bout des ongles.
Es Inglés hasta el meollo.
Er ist bis ins Mark Engländer.
E' inglese fino alle midolla.

CORNER

I'm in a tight corner.
Je me retrouve le dos au mur / Je suis coincé.
Estoy entre la espada y la paréd.
Ich bin in der Klemme / Ich bin in Verlegenheit.
Mi trovo con le spalle al muro.

To turn the corner.
Surmonter le pire.
Pasar lo peor.
Eine Krise überstehen.
Superare il peggio.

COUNSEL

To keep one's own counsel.
Cacher ce que l'on sait.
Callar lo que uno sabe.
Seine Absicht für sich behalten.
Tacere ciò che si sa.

COURSE

To give free course to ...
Donner libre cours à ...
Dar vía libre a ...
Jemandem freien Lauf lassen.
Dare libero sfogo a ...

To let things take their course.
Laisser que les choses suivent leur cours.
Dejar que las cosas tomen su curso natural.
Den Dingen ihren Lauf lassen.
Lasciare andare le cose per il loro corso (verso).

That's a matter of course.
Cela va de soi.
Esto es obvio.
Das ist eine Selbstverständlichkeit.
Questo va da sè.

COURT

You are courting trouble.
Tu cherches les ennuis.

Estás buscando problemas.
Du beschwörst Unheil (Schwierigkeiten) herauf.
Vai in cerca di guai.

To court failure.
Rechercher l'insuccès.
Exponerse al fracaso.
Ein Versagen herausfordern.
Andare in cerca dell'insuccesso.

COVENTRY

To send to Coventry.
Mettre au ban de la société.
Poner en bando a una persona.
Den Verkehr abbrechen / Gesellschaftlich kaltstellen.
Mettere al bando.

CRACK (♦)

To crack a joke.
Faire un mot d'esprit (une boutade).
Soltar un chiste.
Einen Witz reissen.
Dire una battuta / Raccontare una barzelletta.

(♦) To crack up. (p. 120)
Craquer / Faire une dépression nerveuse.
Desmoronarse.
Zusammenbrechen.
Andare a pezzi / Avere un esaurimento nervoso.

CRACKING (♦)

(♦) To get cracking. (p. 121)
Se dépêcher.
Apurarse.
Sich beeilen.
Sbrigarsi.

CRANE

To crane one's neck.
Allonger le cou pour essayer de voir.

119

Estirar el cuello (para ver).
Sich den Hals ausrecken nach . . .
Allungare il collo.

CRANK

He is a crank!
C'est un excentrique!
¡Es un excéntrico!
Er ist ein komischer Kauz.
E' un eccentrico!

CREDIT

To take the credit for something.
Tirer mérite de quelque chose.
Darse crédito por una cosa.
Sich etwas als Verdient anrechnen / Den Ruhm für etwas in
Anspruch nehmen.
Prendersi il merito per una cosa.

CREEP

To give somebody the creeps.
Donner des frissons à quelqu'un.
Hacer espeluznar de miedo a alguien.
Jemandem das Gruseln beibringen / Jemandem eine Gänsehaut
machen.
Far rabbrividire qualcuno.

It makes one's flesh creep.
Donner des frissons.
Es espeluznante.
Es überläuft einen kalt / Eine Gänsehaut davon bekommen.
Far rabbrividire.

CRISS-CROSS

Everything went criss-cross.
Tout alla de travers.
Todo ha ido enrevesado.
Alles ging schief.
Tutto andò di traverso (storto).

CROCK

To crock up.
Tomber malade.
Enfermarse.
Erkranken.
Ammalarsi.

CROOK

By hook or by crook.
De gré ou de force.
Por las buenas o por las malas.
Um jeden Preis / Unter allen Umständen.
Di riffa o di raffa.

He is a bit of a crook.
C'est une personne un peu louche.
Es algo pícaro.
Er ist eine etwas verdächtige Person / Er ist ein kleiner Gauner
(Betrüger).
E' un tipo un po' losco.

CROSSED

It crossed my mind.
Cela traversa mon esprit.
Se me pasó por la cabeza.
Es kam mir in den Sinn / Es fiel mir ein.
Mi passò per la mente.

CROSS

I feel very cross.
Je suis d'une humeur exécrable.
Estoy contrariado.
Ich bin schlechter Laune (schlecht gelaunt).
Sono di pessimo umore.

CRY (♦)

To cry one's eyes out.
Pleurer à chaudes larmes.
Llorar a mares.

124

Sich die Augen ausweinen.
Consumarsi gli occhi dal piangere / Piangere a calde lacrime.

(♦) **It's no use crying over spilt milk!** (p. 124)
Ce qui est fait est fait!
¡A lo hecho, pecho!
Geschehen ist geschehen / Hin ist hin.
E' inutile piangere sul latte versato.

CUP (♦)

(♦) **One's cup of tea.** (p. 126)
Le cheval de bataille.
El caballo de batalla.
Nach jemandes Geschmack sein.
Il proprio cavallo di battaglia.

CURE

To be past cure.
Etre incurable.
Ser incurable / No tener remedio.
Unheilbar sein.
Essere incurabile.

CURSED

To be cursed with . . .
Etre atteint de . . .
Estar afligido por . . .
Mit etwas gestraft (geplagt) sein.
Essere afflitto da . . .

CURSES

Curses come home to roost. (prov.)
Les malédictions retombent toujours sur ceux qui les lancent.
Las maldiciones recaen sobre la cabeza de quien las profiere.
Wer böse Worte säht, wird Fluch ernten / Wie man in den Wald ruft, so kommt es zurück.
Le maledizioni ricadono sul capo di chi le scaglia.

126

CUT (♥)

To be cut up.
Eprouver une grande douleur.
Estar apesadumbrado.
Tief betrübt sein.
Essere molto addolorato.

His father cut him off without a penny.
Son père lui coupa les vivres.
Su padre no le ha dejado ni un centavo.
Sein Vater hinterliess ihm keinen Pfennig.
Suo padre non gli lasciò un soldo.

To cut one's stick.
Couper la corde.
Poner pies en polvorosa.
Sich aus dem Staub machen / Abhauen.
Tagliare la corda.

(♦) To cut corners. (p. 128)
Prendre le raccourci.
Ir por atajos.
Den Weg abkürzen.
Prendere la scorciatoia.

(♦) To cut someone down to size. (p. 129)
Rabaisser le caquet à quelqu'un.
Quitarle las ínfulas a alguien.
Jemanden demütigen / Jemanden herabsetzen.
Umiliare qualcuno / Ridimensionare qualcuno.

To cut to the quick.
Piquer au vif.
Herir en lo más hondo.
Tief verwunden.
Ferire nel vivo.

To cut the knot.
Débrouiller une affaire.
Cortar por lo sano.
Den Knoten durchhauen (lösen).
Risolvere un problema in modo irregolare ma efficace / Tagliare il nodo / Andare per le spicce.

129

CUTS

This cuts both ways.
C'est une arme à double tranchant.
Esta es un arma de doble filo.
Das ist ein zweischneidiges Schwert.
Questa è un'arma a doppio taglio.

CUTTING

A cutting remark.
Une observation cinglante.
Una observación mordáz.
Eine schneidende Bemerkung / Eine scharfe Bemerkung.
Un'osservazione mordace.

A cutting wind.
Un vent tranchant.
Un viento que corta.
Ein schneidender Wind.
Un vento tagliente.

DAGGERS

To look daggers.
Foudroyer du regard.
Traspasar con la mirada.
Mit Blicken durchbohren.
Fulminare con lo sguardo.

DARK

To keep dark.
Garder secret quelque chose.
Tener en secreto.
Geheimhalten.
Tener segreto.

DASH

I must dash off.
Je dois me sauver.
Tengo que huir.
Ich muss abhauen.
Devo scappare via.

DASHED

His hopes were dashed.
Ses espoirs furent anéantis.
Sus esperanzas han sido frustradas.
Seine Hoffnungen waren vernichtet.
Le sue speranze furono distrutte.

DATE

Up to date.
Moderne / D'actualité.
Al día / De actualidad.
Zeitgemäss / Modern / Auf der Höhe / Aktuell.
Moderno / D'attualità / Aggiornato.

Out of date.
Dépassé.
Anticuado / Desusado.
Unmodern / Veraltet / Überholt.
Fuori moda.

DAUNTED

I was daunted.
Je me sentis découragé.
Me desanimé / Me descorazoné.
Ich war entmutigt / Ich fühlte mich entmutigt.
Mi sentii scoraggiato.

DAWDLE

To dawdle over something.
Faire traîner l'affaire en longueur.
Darle largas a un asunto.
Mit etwas trödeln (bummeln).
Tirare per le lunghe.

DAWNED

It never dawned upon me.
Ça ne m'est jamais venu à l'esprit / Ça ne m'est jamais passé
par la tête.

Ni se me ha asomado por la cabeza.
Es ist mir nie in den Sinn gekommen.
Non mi è mai passato per la testa.

DAY

To live from day to day.
Vivre au jour le jour.
Vivir al día.
Von der Hand in den Mund leben.
Vivere alla giornata.

Every dog has its day.
La fortune sourit parfois même aux plus malheureux / Tôt ou
tard la fortune nous sourit.
Todos tienen su pedacito de cielo.
Jeder hat einmal Glück im Leben.
Qualche volta la fortuna sorride anche ai più disgraziati.

DAYS

In those days.
En ce temps-là.
Por aquellos días.
In jenen Tagen / Damals.
A quei tempi.

DEAD (♦)

What a dead town!
Quelle ville monotone! / Quelle ville morte!
¡Que ciudad más aburrida!
Welch eine tote Stadt!
Che città monotona! / Che città morta!

At dead of night.
Au cœur de la nuit.
En el sigílo de la noche.
Mitten in der Nacht.
Nel cuore della notte.

(♦) A dead cert. (p. 133)
Une chose sûre et certaine.
Algo muy cierto.

Eine todsichere Sache.
Una cosa certa.

It's a dead certainty.
C'est absolument sûr.
De plano es seguro / Es completamente seguro.
Es ist todsicher.
E' assolutamente sicuro.

DEADLOCK

Matters were at a deadlock.
L'affaire était au point mort.
Las cosas estaban en un impasse.
Die Dinge waren an einem toten Punkt angelangt.
Le cose erano ad un punto morto.

DEAF

As deaf as a post. (comp.)
Sourd comme un pot.
Sordo como una campana.
Stocktaub.
Sordo come una campana.

To turn a deaf ear.
Faire la sourde oreille.
Hacer oídos de mercader.
Taub sein gegen.
Far orecchie da mercante.

DEALINGS

These are foul dealings!
Ça c'est une trahison!
¡Esta es una traición!
Das sind faule Geschäfte / Das ist Betrug.
Questo è un tradimento!

DEAR

To run for dear life.
Courir comme s'il en allait de la vie / Courir comme un dératé.

DEFICIENT

Mentally deficient.
Fou / Idiot.
Tonto.
Schwachsinnig.
Mentecatto.

DEGREE

In some degree.
Jusqu'à un certain point.
Hasta cierto punto / De alguna manera.
Bis zu einem gewissen Punkt.
Fino ad un certo punto.

DEGREES

By degrees.
Peu à peu.
Poco a poco / Gradualmente.
Allmählich / Mach und nach / Mit der Zeit.
A poco a poco.

DEMAND

Supply and demand.
L'offre et la demande.
La oferta y la demanda.
Angebot und Nachfrage.
Domanda e offerta.

In great demand.
Très recherché / Très prisé.
De mucha demanda.
In grosser Nachfrage / Sehr gefragt.
Ricercatissimo.

DEVIL (♦)

A devil-may-care manner.
Un air de je-m'en-foutiste.
Un aspecto de fresco.
Eine verwegene Art / Eine freche Art.
Un'aria da « me ne infischio » (da strafottente).

(♦) To be a devil. (p. 139)
Etre un diable.
Ser peor que el diablo.
Ein Teufel sein.
Essere un diavolo.

DIAMOND

A rough diamond.
Le bourru bienfaisant.
Un diamante en bruto / Un hombre brusco pero bueno.
Ein ungeschliffener Mensch / Ein Mensch mit rauher Schale
und gutem Kern.
Un burbero benefico.

DIE

Never say die!
Il ne faut jamais se désespérer!
¡Nunca hay que desalentarse!
Nur nicht verzweifeln! / Kopf hoch!
Non bisogna mai disperarsi!

DYING

I'm dying to . . .
Je meurs d'envie de . . .
No puedo aguantar las ganas de . . .
Ich sterbe für . . . / Ich würde schrecklich gern . . .
Muoio dalla voglia di . . .

DIFFER

We agreed to differ.
Chacun décida de rester sur ses positions.
Decidimos mantener nuestras opiniones personales.
Wir einigten uns dahin, dass jeder seine Meinung behalten
konnte.
Ognuno decise di conservare la propria opinione.

139

DIFFERENCE

To split the difference.
En venir à un compromis.
Llegar a un compromiso.
Einen Kompromiss schliessen.
Venire ad un compromesso.

DIFFERENT

They are as different as day and night. (comp.)
C'est le jour et la nuit.
Son dos cosas completamente diferentes.
Sie sind wie Tag und Nacht.
Sono come il giorno e la notte.

DIGGER

He is a gold-digger.
Il est très intéressé.
Es un interesado.
Er ist ein Opportunist.
E' molto interessato / E' un opportunista.

DIRTY (♦)

(♦) A dirty look. (p. 141)
Un regard vicieux.
Una mirada lujuriosa.
Ein schmutziger Blick / Ein dreckiger Blick.
Uno sguardo da sporcaccione.

DISGRACE

It's no disgrace to be poor.
Ce n'est pas une honte d'être pauvre.
No es vergüenza ser pobre.
Armut ist keine Schande.
Non è una vergogna essere povero.

DISLIKE

To take a dislike to ...
Prendre en antipathie.

Tomar aversión por . . .
Eine Abneigung fassen gegen . . .
Prendere in antipatia.

DISPENSE

I can dispense with your help.
Je peux me dispenser de votre aide.
No me hace falta su ayuda.
Ich kann auf Ihre Hilfe verzichten.
Posso fare a meno del vostro aiuto.

DISPUTE

Beyond all dispute.
C'est incontestable.
Fuera de toda disputa.
Ausser Frage / Zweifellos.
E' incontestabile / E' innegabile.

DISTANCE

To keep one's distance.
Prendre ses distances / Rester à sa place.
Mantener las distancias.
Distanz halten / Den Abstand wahren.
Restare al proprio posto.

DIZZY

He got dizzy.
Il fut pris de vertige.
Está mareado / Le dá vueltas la cabeza.
Ihm wurde schwindelig.
Gli venne il capogiro.

DO

That will do!
Ça suffit!
¡Está bien, suficiente!
Das genügt! / Das reicht! / Genug davon!
Va bene, basta!

To do up.
Remettre à neuf / Moderniser.
Limpiar / Arreglar.
Renovieren / Neu herrichten.
Rimodernare.

To do away with ...
Faire disparaître.
Deshacerse de ...
Beseitigen / Abschaffen.
Far sparire.

To do in someone.
Descendre quelqu'un.
Matar a alguien.
Jemanden beiseite schaffen.
Accoppare qualcuno.

DOCTOR

To doctor oneself.
Se soigner soi-même.
Curarse a sí mismo.
Sich selbst verarzten.
Curarsi da sè.

DOG (♦)

A dog in the manger.
Le chien du jardinier / Un égoïste.
El perro del hortelano no come y no deja comer / El perro del
hortelano, ni come las berzas, ni las deja comer al extraño.
Ein Neidhammel.
Uno stupido egoista.

Let sleeping dogs lie. (prov.)
Ne réveillez pas le chat qui dort.
No hay que buscarle cinco pies al gato.
Schlafende Hunde soll man nicht aufwecken.
Non svegliare il can che dorme.

To go to the dogs.
Etre ruiné / Aller au diable.

Arruinarse / Ir en ruina.
Vor die Hunde gehen.
Andare in malora.

Top dog.
Une grosse légume.
Un pájaro gordo.
Der Überlegene / Der Sieger.
Un pezzo grosso.

To be an under dog.
Etre la dernière roue de la charrette.
Ser la última rueda del engranaje.
Das letzte Rad am Wagen sein.
Essere l'ultima ruota del carro.

Dog does not eat dog. (prov.)
Les loups ne se mangent pas entre eux.
Los lobos no se comen entre ellos.
Eine Krähe hackt der anderen kein Auge aus.
Cane non mangia cane / Fra cani grossi non si mordono.

Every dog has his day. (prov.)
La fortune nous sourit tôt ou tard.
Todos tienen su pedacito de cielo.
Jeder hat einmal Glück im Leben.
Per tutti, prima o poi, viene il giorno della fortuna.

Give a dog an ill name and hang him. (prov.)
La calomnie détruit.
Calumnia y calumnia, siempre algo quedará.
Jemanden auf Grund von Gerüchten verurteilen.
La calunnia uccide.

You can't teach an old dog new tricks. (prov.)
Ce n'est pas au vieux singe qu'on apprend à faire la grimace.
La costumbre es vieja como la historia / Al viejo mañoso nada
le puede cambiar.
Man kann einen alten Hund nicht ändern.
E' difficile cambiare abitudini in vecchiaia.

He is a sly dog!
C'est quelqu'un d'astucieux!
¡Es un zorro!

144

Er ist ein schlauer Fuchs.
E' un tipo astuto!

He is a lucky dog!
C'est quelqu'un qui a de la chance!
¡Es un tipo con mucha suerte!
Er ist ein Glückspilz.
E' un tipo fortunato!

To give to the dogs.
Faire du gaspillage.
Desperdiciar / Malgastar.
Vergeuden. / Zum Fenster hinauswerfen / Perlen vor die Säue werfen.
Buttar via / Sprecare qualcosa / Gettar perle ai porci.

To help a lame dog over a stile.
Secourir quelqu'un dans le besoin.
Ayudar a un amigo sea como sea.
Jemandem in der Not helfen.
Dimostrarsi amico di qualcuno / Soccorrere qualcuno in un momento di bisogno.

(♦) In the dog house. (p. 146)
Etre mis au ban.
Estar en desgracia.
Im Unglück sein.
Essere in disgrazia.

(♦) To lead a dog's life. (p. 679)
Mener une vie de chien.
Hacer una vida de perros.
Ein Hundeleben führen.
Far una vita da cani.

Not to have a dog's chance.
N'avoir aucune chance de s'en sortir.
No tener ninguna posibilidad de salir bien parado.
Keinerlei Aussicht haben.
Non avere nessuna possibilità di successo (nessuna probabilità di cavarsela).

To rain cats and dogs.
Il pleut à verse / Il tombe des cordes.
Llover a cántaros.

In Strömen giessen.
Piovere a dirotto; a catinelle.

To be dogged by misfortune.
Etre poursuivi par la malchance.
Estar perseguido por la mala suerte.
Vom Unglück verfolgt sein.
Essere perseguitato dalla sfortuna.

DOING

The patient is doing well.
Le malade est en voie de guérison.
El paciente está mejorando.
Der Patient ist auf dem Wege der Heilung (Genesung).
L'ammalato è in via di guarigione.

DOINGS

Pretty doings these!
C'est du beau!
¡Qué bueno!
Schöne Sache! / Schöne Geschichte!
Bella roba!

DONE

To have done with ...
En finir avec ...
Terminar con ...
Fertig sein mit ...
Farla finita con ...

We are done for!
Nous sommes perdus!
¡Se acabó! / ¡Es el fín! / ¡Estamos despachados!
Wir sind erledigt (geliefert)!
Siamo spacciati!

DOOR

It will be laid at your door!
Ce sera de votre faute!
¡De ustedes será la culpa!

Es wird Ihre Schuld sein!
La colpa sarà vostra!

To open a door to . . .
Ouvrir la route à . . . / Rendre possible.
Allanar el camino a . . .
Möglich machen / Die Möglichkeit eröffnen zu . . .
Aprire la strada a . . . / Rendere possibile.

DOORNAIL

To be as dead as a doornail. (comp.)
Etre raide mort.
Estar muerto y seco.
Mausetot.
Essere morto stecchito.

To be as deaf as a doornail.
Etre sourd comme un pot.
Ser sordo como una campana.
Stocktaub.
Essere sordo come una campana.

DOT

To dot one's i's and cross one t's.
Etre méticuleux / Etre tatillon / Etre vétilleux.
Ser meticuloso.
Mit dem i-Punkt versehen sein / Peinlich genau sein.
Essere meticoloso; pignolo.

DOTES

She dotes on her children.
Elle adore ses enfants.
Idolatra sus niños.
Sie ist vernarrt in ihre Kinder.
Adora i suoi figli.

DOTTY

He is dotty.
Il est un peu sonné (toqué) / Il est devenu gâteux / Il est
tombé en enfance.

Está sonado / Está loco.
Er ist übergeschnappt / Er ist ein bisschen verrückt.
E' un po' tocco / E' rimbambito.

DOUBLE

To talk double Dutch.
Parler hébreu / Parler charabia / Parler petit nègre.
Hablar en jerigonza / Hablar de manera incomprensible.
Kauderwelsch sprechen / Chinesisch sprechen.
Parlare un gergo incomprensibile / Parlare turco.

DOUBLE-FACED

To be double-faced.
Etre hypocrite.
Ser hipócrita / Ser de doble fondo.
Heuchlerisch (scheinheilig, unaufrichtig) sein / Zwei Gesichter haben.
Essere ipocrita.

DOWN (♦)

To be down on someone.
Traiter très sévèrement quelqu'un.
Ser muy severo con alguien.
Jemanden sehr streng behandeln.
Trattare molto severamente qualcuno.

To send a student down.
Renvoyer un étudiant.
Expulsar un estudiante.
Einen Studenten dispensieren.
Espellere uno studente.

(♦) To be down and out. (p. 150)
Etre épuisé.
Estar exhausto / Estar agotado.
Erledigt (ruiniert) sein.
Essere sfinito (esausto).

To be down on one's luck.
Etre malchanceux.
No tener suerte.
Pech haben.
Essere sfortunato.

To be on the down grade.
Etre en décadence.
Estar en decadencia.
Im Verfall sein / Absteigen / Auf einem absteigenden Ast sitzen.
Essere in decadenza.

To run down . . .
Dire du mal de . . .
Hablar mal de . . . / Hablar barbaridades de . . .
Schlecht sprechen von . . .
Sparlare di . . .

(♦) I'm rather run down. (p. 492)
Je suis un peu las / J'ai les nerfs fatigués.
Me siento deprimido.
Ich bin ziemlich erschöpft (abgespannt).
Ho un po' di esaurimento.

To write it down.
Prendre note.
Tomar nota.
Aufschreiben / Eine Notiz machen.
Prendere un appunto.

To be down in the mouth.
Etre abattu.
Estar descorazonado.
Niedergeschlagen sein.
Essere abbattuto.

DOWNRIGHT

He's a downright scoundrel!
C'est un sacré vaurien! / C'est un sacré chenapan!
¡Es un bribón de pacotilla!
Er ist ein Erzschurke (Schlawiner).
E' un furfante di tre cotte!

151

DOWNS (♦)

(♦) The ups and downs of life. (p. 637)
Les hauts et les bas de la vie.
Las vueltas de la vida.
Das Auf und Ab im Leben / Die Höhne und Tiefen des Lebens.
Gli alti e bassi della vita.

DOZEN

To talk nineteen to the dozen.
Parler sans arrêt.
Hablar sin parar.
Wie ein Buch reden.
Parlare senza tregua / Parlare rapidamente.

DRAW

To draw up a programme.
Se montrer prudent.
Ser prudente.
Vorsichtig sein.
Farsi prudente.

To draw in one's horns.
Mettre sur pied un programme.
Redactar un programa.
Ein Programm aufstellen.
Compilare un programma.

DREGS

To drain the cup of misery to the dregs.
Boire le calice jusqu'à la lie.
Beber la copa hasta la última gota amarga.
Den Unglücksbecher bis zur Neige leeren.
Bere il calice sino all'ultima goccia.

DRINK

To drink to . . .
Boire à la santé de . . . / Trinquer.
Tomar a la salud de . . .

152

Anstossen auf das Wohl von . . .
Bere alla salute di . . .

DRIVE (♦)

To drive crazy.
Devenir fou / Faire tourner en bourrique.
Hacer enloquecer.
Verrückt machen.
Fare impazzire.

(♦) To drive at something. (p. 154)
Mirer à quelque chose.
Tener un objetivo.
Auf etwas gerichtet sein / Auf etwas abzielen.
Mirare a qualcosa.

(♦) To drive someone up the wall. (p. 155)
Faire devenir fou.
Hacer enloquecer a alguien.
Jemanden auf die Palme bringen.
Far impazzire qualcuno.

DROP (♦)

Prices dropped.
Les prix baissèrent.
Los precios bajaron.
Die Preise fielen (sanken).
I prezzi diminuirono.

(♦) To drop in. (p. 156)
Se pointer chez quelqu'un / Entrer chez quelqu'un en passant / Arriver à l'improviste.
Hacer una visíta de improviso.
Einen kurzen Besuch machen.
Fare una visitina / Piombare in casa di qualcuno.

DRUM

To drum a lesson into a boy's head.
Faire entrer une leçon dans la tête d'un enfant à force de rabâchage.

154

Meter una lección en la cabeza de un muchacho.
Einem Jungen eine Lektion einpauken.
Inculcare una lezione in testa a un ragazzo.

DRUNK

As drunk as a lord. (comp.)
Ivre mort.
Estar tan borracho como el aguardiente / Estar muy borracho.
Total blau (betrunken / besoffen).
Ubriaco fradicio.

DRY

As dry as a bone. (comp.)
Très sec.
Tener la garganta seca / Seco como el desierto.
Trocken wie Heu.
Molto asciutto / Secco come un chiodo.

Dry up!
Taisez-vous! Arrête!
¡Cállese! / ¡Basta! / ¡Pare allí!
Hör auf! / Sei still! / Halt die Klappe!
Sta' zitto! / Smettila! / Piantala!

DUCK

To take to something like a duck to water.
Etre à l'aise pour faire quelque chose.
Hacer algo sin ninguna dificultad.
Aus dem Ärmel schütteln.
Fare qualcosa facilmente come bere un bicchiere d'acqua.

DUCKS

To play ducks and drakes with one's money.
Gaspiller son argent.
Malgastar el dinero.
Sein Geld vergeuden.
Sperperare il proprio denaro.

DUDGEON

To be in high dudgeon.
Etre très en colère / Etre vexé.
Estar muy enojado / Sentirse ofendido.
Vor Wut kochen.
Essere molto in collera / Essere offeso.

DUE

Give the devil his due. (prov.)
Il faut savoir reconnaître ce qui est juste.
Dar al diablo lo que le es debido.
Gebt dem Kaiser, was des Kaisers ist.
Date a Cesare quel che è di Cesare.

DULL

As dull as ditchwater.
Ennuyeux à mourir.
Muy aburrido / Tan aburrido como una cabra.
Stinklangweilig.
Estremamente noioso.

DUMPS

To be down in the dumps.
Ne pas avoir le moral.
Estar deprimido.
Niedergeschlagen sein / Trübsinnig sein.
Essere giù di morale (giù di corda).

DUST (♦)

To make the dust fly.
Se donner du mal.
Ponerse a trabajar de veras.
Sich ins Zeug legen.
Darsi da fare.

(♦) To throw dust in someone's eyes. (p. 159)
Embrouiller quelqu'un / Jeter de la poudre aux yeux de quelqu'un.

Taparle los ojos a alguien / Embrollar.
Jemandem Sand in die Augen streuen.
Gettare fumo negli occhi a qualcuno.

DUTY

To be on duty.
Etre de service.
Estar de turno / Estar en servicio.
Dienst haben.
Essere di servizio.

DWELL

Don't let's dwell upon this subject.
N'insistons pas sur ce sujet.
No insistamos sobre este tema.
Lassen Sie uns nicht länger bei diesem Thema verweilen.
Non insistiamo su questo argomento.

DYE

A scoundrel of the deepest dye.
Un vaurien de la pire espèce.
Un pícaro de la peor especie / Un vividor.
Ein Schurke übelster Sorte.
Un furfante della peggiore specie.

EAR (♦)

(♦) To go in one ear and out the other. (p. 161)
Entrer par une oreille et sortir de l'autre.
Entrarle a uno una cosa por un oído y salirle por el otro.
In ein Ohr hineingehen und zum anderen hinaus.
Entrare da un orecchio ed uscire dall'altro.

To turn a deaf ear.
Ne pas prêter attention à . . .
Escuchar solamente por un oído.
Taub sein / Sich taub stellen.
Non dare ascolto / Fare orecchi da mercante.

To send someone on his way with a flea in his ear.
Dire ses quatre vérités à quelqu'un.
Decir una cuantas verdades.
Jemanden zusammenstauchen.
Dire delle verità spiacevoli a qualcuno.

(♦) To have one's ears burning. (p. 163)
Avoir les oreilles qui sifflent.
Arderle a uno los oídos.
In den Ohren pfeifen.
Avere le orecchie che fischiano.

EARLY (♦)

To be an early riser.
Etre matinal.
Ser madrugador.
Ein Frühaufsteher sein.
Essere mattiniero.

An early bird.
Une personne matinale.
Una persona que se levanta muy temprano.
Ein Morgenmensch.
Un tipo mattiniero.

(♦) The early bird gets the worm. (prov.) (p. 164)
Le dernier arrivé est le plus mal servi.
A quien madruga Dios le ayuda.
Morgenstund hat Gold in Mund.
Chi tardi arriva male alloggia.

EARNEST

To be in earnest.
Parler sérieusement.
Hablar en serio.
Ernst sein / Es ernst meinen / Mit Ernst sprechen.
Parlare sul serio.

EARSHOT

Within earshot.
Très près de l'oreille / Collé à l'oreille.

Al alcance del oído.
In Hörweite.
A portata d'orecchio.

EARTH

Why on earth do you say so?
Comment pouvez-vous parler ainsi?
¿Por cual motivo tiene que decir eso?
Warum in aller Welt sagen Sie das.
Perché mai dite così?

EASE

To set at ease.
Rassurer.
Asegurar / Dar por seguro.
Beruhigen.
Rassicurare.

EASY

To take things easy.
Prendre les choses comme elles viennent.
Tomar las cosas como Dios nos las manda.
Dinge leicht nehmen / Sich nicht aufregen.
Prendere il mondo come viene.

As easy as lying. (comp.)
Simple comme bonjour.
Muy fácil / Tan fácil como tomar agua.
Sehr leicht / Kinderleicht / Mühelos.
Facilissimo / Facile come bere un bicchier d'acqua.

As easy as A.B.C. (comp.)
Simple comme bonjour.
Muy fácil / Tan fácil como el A.B.C.
Leicht wie das ABC.
Facile come l'A.B.C.

An easy going father.
Un père coulant.
Un padre muy acondicendiente.
Ein grosszüger Vater.
Un padre di manica larga.

EAT

To eat one's heart out.
Se faire du mauvais sang.
Comerse el hígado / Roerse las entrañas.
Sich aufregen. ·
Rodersi il fegato.

To eat one's words.
Se rétracter / Revenir sur sa promesse.
Tragarse la palabra / Hacerse para atrás.
Seine Worte verschlingen.
Rimangiarsi la parola.

You can't eat your cake and have it. (prov.)
On ne fait pas d'omelette sans casser les œufs.
No es posible obtenerlo todo sin dar nada.
Sie können nur eines von beiden tun (haben) / Man kann nicht
alles haben / Man kann nicht auf zwei Hochzeiten tanzen.
Non si può avere la botte piena e la moglie ubriaca.

EGGS (♦)

To teach one's grandmother to suck eggs.
Apprendre au vieux singe à faire la grimace.
Enseñar a las gallinas a poner huevos.
Den Fischen das Schwimmen beibringen.
Insegnare ai pesci a nuotare / Insegnare ai gatti ad arrampi-
carsi.

(♦) To put all one's eggs in one basket. (p. 167)
Jouer le tout pour le tout / Mettre tous les œufs dans le
même panier.
Jugar el todo por el todo.
Alles auf eine Karte setzen.
Giocare il tutto per tutto.

To egg on.
Inciter.
Incitar.
Anreizen / Anstacheln / Aufhetzen.
Incitare.

166

EKE

To eke out an existence.
Gagner péniblement son pain (sa vie).
Ganar apenas lo suficiente para vivir / Ganarse apenas la vida.
Sich kümmerlich durchschlagen.
Guadagnarsi a stento la vita.

ELBOW

To have elbow room.
Ne pas avoir les mains liées.
Tener suficiente espacio para moverse.
Ellenbogenfreiheit haben.
Avere spazio per muoversi.

ELBOWS

Out at elbows.
Qui a des difficultés financières.
Estar en una situación difícil.
Schäbig / Heruntergekommen.
In dissesto.

EMERGENCY

In an emergency.
En cas de nécessité.
En una emergencia.
Im Notfall / Notfalls.
In caso di necessità; di emergenza.

EMOTIONAL

To be emotional.
Etre émotif / Etre impressionable.
Ser emotivo / Ser emocionable.
Emotional (gefühlsbetont) sein.
Essere impressionabile.

EMPTY

Empty-headed!
Ecervelé! / Idiot!

¡Bobo! / ¡Tonto! / ¡Cabezahueca!
Hohlköpfig.
Sciocco! / Testa vuota!

END (♦)

To be at the end of one's tether.
Etre à bout de patience.
Estar al límite de las propias capacidades / Estar al límite de
la paciencia.
Am Ende seiner Kräfte (oder Geduld) sein / Sich nicht mehr
zu helfen wissen.
Essere al limite delle proprie capacità; della propria pazienza.

(♦) To have one's hair stand on end. (p. 253)
Faire se dresser les cheveux sur sa tête.
Erizarsele a uno el pelo en la cabeza.
Einen Schock versetzen.
Far rizzare a uno i capelli.

To be at one's wits' end.
Ne savoir que faire.
No saber que hacer.
Mit seiner Weisheit zu Ende sein / Sich nicht mehr zu helfen
wissen.
Non sapere più che pesci pigliare.

This is an end of the matter!
Qu'on en finisse!
¡El argumento se ha agotado! / ¡No volvamos sobre lo mismo! /
¡Qué no se hable más de lo mismo!
Schluss mit der Sache!
Non se ne parli più!

He has no end of friends.
Il a un tas d'amis.
Tiene un montón de amigos / Tiene muchos amigos.
Er hat eine Unmenge von Freunden.
Ha un'infinità di amici.

(♦) The end of the line! (p. 170)
C'est la fin!
¡Es el fín!
Das ist das Ende!
E' la fine!

ENDS

To the ends of the earth.
Jusqu'au bout du monde.
Hasta el pico del mundo / Hasta el culo del mundo.
Bis ans Ende der Welt.
Fino in capo al mondo.

To make both ends meet.
Equilibrer la balance.
Igualar el balance.
Mit seinem Geld auskommen.
Pareggiare il bilancio.

ENGLISH

I told him in plain English.
Je le lui ai dit clair et net.
Se lo dije claro y tendido.
Ich sagte ihm klar und deutlich (Klipp und klar).
Glielo dissi chiaro e tondo.

ENOUGH

That's enough!
Ça suffit!
¡Es suficiente! / ¡Estoy hasta aquí de eso!
Das genügt / Schluss damit!
Basta!

Enough is as good as a feast. (prov.)
Ni trop, ni trop peu.
Mejor lo suficiente que lo demasiado.
Allzuviel ist ungesund.
La giusta misura è meglio del troppo.

ENTERTAIN

To entertain a lot.
Recevoir beaucoup.
Tener muchas reuniones en casa.
Viele Gäste empfangen.
Ricevere molto.

ENTITLED

I'm entitled to this money.
Cet argent me revient de droit.
Tengo derecho a este dinero.
Ich habe Anspruch auf dieses Geld.
Ho diritto a questo denaro.

ESCAPE

To have a narrow escape.
L'échapper belle.
Salvarse por milagro / Salvarse por un pelo.
Mit knapper Not entkommen.
Scamparla per miracolo.

ESTRANGED

To become estranged.
Ne plus être amis.
Distanciarse de un amigo / No relacionarse más con alguien.
Sich abwenden von . . .
Non essere più amici.

EVEN

To break even.
Terminer à égalité.
Empatar con alguien.
Ohne Gewinn (oder Verlust) abschliessen.
Finire alla pari.

To get even with somebody.
Régler les comptes / Se venger de quelqu'un.
Estar empatados con alguien / Vengarse de alguien.
Mit jemandem abrechnen / Sich rächen.
Pareggiare i conti con qualcuno / Vendicarsi.

EVENTS

At all events.
En tout cas.
De cualquier manera / De todos modos.
Auf alle Fälle / Jedenfalls.
In ogni caso.

172

EVERY

Every now and then.
De temps en temps.
De vez en cuando.
Gelegentlich / Hin und wieder.
Di quando in quando.

EVIDENCE

To give evidence.
Témoigner.
Atestiguar.
Bezeugen / Als Zeuge aussagen.
Testimoniare.

EXCEPTION

The exception proves the rule.
L'exception confirme la règle.
La excepción confirma la regla.
Die Ausnahme bestätigt die Regel.
L'eccezione conferma la regola.

EXERCISE

To take exercise.
Se mettre un peu en mouvement / Faire un peu d'exercice.
Hacer un poco de ejercicio.
Sich Bewegung machen.
Fare un po' di moto.

EXHIBITION (♦)

(♦) To make an exhibition of oneself. (p. 174)
Se rendre ridicule.
Hacer el ridículo.
Sich lächerlich machen / Sich zum Gespött machen.
Rendersi ridicolo.

EXTENT

To a certain extent.
Jusqu'à un certain point.

173

Hasta cierto punto.
Bis zu einem gewissen Grade.
Fino ad un certo punto.

EXISTENCE

To lead a wretched existence.
Avoir une vie malheureuse.
Llevar una vida infelíz.
Ein kümmerliches Dasein führen.
Condurre una vita infelice.

EXTRA

No extras.
Tout compris.
Sin extras.
Keine Nebenkosten / Alles eingeschlossen (inbegriffen).
Tutto compreso.

EXTRAORDINARY

How very extraordinary!
Comme c'est étrange!
¡Es muy extraño!
Seltsam / Merkwürdig! / Wie ungewöhnlich!
Stranissimo!

A man of extraordinary genius.
Un homme d'une rare intelligence.
Un hombre de genio extraordinario.
Ein Mann von ungewöhnlicher Begabung.
Un uomo di rara intelligenza.

EXTRAVAGANCY

His wife's extravagancy ruined him.
La prodigalité de sa femme le mena à la ruine.
Las extravagancias de su mujer lo llevaron a la ruina.
Die Verschwendungssucht seiner Frau ruinierte ihn.
La prodigalità di sua moglie lo mandò in rovina.

EYE (♦)

(♦) To see eye to eye with somebody. (p. 677)
Etre parfaitement d'accord avec quelqu'un.
Estar perfectamente de acuerdo con alguien.
Mit jemandem übereinstimmen.
Essere perfettamente d'accordo con qualcuno.

An eye for an eye and a tooth for a tooth. (prov.)
Œil pour œil, dent pour dent.
Ojo por ojo, diente por diente.
Auge um Auge, Zahn um Zahn.
Occhio per occhio e dente per dente.

EYES (♦)

(♦) To be up to one's eyes in work. (p. 177)
Avoir beaucoup à faire / Avoir du travail par-dessus la tête.
Tener mucho que hacer.
Ich bin bis zum Kopf in Arbeit / Bis über die Ohren in Arbeit
stecken.
Essere molto indaffarato.

FACE (♦)

To put a good face on.
Faire contre mauvaise fortune bon cœur.
Poner cara de contento aunque la situación no sea favorable.
Gute Miene zum bösen Spiel machen.
Far buon viso a cattivo gioco.

(♦) To face the music. (p. 178)
Affronter avec courage un danger, une situation difficile.
Encararse al peligro o a una situación difícil.
Der Gefahr ins Auge sehen.
Affrontare coraggiosamente un pericolo (una situazione dif-
ficile).

To set one's face against ...
S'opposer résolument à ...
Oponerse con resolución.
Sich widersetzen / Sich wenden gegen ...
Opporsi risolutamente a ...

178

FACES

To make faces.
Faire des grimaces.
Hacer caras / Hacer muecas.
Fratzen schneiden.
Fare smorfie.

FACT

In point of fact.
A vrai dire.
A decir verdad.
In der Tat / Tatsächlich / Eigentlich / Offen gesagt.
A dire il vero.

FACTS

The facts of life.
Les faits se rapportant à la vie sexuelle.
Lo que es la vida (sexual).
Die die Sexualität betreffenden / Tatsachen des Lebens.
I fatti riguardanti la vita sessuale.

FAGGED

To be fagged out.
Etre épuisé.
Estar. agotado.
Erschöpft sein / Kaputt sein.
Essere sfinito.

FAINT

To feel faint.
Se sentir défaillir.
Sentirse desfallecer.
Sich matt fühlen.
Sentirsi venir meno.

I haven't the faintest idea.
Je n'en ai pas la moindre idée.
No tengo la mínima idéa.
Ich habe nicht die geringste (leiseste) Ahnung.
Non ne ho la più pallida idea.

He was faint with hunger.
La faim l'avait épuisé (diminué).
Él estaba extenuado por el hambre.
Er war schwach vor Hunger.
Era stremato per la fame.

Faint heart never won fair lady.
Une personne timide n'aura jamais de succès.
El que es timido no triunfa en la vida.
Wer nicht wagt, gewinnt nicht.
Un timido non avrà mai successo.

FAIR

As fair as a rose. (comp.)
Fraîche comme une rose / Très belle.
Hermosa como una rosa.
Wunderschön.
Bella come un fiore.

By fair means or foul.
De gré ou de force.
Por las buenas o por las malas.
Entweder oder.
Per amore o per forza.

A fair-weather friend.
Amitié passagère.
Un amigo que voltea las espaldas cuando las cosas no van
bien / Amigo de buenos tiempos, la lluvia se lo lleva.
Ein Freund im Glück.
Amico finché dura la fortuna.

All's fair in love and war. (prov.)
En amour comme à la guerre tout est permis.
Todo está permitido en la guerra y en el amor.
In Liebe und Krieg ist alles gestattet.
In amore e in guerra tutto è lecito.

FALL

To fall in love.
Tomber amoureux.
Enamorarse.

180

Sich verlieben (verknallen).
Innamorarsi.

A fall in prices.
Une baisse des prix.
Una caída de los precios.
Ein Fallen der Preise / Ein Preissturz.
Un ribasso dei prezzi.

To fall out.
En venir aux mots.
Enfrentarse a palabras.
Ausfallend sein.
Venir a parole.

To fall short of . . .
Etre inférieur à . . .
Ser inferior a . . . / Ser menos de . . .
Zurückbleiben hinter . . . / Nachstehen.
Essere inferiore a . . .

To fall ill.
Tomber malade.
Enfermarse.
Erkranken.
Ammalarsi / Cadere ammalato.

He has nobody to fall back upon.
Il n'a personne sur qui compter.
No tiene a nadie a quien recurrir / No tiene donde caer muerto.
Er hat niemanden, auf den er zurückgreifen kann.
Non ha nessuno a cui ricorrere.

FALSE
To sail under false colours.
Passer pour ce que l'on n'est pas / Se montrer sous un mauvais jour.
Hacerse pasar por lo que no se es / Mostrarse pavo siendo gallina.
Unter falscher Flagge segeln / Sich für jemanden ausgeben, der man nicht ist.
Spacciarsi per quello che non si è.

FAMILIAR

To be on familiar terms with someone.
Etre familier avec quelqu'un / Etre en bons termes.
Tener relaciones de confianza con alguien.
Mit jemandem gut bekannt sein / Gut kennen.
Avere familiarità con qualcuno / Essere in confidenza con qualcuno.

To be too familiar.
Avoir trop de familiarités.
Ser demasiado confianzudo / Ser muy abusivo.
Zu familiär sein / Zu sehr vertraulich sein.
Prendersi troppa confidenza.

FAMILIARITY

Familiarity breeds contempt. (prov.)
L'excès de familiarité nuit au respect.
Si no se toman las distancias debidas, se pierde el respecto de los demás.
Übermässige Vertrautheit (plumpe Vertraulichkeit) erzeugt Respektlosigkeit.
Confidenza toglie riverenza / L'eccessiva familiarità fa perdere il rispetto.

FAMISHING

To be famishing.
Avoir une faim de loup.
Estar famélico / Tener un hambre de lobos.
Heisshunger haben.
Avere una fame da lupo.

FAMOUSLY

To get on famously.
Faire de grands progrès.
Progresar mucho.
Riesige Fortschritte machen / Ausgezeichnet vorankommen.
Fare grandissimi progressi.

182

FAN

To fan the fire.
Souffler sur le feu / Attiser le feu.
Soplar sobre el fuego / Dar leña al fuego.
Das Feuer anfachen (anschüren).
Soffiare sul fuoco.

FANCY

Fancy that!
Ça alors!
¡Qué raro!
Stell Dir vor! / Nicht zu glauben!
Ma guarda un po'!

I don't fancy this salmon.
Ce saumon ne m'inspire pas (confiance).
Este salmón no me gusta / Ésto me huele mal.
Dieser Lachs gefällt mir nicht.
Questo salmone non m'ispira fiducia.

To take a fancy to someone.
Prendre quelqu'un en sympathie.
Simpatizar con . . . / Gustarse mutuamente.
Gefallen finden an . . . / Schwärmen für . . .
Prendere in simpatia qualcuno.

FAR

A far away look.
Un regard lointain.
Una mirada ausente.
Ein abwesender Blick.
Uno sguardo assente.

From far and wide.
De tous les côtés.
De todas partes.
Von weit und breit.
Da tutte le parti.

Far from beautiful.
Loin d'être belle.
Lejos de ser bella.

Alles andere als schön.
Tutt'altro che bella / Ben lungi dall'esser bella.

To be a far cry from . . .
Il y a une belle différence.
Existir una buena diferencia.
Weit entfernt sein von . . .
Esserci una bella differenza.

So far so good.
Jusque là ça va.
Hasta aquí todo bien.
So weit, so gut.
Fin qui va bene.

FAST

To play fast and loose.
Hésiter / Ne pas savoir sur quel pied danser.
Jugar a las escondidas / Ganar tiempo.
Zeit schinden / Verzögern.
Fare a tira e molla.

Hard and fast rules.
Règlements sévères.
Reglas muy rígidas.
Strenge und starre Regeln.
Regolamenti rigidi.

A fast girl.
Une fille frivole.
Una muchacha ligéra.
Ein leichtes Mädchen.
Una ragazza poco seria.

Fast bind, fast find. (prov.)
Méfiance est mère de sûreté.
Confiar es bueno, no confiarse es mejor.
Vertrauen ist gut, Misstrauen ist besser.
Fidarsi è bene, non fidarsi è meglio.

FAT

As fat as a porpoise. (comp.)
Gros comme une vache.

Gordo como un tonél.
Fett wie ein Schwein.
Molto grasso (di persona).

As fat as butter. (comp.)
Très gras.
Gordo como la manteca.
Fett wie Öl.
Molto grasso (di condimento).

As fat as a pig. (comp.)
Gras comme un porc.
Gordo como un cerdo.
Fett wie ein Schwein.
Grasso come un maiale.

FATE

As sure as fate. (comp.)
Très sûr.
Absolutamente seguro.
Ganz sicher.
Certissimo.

FAT-HEAD

Fat-head.
Têtu / Tête dure.
Cabeza de aserrín.
Dickkopf / Sturer Kopf.
Zuccone / Testa dura.

FATHOM

I cannot fathom his meaning.
Je n'arrive pas à saisir le sens de ses mots.
No logro comprender lo que quiere decir.
Ich verstehe nicht, was er meint.
Non riesco a cogliere il significato delle sue parole.

FAULT

Generous to a fault.
Généreux jusqu'à l'excès.

Generoso hasta el exceso / Tan generoso que pierde hasta la camisa.
Bis zum Übermass grosszügig.
Generoso fino all'eccesso.

FAULT-FINDER

Fault-finder.
Critiqueur.
Criticón.
Besserwisser / Nörgler / Meckerer.
Criticone.

FAVOUR

To curry favour with someone.
Etre dans les bonnes grâces de quelqu'un.
Ganarse los favores de alguien.
Sich bei jemandem lieb Kind machen.
Entrare nelle grazie di qualcuno.

FEASTED

He feasted his eyes on her.
Il la dévorait des yeux.
Se la comía con los ojos.
Er frisst sie mit seinen Augen auf.
Se la divorava con gli occhi.

FEATHER

To show the white feather.
Se montrer vil.
Demostrarse cobarde.
Sich feig zeigen.
Mostrarsi vile.

Birds of a feather.
Gens de la même espèce.
Génte de la misma especie / Génte de igual calaña.
Leute gleicher Art / Gleich und gleich.
Gente della stessa sorta (risma).

FED

To be fed up.
En avoir assez.
Estar cansado de . . . (una situación, de una persona).
Satt haben / Die Nase voll haben.
Essere stufo / Averne abbastanza / Non poterne più.

FEEL

I feel sorry for you.
Je vous plains.
Lo siento por tí.
Ich habe Mitgfühl mit Ihnen / Ich bedauere Sie.
Vi compiango.

I don't feel quite myself.
Je ne me sens pas bien.
No me siento muy bien.
Ich bin nicht auf dem Posten.
Non mi sento troppo bene.

FEELINGS

She hurt my feelings.
Elle blessa mon amour-propre / Elle me vexa.
Ella lastimó mis sentimientos.
Sie verletzte meine Gefühle.
Mi offese.

FELLOW

A jolly good fellow.
Un bon petit diable.
Un buen diablo.
Ein prima Kerl.
Un buon diavolo.

FENCE

To sit on the fence.
Rester neutre.
Permanecer neutral / No tomar partido.
Sich abwartend (neutral) verhalten.
Rimanere neutrale.

FEND

To fend off a blow.
Parer un coup.
Parar un golpe.
Einen Schlag abwenden.
Parare un colpo.

FERRET

To ferret out.
Arracher un secret avec habileté.
Escudriñar / Buscar hasta el minimo detalle.
Herausfinden.
Strappare abilmente un segreto a qualcuno.

FEW

A good few people.
Pas mal de gens.
Un buen número de gente.
Eine ganze Menge Leute.
Un bel po' di gente.

FIDDLESTICKS

Fiddlesticks!
Des blagues!
¡Son mentiras! / ¡Son cuentos!
`Unsinn! / Blödsinn! / Quatsch!
Frottole!

FIERCE

As fierce as a tiger.
Féroce comme un lion.
Feroz como un tígre.
Wild wie ein Tiger.
Molto feroce / Feroce come una tigre.

FIFTY

To go 50-50.
Chacun paye sa part / Faire « fifty-fifty ».

188

Pagar a mitad / Hacer a mitades.
Halb und halb machen.
Pagare metà per uno.

FIGURE

To keep one's figure.
Garder la ligne / Tenir la ligne.
Mantener la línea.
Seine Figur halten / Schlank bleiben.
Conservare la linea.

To figure out a problem.
Résoudre un problème.
Resolver un problema.
Ein Problem lösen.
Risolvere un problema.

To cut a brilliant figure.
Bien figurer / Avoir de la prestance.
Hacer un buen papel.
Einen guten Eindruck machen / Eine gute Figur abgeben.
Fare una bella figura.

To cut a poor figure.
Faire piètre figure.
Hacer un mal papel.
Eine traurige Figur abgeben.
Fare una brutta figura.

A figure of speech.
Une figure réthorique.
Una imágen retórica / Una imágen metafórica / Figura de dicción.
Eine Redewendung.
Una figura retorica.

FILL

To cry one's fill.
Pleurer toutes les larmes de son corps / Pleurer à chaudes larmes.
Llorar todas las lagrimas que le han quedado a uno.
Sich ausweinen.
Piangere tutte le proprie lacrime.

To have one's fill of bad luck.
Avoir sa part de malchance.
Tener la mala suerte que le corresponde a uno.
Genug vom Unglück haben.
Avere la propria parte di sfortuna.

To eat one's fill.
Manger à satiété.
Comer hasta saciarse.
Sich satt essen.
Mangiare a sazietà.

FIND

To find fault with . . .
Trouver à redire.
Criticar a . . .
Etwas auszusetzen haben an . . . / Nörgeln.
Trovare da ridire su qualcosa (o con qualcuno).

I've found you out!
Je t'ai pris sur le fait!
¡Te he descubierto!
Ich habe dich ertappt (entlarvt).
Ti ho colto in fallo!

FINGERS

He's all fingers and thumbs!
Il est maladroit!
¡Es torpe! / ¡Es chambón!
Er ist ungeschickt / Er hat zwei linke Hände.
E' maldestro!

My fingers itch.
Je suis impatient / Les doigts me démangent.
Estoy impaciente / Me arden los pies por la impaciencia.
Es juckt mir (mich) in den Fingern.
Sono impaziente / Mi prudono le dita.

I'll cross my fingers for you!
Bonne chance!
¡Buena suerte!

Ich werde Ihnen die Daumen drücken / Hals- und Beinbruch! /
Viel Glück!
In bocca al lupo! / Buona fortuna!

FIRE

There's no smoke without fire. (prov.)
Il n'y a pas de fumée sans feu.
No hay humo sin fuego.
Kein Rauch ohne Feuer.
Non c'è fumo senza arrosto.

To pour oil on the fire.
Souffler sur le feu / Jeter de l'huile sur le feu / Fomenter
des discordes.
Promover discordias / Echar leña al fuego.
Öl ins Feuer giessen.
Soffiare sul fuoco / Fomentare discordie.

To set the Thames on fire.
Faire une chose extraordinaire.
Hacer algo sensacional.
Eine sensationelle Sache machen.
Fare una cosa sensazionale.

Out of the frying pan into the fire.
Tomber de Charybde en Scylla.
De la sartén a las brazas.
Aus dem Regen in die Traufe.
Dalla padella nella brace.

FIRM

As firm as a rock. (comp.)
Solide comme un roc.
Sólido como una roca.
Hart (stark) wie ein Felsen.
Molto solido / Saldo come una roccia.

FIRST

A first-rate show.
Un spectacle de premier ordre.
Un espectáculo de primera clase.

Eine erstklassige Aufführung.
Uno spettacolo di prim'ordine.

First and foremost.
Avant tout.
Antes que nada.
Zu allererst / Vor allem.
Prima di tutto.

FISH (♦)

(♦) A queer fish. (p. 193)
Une personne étrange / Un drôle de type!
Una persona muy rara.
Ein komischer Kauz.
Una strana persona.

(♦) To feel like a fish out of water. (p. 194)
Se sentir comme un poisson hors de l'eau.
Sentirse como un pez fuera del agua.
Nicht im eigenen Element sein.
Sentirsi come un pesce fuor d'acqua.

I have better fish to fry.
J'ai mieux à faire.
Tengo algo mejor que hacer.
Ich habe Besseres zu tun.
Ho di meglio da fare.

All's fish that comes to his net.
Pour lui tout est bon.
Para él todo es bueno.
Er nimmt unbesehen alles (mit) / Ihm ist alles recht.
Per lui tutto va bene.

As drunk as a fish. (comp.)
Ivre mort.
Borracho perdido.
Stockbesoffen.
Ubriaco fradicio.

I've another fish to fry.
Avoir d'autres chats à fouetter.

Tengo otros problemas que resolver / Ya tengo suficientes problemas.
Ich habe Wichtigeres zu tun.
Ho un'altra gatta da pelare.

(♦) **A pretty kettle of fish!** (p. 196)
Une belle salade! / Un beau gâchis!
¡Es un buen lío!
Eine schöne Bescherung!
Un bel pasticcio!

FISHY

A fishy business.
Une affaire louche.
Un asunto sospechoso.
Ein faules Geschäft / Ein anrüchiges Geschäft.
Un affare sospetto.

FIT

A fit of anger.
Un excès de colère.
Un arrebato de cólera.
Ein Wutanfall.
Uno scatto d'ira.

As fit as a fiddle. (comp.)
Etre en parfaite santé.
Sano como un pez.
Kerngesund / Frisch wie ein Fisch.
Sano come un pesce.

FITS

By fits and starts.
Par à-coups.
A sobresaltos / Espasmódicamente.
Stossweise / Ruckweise / Nach und nach.
A sbalzi.

FIX

To fix something up.
Fixer quelque chose.

Establecer algo / Arreglar algo.
Etwas festsetzen (arrangieren).
Stabilire qualche cosa.

To fix on something.
Se décider pour quelque chose.
Decidirse por algo.
Sich für etwas entscheiden.
Decidersi per qualche cosa.

FIZZLED

His enthusiasm fizzled out.
Son enthousiasme s'évanouit.
Su entusiasmo desapareció de improviso.
Seine Begeisterung verpuffte.
Il suo entusiasmo si dileguò.

FLAIR

To have a flair for music.
Avoir un penchant pour la musique.
Tener disposición para la música / Tener oído para la música.
Eine Begabung für Musik haben.
Essere portato per la musica.

FLARE

To flare up.
Se mettre en colère.
Enojarse / Enfurecerse.
Aufbrausen / Platzen.
Andare in collera.

FLASHED

It flashed across my mind.
Cela me sauta à l'esprit.
Se me vino a la mente como un relámpago.
Es schoss mir durch den Kopf.
Mi balenò per la mente.

197

FLASHY

A flashy suit.
Un habit voyant.
Un vestido llamativo.
Ein auffälliges Kleid.
Un vestito appariscente.

FLAT

As flat as a pancake. (comp.)
Plat comme une sole.
Aplastado como una tortilla.
Flach wie ein Brett.
Completamente schiacciato / Piatto.

As flat as a board.
Plat comme une planche.
Aplastado como una tortilla.
Platt wie ein Brett.
Completamente schiacciato / Piatto.

To fall flat.
Faire « fiasco » / Echouer.
Fracasar.
Ein Fiasko erleben.
Far fiasco.

FLATLY

To flatly refuse.
Refuser catégoriquement.
Rehusarse absolutamente.
Eine glatte Absage geben.
Rifiutare nettamente.

FLEA

(♦) A flea in someone's ear (p. 199)
La puce à l'oreille / Un reproche.
Un reproche.
Ein Floh im Ohr.
Una pulce nell'orecchio / Un rimprovero.

FLEECE

To fleece someone of all his money.
Dépouiller quelqu'un de son argent.
Despojar a alguien de todo su dinero / Estafar a alguien.
Jemanden um sein ganzes Geld bringen.
Spogliare qualcuno di tutto il suo denaro.

FLEECED

I was fleeced at the market.
Je me suis fait plumer au marché.
Me trasquilaron al mercado / Me han quitado todo mi dinero al mercado.
Ich wurde auf dem Markt geschröpft (ausgenommen).
Mi hanno pelato al mercato.

FLEET

As fleet as a deer. (comp.)
Très agile / Etre comme une gazelle.
Tan ágil como una liebre / Tan ágil como un mono.
Flink wie ein Wiesel.
Molto agile / Agile come una gazzella.

FLESH

A flesh wound.
Une blessure superficielle.
Una herida superficial.
Eine Fleischwunde / Eine leichte Wunde.
Una ferita superficiale.

FLEW

The door flew open.
La porte s'ouvrit subitement.
La puerta se abrió de improviso.
Die Tür flog auf.
La porta si spalancò!

FLINT

To skin a flint.
Demander une chose impossible.
Pelar una piedra / Sacar agua del desierto.
Ein Pfenningfuchser sein / Geizig sein.
Cavar sangue da una rapa.

FLOAT (♦)

(♦) To float around. (p. 202)
Vadrouiller.
Holgazanear / Vagar.
Bummeln.
Bighellonare.

FLUSTER

To be all in a fluster.
Etre excité.
Estar excitado.
Ganz verwirrt sein.
Essere tutto eccitato.

FLY (♦)

To let fly at a person.
Lui en dire des vertes et des pas mûres / Lui en dire de toutes les couleurs.
Lanzarse verbalmente contra de una persona / Sacarle a una persona los paños al sol.
Mit einer Person grob werden / Den Kopf waschen / In Wut geraten.
Dirne un sacco e una sporta a una persona.

To fly into a rage.
Etre dans une rage folle.
Enfurecerse / Dejarse ir en escandecencias.
Wütend werden.
Andare su tutte le furie.

(♦) I must fly! (p. 203)
Je dois me sauver!
¡Tengo que irme!

Ich muss fliehen! / Ich muss weg.
Devo scappare! / Devo volare!

FOGEY

An old fogey.
Un vieux fossile.
Un viejo fósil / Una persona fosilizada.
Ein alter Spiesser / Ein komischer Kauz.
Una vecchia fossile.

FOGGIEST

I haven't the foggiest.
Je n'ai pas la moindre idée.
No tengo la mínima idea.
Es ist mir schleierhaft.
Non ho la minima idea.

FOND

I'm fond of music.
J'aime la musique.
Soy un amante de la música.
Ich liebe Musik / Ich schwärme für Musik.
Sono amante della musica.

FONDEST

My fondest wish.
Mon plus cher désir.
Mi más ardiente deseo.
Mein brennenster Wunsch.
Il mio più ardente desiderio.

FOOD

To be off one's food.
Souffrir d'inappétence.
No tener hambre / Ser anoréxico.
An Appetitlosigkeit leiden.
Soffrire d'inappetenza.

FOOL (♦)

To make a fool of somebody.
Se moquer de quelqu'un.
Burlarse de alguien.
Jemanden zum Narren halten / Jemanden auf den Arm nehmen.
Prendere in giro qualcuno.

A fool's bolt is soon shot. (prov.)
Les personnes stupides ont peu de flèches à leur arc.
El tonto tarde o temprano viene cazado.
Dummheit entblösst sich selbst.
Gli sciocchi hanno poche frecce al loro arco.

(♦) To play the fool. (p. 206)
Faire le fou / Faire l'imbécile.
Hacerse el loco.
Den Narren spielen / Verrückt spielen.
Fare il matto / Fare lo scemo.

Man is a fool, or a physician at thirty. (prov.)
Un homme sensé n'a pas besoin de médecin.
El hombre sabio es médico de si mismo.
Ein Mann mit Verstand braucht keinen Arzt.
Un uomo assennato non ha bisogno di medico.

To fool one's time away.
Gâcher le temps.
Botar el propio tiempo.
Seine Zeit vertrödeln.
Sciupare il proprio tempo.

There's no fool like an old fool. (prov.)
Il n'y a pas de pire sourd que celui qui ne veut pas entendre.
El peor loco es aquél con experiencia.
Es gibt keinen schlimmeren Narren als einen alten Narren.
Non c'è peggior pazzo di un vecchio pazzo.

FOOL'S

A fool's paradise.
Un bonheur éphémère.
Una felicidad ilusoria.

206

Ein Wolkenkuckucksheim / Eine Illusion.
Una felicità illusoria.

FOOT (♦)

(♦) **To have one foot in the grave.** (p. 243)
Avoir un pied dans la tombe.
Tener un pie en la tumba.
Mit einem Fuss im Grabe stehen.
Avere un piede nella fossa.

(♦) **To put one's foot down.** (p. 208)
S'arc-bouter / Se buter / S'entêter.
Puntar los pies.
Energisch werden / Ein Machtwort sprechen.
Puntare i piedi / Impuntarsi / Intestardirsi.

To put one's foot in it.
Faire une gaffe.
Meter la pata.
Sich danebenbenehmen / Ins Fettnäpfchen treten.
Fare una « gaffe ».

(♦) **To start off on the wrong foot.** (p. 209)
Partir du mauvais pied.
Comenzar mal.
Schlecht beginnen (anfangen).
Cominciare male.

FORBIDDEN

Forbidden fruit.
Fruit interdit.
Fruto prohibido.
Verbotene Frucht.
Frutto proibito.

FORCE

The laws in force.
Les lois en vigueur.
Las leyes vigentes.
Die gültigen Gesetze / Die Gesetze in Kraft.
Le leggi vigenti.

THIS TIME I'M PUTTING MY FOOT DOWN

FORGIVING

He has a forgiving nature.
Il est toujours prêt à pardonner.
Él está siempre dispuesto a perdonar / Es muy elástico.
Er hat einen versöhnlichen Charakter.
E' sempre disposto a perdonare.

FORK

To fork out the money.
Débourser de l'argent.
Desembolsar dinero.
Das Geld herausrücken.
Sborsare il denaro.

FORM

To lose one's form.
Perdre la forme.
Perder la propia forma.
Nicht in Form sein.
Andare giù di forma.

FORMAL

To be formal.
Etre cérémonieux.
Ser formal.
Förmlich sein / Formell sein.
Essere cerimonioso.

FORTE

French is my forte.
Le français est mon fort.
El francés es mi fuerte.
Französisch ist meine Stärke.
Il francese è il mio forte.

FORTUNE

To have one's fortune told.
Etre réprimandé.

210

Ser regañado.
Gescholten werden.
Essere rimproverato.

A fortune-hunter.
Un chasseur de dotes.
Un cazador de fortunas.
Ein Mitgiftjäger.
Un cacciatore di dote.

To spend a small fortune.
Dépenser un capital.
Gastarse una fortuna.
Ein kleines Vermögen ausgeben.
Spendere un capitale.

FORTY
To have 40 winks.
Faire un somme.
Hacer una siesta.
Ein Nickerchen machen.
Fare un sonnellino.

FOX
A sly old fox.
Un vieux renard.
Un viejo zorro / Un viejo taimado.
Ein schlauer Fuchs / Ein alter Fuchs.
Un vecchio volpone.

FRAME
To frame somebody.
Faire tomber quelqu'un dans le piège.
Meterle la zancadilla a alguien / Engañar a alguien.
Jemandem eine Falle stellen.
Far cadere qualcuno in un tranello.

FREE
To make free with something.
Prendre des libertés / Faire quelque chose qui n'est pas permis.

Usar algo abusivamente.
Sich die Freiheit herausnehmen, etwas zu benutzen.
Usare qualcosa senza permesso.

As free as the air. (comp.)
Libre comme l'air.
Libre como los pájaros.
Frei wie ein Vogel.
Libero come l'aria; come un uccello.

To be free with one's money.
Prodiguer son argent.
Ser pródigo con el dinero.
Freigebig sein.
Essere prodigo (del proprio denaro).

Free and easy.
Désinvolte.
Desenvuelto.
Ungeniert / Zwanglos / Ungezwungen.
Disinvolto.

FREEZE

To freeze somebody's blood.
Glacer le sang à quelqu'un.
Helarsele a uno la sangre de las venas.
Jemandem das Blut in den Adern erstarren lassen.
Far gelare il sangue a qualcuno.

FRENCH

To take French leave.
Couper la corde.
Huir.
Sich französisch empfehlen.
Tagliare la corda.

FRIEND

A friend in need is a friend indeed. (prov.)
C'est dans le besoin qu'on reconnaît un ami.
Un amigo en la necesidad es un amigo para siempre.
Den Freund erkennt man in der Not.
L'amico si conosce nel bisogno.

212

FRIGHT

He's a regular fright.
Il est laid comme un pou.
Es feo como nadie.
Er ist hässlich wie eine Vogelscheuche / Er ist ein richtiges Scheusal.
E' brutto da fare spavento.

FRO

To go to and fro.
Monter et descendre.
Ir de un lado para otro.
Hin und her gehen / Auf und ab gehen.
Andare su e giù / Andare avanti e indietro.

FROG (♦)

(♦) To have a frog in one's throat. (p. 214)
Avoir la voix rauque.
Estar ronco.
Eine heisere Stimme haben.
Avere la voce rauca.

FULL

To know full well.
Savoir très bien.
Saber muy bien.
Sehr wohl wissen / Ganz gut wissen.
Sapere benissimo.

FUME (♦)

(♦) To fume. (p. 215)
Etre furieux.
Estar enojado.
Wütend sein / Kochen vor Wut.
Essere furioso.

FUN

For fun.
Pour rire.
Por broma.
Aus Spass.
Per scherzo.

To make fun of somebody.
Se moquer de quelqu'un.
Bromear con alguien / Burlarse de alguien.
Jemanden verulken / Jemanden zum besten haben / Sich über jemanden lustig machen / Jemanden auf den Arm nehmen.
Prendere in giro qualcuno / Prendere qualcuno per il naso.

FUNNY (♠)

How funny!
Comme c'est drôle! / Comme c'est amusant!
¡Muy divertido!
Wie lustig! / Wie ulkig!
Che divertente!

(♠) Funny business. (p. 217)
Une embrouille / Quelque chose d'étrange.
Una estafa / Algo extraño.
Faules Geschäft / Faule Sache.
Un imbroglio / Qualcosa di strano.

FURTHER

Till further orders.
Jusqu'à nouvel ordre.
Hasta nueva orden.
Bis auf weitere Anordnungen.
Fino a nuovo ordine.

FUSS

You fuss too much.
Vous vous agitez sans raison.
Usted se agíta sin razón.

216

217

Sie regen sich viel zu viel auf / Sie machen zuviel Aufhebens (darum).
Vi agitate senza ragione.

GAB

To have the gift of the gab.
Parler avec « brio ».
Tener el don de la palabra / Hablar con propiedad.
Ein gutes Mundwerk haben.
Saper parlare con brio (con spirito).

GAD

To gad about.
Vadrouiller.
Vagar / Dar una vuelta / Callejear.
Sich herumtreiben / Bummeln.
Gironzolare / Andare a zonzo.

GAGE

To throw down the gage.
Jeter le gant / Lancer un défi.
Desafiar.
Herausfordern / Den Fehdehandschuh hinwerfen.
Gettar il guanto / Lanciare una sfida.

GAIN

To gain the upper hand.
Avoir le dessus.
Ser el ganador.
Die Oberhand gewinnen / (An) Boden gewinnen.
Aver la meglio.

To gain ground.
Gagner du terrain.
Ganar terreno.
An Boden gewinnen.
Guadagnar terreno.

GALLERY

To play to the gallery.
Jouer pour la galerie.
Recitar para las masas.
Den niederen Geschmack ansprechen / Nach Effekt haschen.
Recitare per le masse.

GALLIVANT

To gallivant.
Se balader.
Vagar.
Sich herumtreiben / Bummeln.
Andare a zonzo / Gironzolare.

GALLOP

To gallop through one's work.
Bâcler son travail.
Trabajar de prisa / Trabajar a toda máquina.
Seine Arbeit im Galopp erledigen.
Fare il proprio lavoro in gran fretta.

GALORE

There was beer galore.
Il y avait de la bière à gogo.
Había un montón de cerveza.
Dort war jede Menge Bier / Dort gab es Bier in Hülle und Fülle.
C'era birra a profusione.

GAME

The game is up.
Le plan a échoué.
El plan ha fracasado.
Das Spiel ist aus (oder verloren).
Il piano è fallito.

To play the game.
Jouer le jeu.
Comportarse con dignidad.

Sich an die Spielregeln halten.
Comportarsi onorevolmente.
I am game for anything.
Je suis prêt à tout.
Estoy listo para cualquier cosa.
Ich bin bereit, alles mitzumachen / Ich bin mit von der Partie.
Sono pronto a tutto.

GAOL

Gaol bird.
Individu peu recommandable.
Galeote / Una persona poco limpia.
Zuchthäusler / Galgenvogel.
Individuo da galera.

GAPE

To gape at . . .
Regarder bouche-bée.
Estar boquiabierto.
Anstarren / Angaffen / Mit offenem Mund anschauen.
Guardare a bocca aperta.

GARDEN (♦)

(♦) To lead someone up the garden path. (p. 221)
Tromper, embrouiller quelqu'un.
Engañar a alguien.
Jemanden an der Nase herumführen.
Ingannare qualcuno.

GAS-BAG

To be a gas-bag.
Etre blagueur / Avoir du bâgout.
Decir bolas / Ser un exagerado al hablar.
Ein Schwätzer sein.
Essere un chiacchierone.

GASP

To gasp for breath.
Faire des efforts pour respirer.

221

Esforzarse para respirar / Boquear / Jadear.
Nach Luft schnappen.
Respirare a stento.

At the last gasp.
Moribond.
Estar agonizando.
In den letzten Zügen / Sterbend.
Moribondo.

GATE

To give someone the gate.
Mettre quelqu'un à la porte.
Sacar alguien afuera.
Jemandem die Tür weisen / Hinauswerfen.
Mettere qualcuno alla porta.

GATE-CRASH

To gatecrash.
S'inviter.
Colarse en una fiesta.
Ungeladen erscheinen.
Autoinvitarsi.

GATHER

A rolling stone gathers no moss. (prov.)
Pierre qui roule n'amasse pas mousse.
Quien mucho abraza nada abarca.
Ein rollender Stein wird nicht moosig.
Chi tenta troppe vie non raggiunge nessuna meta / Pietra mossa, non fa muschio.

GAUDY

As gaudy as a butterfly. (comp.)
Très fastueux.
Muy fastuoso.
Prächtig wie ein Pfau.
Molto fastoso.

As gaudy as a peacock.
Très fastueux.
Muy fastuoso.
Prächtig wie ein Pfau.
Molto fastoso.

GAUNTLET

To throw down the gauntlet.
Lancer un défi.
Lanzar el guante / Desafiar.
(Jemandem) den Fehdehandschuh hinwerfen / (Jemanden) herausfordern.
Lanciare una sfida.

GAY

As gay as a lark. (comp.)
Gai comme un pinson.
Alegre como un pajarito.
Sehr fröhlich.
Molto gaio / Contento come una pasqua.

GENTLE

As gentle as a lamb. (comp.)
Très délicat.
Muy amable.
Sanft wie ein Lamm.
Molto delicato.

GET (♦)

To get the sack.
Etre licencié.
Ser despedido.
Fliegen / Entlassen werden / An die Luft gesetzt werden.
Venire licenziato in tronco.

To get wind of ...
Avoir vent de ...
Venir a saber que ...
Wind bekommen von ...
Venire a sapere ...

(♦) To get the hang of something. (p. 225)
S'habituer à quelque chose.
Acostumbrarse a algo.
Sich gewöhnen an ...
Abituarsi a qualche cosa.

To get on with ...
Etre d'accord avec ...
Ir de acuerdo con ...
Übereinstimmen mit / Gut auskommen mit / Sich vertragen mit.
Andare d'accordo con ...

To get on.
Faire des progrès.
Hacer progresos.
Fortschritte machen.
Fare progressi.

To get one's back up.
S'arc-bouter / S'entêter.
No ceder.
Sich auf die Hinterbeine stellen.
Impuntarsi.

To get the upper hand of ...
Avoir le dessus.
Tener razón sobre alguien.
Die Oberhand gewinnen.
Avere la meglio su ...

To get nowhere.
N'obtenir aucun résultat.
No concluir nada.
Nichts zuwege bringen / Nichts erreichen.
Non concludere niente.

To get rid of ...
Se débarrasser de ...
Desembarazarse de ...
Jemanden oder etwas loswerden.
Sbarazzarsi di ...

To get wise to something.
S'apercevoir de quelque chose.

Darse cuenta de algo.
Etwas spitzkriegen / Etwas in Erfahrung bringen.
Accorgersi di qualcosa.

To get over something.
Se remettre (d'une maladie) / Reprendre le dessus / Se consoler.
Restablecerse (de una enfermedad) / Consolarse.
Über etwas hinwegkommen - Sich trösten.
Rimettersi (da una malattia) / Consolarsi.

(♦) To get the point of something. (p. 227)
Saisir l'essence de quelque chose.
Comprender una cuestión / Dar en el blanco.
Das Beste erhalten / Den Kern einer Sache treffen.
Cogliere il nocciolo di qualcosa / Afferrare qualcosa.

Get out of the way!
Laissez le passage libre!
¡Déjen libre el paso!
Raus aus dem Weg / Machen Sie den Weg frei!
Lasciate libero il passaggio! / Sgomberate!

Get a move on!
Allons!
¡Muevanse!
Rühr dich / Beweg dich! / Setz dich in Bewegung!
Muoviti!

(♦) To get away with something. (p. 228)
Faire le coup à l'as.
Salvarse por un pelo.
Unbehelligt davon kommen.
Farla franca.

(♦) To get under someone's feet. (p. 229)
Casser les pieds à quelqu'un.
Romperle los cascos a alguien.
Auf die Nerven gehen.
Rompere le scatole a qualcuno.

GHOST

There is not the ghost of a chance!
Il n'a pas la moindre chance de réussir!
¡No hay manera que resulte!

Da ist nicht die geringste Aussicht.
Non c'è neanche un filo di speranza!

To give up the ghost.
Rendre l'âme.
Rendir el alma.
Den Geist aufgeben / Sterben.
Rendere l'anima.

GIDDY

To play the giddy goat.
Faire l'imbécile.
Hacerse el tonto.
Sich närrisch benehmen.
Fare lo stupido / Fare lo scemo.

GIFT

To have the gift of the gab.
Avoir le don de la plaisanterie.
Tener el don de la palabra.
Ein gutes Mundwerk haben.
Saper parlare con brio (con spirito).

Never look a gift horse in the mouth. (prov.)
A cheval donné on ne regarde pas à la dent.
A caballo regalado no se le mira el diente.
Einem geschenkten Gaul schaut man nicht ins Maul.
A caval donato non si guarda in bocca.

GIG

As merry as a gig. (comp.)
Heureux comme un poisson dans l'eau.
Felíz como unas pascuas.
Sehr lustig.
Allegro come un grillo.

GIST

That's the gist of what she said.
Voilà la substance de son discours.
Esto es la esencia de lo que dijo.

Das ist das der Kern, von dem, was sie sagte.
Questo è il succo di quel che ha detto.

GIVE

To give way.
Céder le pas.
Ceder terreno / Entregarse.
Platzmachen / Nachgeben.
Cedere terreno.

To give oneself away.
Se trahir.
Ponerse en luz / Traicionarse.
Sich verraten / Sich verplappern.
Tradirsi.

To give notice.
Prendre congé / Se retirer.
Despedirse.
Kündigen.
Congedarsi.

To give in.
Céder au désespoir.
Darse por vencido.
Sich geschlagen geben / Aufgeben.
Cedere alla disperazione.

To give tit for tat.
Rendre la pareille.
Responder por las suyas.
Mit gleicher Münze heimzahlen.
Rendere pan per focaccia.

To give the glad eye.
Faire un clin d'œil / Cligner de l'œil à quelqu'un.
Guiñar el ojo.
Schöne Augen machen.
Fare l'occhiolino.

Give me a call!
Téléphonez-moi! / Passez-moi un coup de fil!
¡Telefonéeme!

Rufen Sie mich an!
Telefonatemi!

Mr. Brown gave his daughter away.
Mr. Brown donna sa fille en mariage.
Mr. Brown llevó su hija al altar.
Mr. Brown gab die Hand seiner Tochter.
Mr. Brown concesse la mano di sua figlia.

GIVEN

I'd almost given you up.
Je commençais à croire que tu ne serais plus venu.
Comenzaba a pensar que ya no vendrías.
Ich hatte Sie fast aufgegeben.
Cominciavo a credere che non sareste più venuto.

GLARING

A glaring mistake.
Une faute qui saute aux yeux.
Un error lampante.
Ein krasser Fehler.
Un errore che salta agli occhi (vistoso).

GLASS

To be fond of one's glass.
Aimer boire.
Ser adicto a la bebida.
Gern tief ins Glas schauen / Gerne trinken.
Essere amante del bere.

GLEAM

A gleam of hope.
Une lueur d'espoir.
Un destello de esperanza.
Ein Hoffnungsschimmer.
Un barlume di speranza.

GLEE

In high glee.
Au comble de la joie.

En el ápice del regocijo.
In Hochstimmung.
Al colmo della gioia.

GLIB

A glib talker.
Une personne qui a la langue déliée.
Una persona de mucha labia / Una persona muy locuáz.
Ein gewandter Redner / Ein schlagfertiger Redner.
Una persona dalla lingua sciolta.

GLIMPSE

To catch a glimpse of...
Entrevoir.
Entrever / Vislumbrar.
Einen flüchtigen Blick erhaschen von...
Intravedere...

GLOAT

To gloat over something.
Eprouver un malin plaisir à...
Relamerse de gusto.
Sich hämisch über etwas freuen.
Provare un piacere maligno per qualcosa.

GLOVES

To handle without gloves.
Traiter sans égards.
Tratar con poca delicadeza.
Rücksichtslos (be)handeln.
Trattare con poco tatto.

GLOW

To be glowing with enthusiasm.
Brûler d'enthousiasme.
Brillar de entusiasmo.
Vor Begeisterung strahlen.
Ardere dall'entusiasmo.

GNAT

To strain at a gnat.
Chercher la petite bête.
Hacerse el difícil por cosas de poco.
Haarspalterei betreiben.
Fare il difficile per cose da nulla.

GNAW

Anxiety was gnawing at my heart.
L'anxiété me dévorait.
La angustia le devoraba.
Angst zehrte (nagte) an meinem Herzen / Angst quälte mein Herz.
L'ansia mi rodeva il cuore.

GO

To go to the dogs.
Courir à la ruine.
Arruinarse.
Vor die Hunde gehen.
Andare in rovina.

To go to pot.
Tomber en morceaux.
Irse cuesta abajo.
Kaputtgehen.
Andare a rotoli.

To go to pieces.
Tomber en morceaux / Craquer.
Hacerse pedazos.
In Stücke gehen / Zusammenbrechen.
Andare in pezzi / Andare in frantumi.

To go to Canossa.
Aller à Canossa.
Humillarse / Reconocer un error.
Sich demütigen / Nach Canossa gehen.
Umiliarsi / Andare a Canossa.

To go through thick and thin.
Affronter tous les risques.
Enfrentarse a cualquier situación.
Durch dick und dünn gehen.
Affrontare ogni rischio.

To go back on one's word.
Reprendre sa parole.
Echarse para atrás / Retirar la palabra dada.
Sein Wort nicht halten.
Ritirare la parola data.

To go one better than everyone else.
Faire plus que les autres.
Hacer algo mejor que los demás.
Mehr machen als die anderen.
Fare di più degli altri.

To go one's way.
N'en faire qu'à sa tête.
Hacer lo que a uno se le dá la gana.
Seinen eigenen Weg gehen / Nach seinem eigenen Kopf handeln.
Fare di testa propria.

To go over to the other side.
Passer de l'autre côté.
Pasarse al otro lado.
Zur anderen Seite übertreten / Sich auf die andere Seite stellen.
Passare dall'altra parte.

To go to law.
S'en remettre à la loi.
Demandar.
Den Rechtsweg beschreiten / Prozessieren.
Fare causa.

To go the whole hog.
Aller jusqu'au bout.
Ir hasta el fondo de un asunto.
Aufs Ganze gehen.
Andare fino in fondo.

It goes without saying.
Cela va de soi.

Es obvio / ¡Desde luego!
Es geht von selbst.
Va da sè.

It's no go.
Il n'y a rien à faire.
No hay nada que hacer / No hay remedio.
Da kann man nichts machen / Da ist nichts zu machen.
Non c'è niente da fare.

Do you think the story will go down well?
Vous pensez qu'ils vont avaler l'histoire?
¿Ustedes creen que se tragarán el cuento?
Glauben Sie, dass die Geschichte gut aufgenommen wird?
Credete che la storia sarà accolta bene?

To go against the grain.
Blesser.
Herir o lastimar (sentimientos).
Zuwiderhandeln.
Urtare / Ferire.

To go ahead.
Aller de l'avant.
Ir adelante / Proseguir.
Vorangehen / Fortfahren.
Andare avanti.

A go-getter.
Un arriviste.
Un aprovechador.
Ein Draufgänger / Jemand der weiss, was er will.
Un arrivista.

A go-between.
Un intermédiaire.
Un mediador.
Ein Vermittler / Ein Mittelsmann.
Un intermediario.

To go out of one's mind.
Devenir fou.
Enloquecerse.
Verrückt werden.
Impazzire / Uscire di senno.

236

You can't go by what he says.
Vous ne pouvez vous fier de ce qu'il dit.
No confíen en lo que dice.
Sie können nicht danach gehen, was er sagt.
Non potete fare affidamento su ciò che dice.

GOAT

To separate the sheep from the goats.
Séparer les bons des mauvais.
Separar los malos de los buenos.
Die Schafe von den Böcken trennen / Das Gute vom Schlechten trennen.
Separare i buoni dai cattivi.

GOD

God-forsaken.
Mauvais.
Malvado / Mal hombre.
Von Gott verlassen / Gottverlassener.
Malvagio.

GOLD

All that glitters is not gold. (prov.)
Tout ce qui brille n'est pas or.
No es oro todo lo que reluce.
Es ist nicht alles Gold, was glänzt.
Non è tutto oro quello che luccica.

GONE

He's far gone.
Il est fichu!
¡Está acabado!
Er ist schlimm dran.
E' spacciato!

To be gone on somebody.
Etre amoureux de quelqu'un.
Estar enamorado de alguien / Estar colgado de alguien.
In jemanden verliebt sein.
Essere innamorato di qualcuno.

GOOD

As good as gold. (comp.)
Bon comme le pain.
Una persona buena como el pan.
Sehr gut / Goldrichtig.
Buono come il pane / Molto buono.

To be good at . . .
Etre bon en . . .
Ser bueno para . . .
Gut sein in . . . / Geschickt sein in . . .
Essere bravo in . . .

A good person.
Une brave personne.
Una persona de bien.
Ein guter Mensch.
Una persona per bene.

He as good as told me.
C'est comme s'il me l'avait dit.
Es como si me lo hubiera dicho.
Er hat es mir so gut wie gesagt.
E' come se me l'avesse detto.

Good breeding.
Bonne éducation / Bonnes manières.
Buenas costumbres.
Gute Erziehung / Gute Kinderstube.
Buona creanza.

So much to the good!
Autant de gagné!
¡Tanto mejor!
Soviel extra / Soviel als Gewinn.
Tanto di guadagnato!

I'll make good the loss.
Je paierai les dégâts.
Repondré los daños.
Ich werde den Schaden ersetzen.
Risarcirò i danni.

To have a good mind to . . .
Avoir une envie folle de . . .

238

Tener muchas ganas de ...
Grosse Lust haben zu ...
Avere una gran voglia di ...

I'm not a good sailor.
Je n'ai pas le pied marin.
Sufro de mareos.
Ich leide an der Seekrankheit / Ich werde (bin) seekrank.
Soffro il mal di mare.

In good spirits.
De bonne humeur.
De buen humor / Estar de buenas.
In guter Laune.
Di buon umore.

All in good time.
Chaque chose en son temps.
Cada cosa a su tiempo.
Alles zu seiner Zeit.
Ogni cosa a suo tempo.

To do a good turn.
Rendre service.
Hacer un favor / Hacer una campaña.
Einen Gefallen tun.
Rendere un servizio.

It was as good as play. (comp.)
Ce fut très amusant.
Fué muy divertido / Estuvo muy alegre.
Es war äusserst amüsant.
Fu divertentissimo.

Good looks.
Beauté physique.
Belleza física.
Gutes Aussehen / Schönheit.
Bellezza fisica.

What's the good of it?
Qu'est-ce que ça vaut? / A quoi bon?
¿Que hay de bueno en ello?
Was nützt es?
Che vale? / A che serve?

GOODNESS

Thank goodness!
Grâce à Dieu! / Grâce au Ciel!
¡Gracias a Dios!
Gott sei Dank!
Grazie al cielo!

GOOSE

All his geese are swans. (prov.)
Il voit tout en rose.
Mira el mundo color de rosa.
Er sieht alles durch die rosa Brille.
Vede il mondo con gli occhiali rosa.

To kill the goose that lays the golden eggs. (prov.)
Manger la poule aux œufs d'or.
Matar la gallina de los huevos de oro.
Eine gute Zukunft einer unmittelbaren Notwendigkeit opfern.
Sacrificare un bene futuro per una necessità immediata.

What is sauce for the goose is sauce for the gander. (prov.)
Ce qui vaut pour l'un vaut pour l'autre.
Lo que es bueno para uno es bueno para el otro.
Was dem einen recht ist, ist dem anderen billig.
Ciò che vale per l'uno vale anche per l'altro.

To be unable to say boo to a goose.
Etre très timide.
Ser tímido como un conejo.
Sehr schüchtern sein.
Essere timidissimo / Essere incapace di spiccicare una parola.

To cook somebody's goose.
Faire tout tomber à l'eau.
Molestar a alguien / Entrometerse en lo que a uno no le concierne.
Es jemandem besorgen / Jemanden fertigmachen.
Romper le uova nel paniere a qualcuno.

GOOSEBERRY

To play gooseberry.
Tenir la chandelle.

Halagar / Sobar la leva.
Anstandswauwau spielen.
Reggere il moccolo.

GRABBER

Money - grabber.
Faiseur d'argent.
El que quiere hacer dinero / Codicioso.
Geldgierige(r).
Un arraffone.

GRACE

To be in somebody's good graces.
Etre dans les bonnes grâces de quelqu'un.
Estar en las gracias de alguien.
In jemandes Gunst stehen.
Essere nelle grazie di qualcuno.

GRACEFUL

As graceful as a swan. (comp.)
Elégant comme un cygne / Gracieux.
Con la gracia de un cisne.
Anmutig wie ein Schwan / Sehr graziös.
Molto aggraziato / Elegantissimo.

GRANTED

To take for granted.
Tenir pour sûr.
Tomar por cierto.
Als erwiesen annehmen.
Dare per scontato.

GRASP

It's beyond my grasp.
C'est au-delà de mes moyens.
Está más allá de mis capacidades.
Es geht über meinen Verstand.
E' oltre il mio comprendonio / E' al di là delle mie capacità.

Grasp all, lose all. (prov.)
Qui trop embrasse mal étreint.
Quien mucho abarca, nada aprieta.
Wer zuviel will, wird nichts haben.
Chi troppo vuole, nulla stringe.

To grasp the nettle.
Prendre le taureau par les cornes.
Tomar el toro por los cuernos.
Die Schwierigkeit anpacken.
Prendere il toro per le corna.

GRASPING

As grasping as a miser. (comp.)
Un rafleur.
Tan aprovechado como un mendigo.
Ein Habgieriger / Ein Raffgieriger.
Un arraffone.

GRASS

He doesn't let the grass grow under his feet.
Ne pas perdre une minute.
No deja tiempo al tiempo.
Er verschwendet keine Zeit.
Non perde tempo nel fare le cose.

A grass-widower.
Mari momentanément célibataire.
Viudo de ocasión.
Ein Strohwitwer.
Un marito che ha la moglie in vacanza (vedovo temporaneo).

A grass-widow.
Femme momentanément célibataire.
Viuda de ocasión.
Eine Strohwitwe.
Una moglie che ha il marito in vacanza (vedova temporanea).

GRAVE (♦)

(♦) **To have one foot in the grave.** (p. 243)
Avoir un pied dans la tombe.

Tener un pie en la tumba.
Mit einem Fuss im Grabe stehen.
Avere un piede nella fossa.

To make someone turn in his grave.
Faire se retourner quelqu'un dans la tombe.
Hacer que un muerto se revuelque en la tumba.
Jemanden sich im Grabe umdrehen lassen.
Fare rivoltare qualcuno nella tomba.

As grave as a judge. (comp.)
Très solennel.
Tan solemne como un Pontifice.
Sehr feierlich.
Molto solenne.

To be as secret as a grave. (comp.)
Etre muet (secret) comme une tombe.
Ser mudo como una tumba.
Verschwiegen wie ein Grab.
Essere una tomba.

GREASE

To grease the palm of . . .
Graisser la patte à quelqu'un.
Corromper (con dinero) / Dar una mordida.
Mit einem Trinkgeld bestechen / Schmiergeld zahlen.
Corrompere / Ungere le ruote.

GREASED

Like greased lightning.
En un éclair.
Como un relámpago / Volado.
Wie der Blitz.
In un baleno / In un batter d'occhio.

GREEDY

As greedy as a dog. (comp.)
Gourmand (goinfre).
Goloso / Hartón.
Sehr gefrässig / Gierig.
Molto vorace / Affamato come un lupo.

244

GREEN

He is still green to his job.
Il n'est pas encore expert dans son travail.
Está aún muy verde para su trabajo.
Er ist noch unerfahren in seiner Arbeit.
E' ancora inesperto nel suo lavoro.

Do you see any green in my eye?
Je te semble si naïf?
¿Me crees tan ingénuo?
Erscheine ich dir noch etwas grün hinter den Ohren?
Ti sembro proprio tanto ingenuo? / Ho scritto in fronte Giocondo?

As green as grass. (comp.)
Vert comme l'herbe.
Verde como las montañas.
Grasgrün.
Molto verde.

GREY

The future looks grey.
Le futur s'annonce sombre.
El futuro no es muy risueño.
Die Zukunft sieht grau aus.
Il futuro si presenta grigio.

The grey mare is the better horse. (prov.)
C'est la femme qui porte la culotte.
La esposa es quien lleva los pantalones.
Die Frau ist der Herr im Hause / Die Frau hat die Hosen an.
Chi porta i pantaloni è la moglie.

GRIEF

To come to grief.
Echouer.
Fracasar / Sobrevenirle a uno una desgracia.
Schaden nehmen / In Schwierigkeiten geraten / Fehlschlagen / Scheitern.
Fare fiasco / Andare in malora.

To die of grief.
Mourir de douleur.
Morir de dolor / Morir por la aflicción.
Vor Gram (Kummer) sterben.
Morire di dolore.

GRIN

To grin and bear it.
Souffrir sans se plaindre.
Sufrir sin quejarse / Sufrir en silencio.
Gute Miene zum bösen Spiel machen.
Soffrire senza lagnarsi.

To grin like a Cheshire cat.
Avoir un sourire stéréotypé.
Sonreír sin motivo / Sonreír como un bobo.
Übers ganze Gesicht grinsen.
Sorridere scioccamente.

To grin from ear to ear.
Sourire jusqu'aux oreilles.
Sonreír abiertamente.
Übers ganze Gesicht grinsen.
Avere un largo sorriso (che va da un orecchio all'altro).

GRIND

To have an axe to grind with someone.
Avoir un intérêt particulier envers quelqu'un.
Tener un interés personal hacia alguien.
Bei jemandem eigennützige Zwecke verfolgen.
Avere un interesse personale verso qualcuno.

To grind something into a boy's head.
Souffrir les peines de l'enfer pour lui faire entrer l'histoire dans la tête.
Meter, a fuerza de repetir, algo en la cabeza de un muchacho.
Einem Jungen etwas einpauken.
Sudare sette camicie per insegnare una cosa a un ragazzo.

GRIST

To bring grist to the mill.
Faire venir l'eau à son moulin.

Arrimar el ascua a su sardina.
In die eigene Tasche arbeiten.
Tirare acqua al proprio mulino.

All is grist that comes into the mill.
Tout sert / Tout peut servir.
Todo es bueno para el caldo de gallina / Bienvenido sea todo
lo que viene.
Alles ist von Nutzen.
Tutto fa brodo (può tornare utile).

GRIT

To have grit.
Etre courageux.
Tener hígado / Tener valor.
Mumm haben / Mut haben!
Avere del fegato.

GROOMED

A well groomed young man.
Un jeune homme tiré à quatre épingles.
Un jóven empomadado / Un catrín.
Ein gepflegter junger Mann.
Un giovanotto tutto azzimato.

GROPE

To grope for something.
Chercher quelque chose à tâtons.
Buscar a tientas.
Tasten nach . . .
Cercare qualcosa a tastoni.

GROUND

Without grounds.
Sans raison.
Sin motivo.
Ohne Grund.
Senza motivo.

That suits me to the ground.
Il vous va comme un gant.
Me vá a pedir de boca.
Das passt mir (in den Kram).
Mi va proprio a pennello.

To get in on the ground floor.
Entrer dans une société avec les mêmes droits que les fondateurs.
Estar sobre el mismo plano / Tener iguales derechos en una compañia.
Von Anfang an mit dabei sein.
Entrare in una società con diritti pari a quelli dei fondatori.

To shift one's ground.
Changer de position.
Cambiar de posiciones.
Seinen Standpunkt ändern.
Mutare la propria posizione (nei riguardi di un problema).

GROUNDED

Well-grounded.
Bien préparé.
Muy preparado / Muy capáz.
Mit guten (Vor)Kenntnissen.
Ben preparato.

GRUDGE

I bear him no grudge.
Je ne lui en tiens pas rigueur.
No le tengo rencor.
Ich hege keinen Groll gegen ihn.
Non gli porto rancore.

GRUFF

As gruff as a bear. (comp.)
Etre ours.
Ronco.
Sehr rauh.
Molto rauco / Rauco come una rana.

248

GUARD

To be on one's guard.
Etre sur ses gardes.
Estar en guardia / Estar a la quien vive.
Auf der Hut sein.
Stare all'erta / Stare sul chi va là.

To be caught off one's guard.
Etre pris au dépourvu.
Ser tomado desprevenido.
Unvermutet erwischt werden.
Essere preso alla sprovvista.

GUARDED

To use guarded language.
Avoir de la retenue dans son langage.
Usar un lenguaje muy medido / Medir las palabras.
Zurückhaltend im Sprechen sein / Wenige Worte sprechen /
Wenig Worte machen.
Adoperare parole molto misurate.

GUESS

To make a good guess.
Faire mouche / Tomber juste.
Dar en el punto / Acertar.
Gut schätzen.
Azzeccare.

GUILE

To say without guile.
Parler avec naïveté.
Decir ingenuamente.
Ohne Arglist sprechen.
Dire ingenuamente (senza volerlo).

GUM (♦)

(♦) To be up a gum-tree. (p. 250)
Etre dans de mauvais draps.
Estar en problemas / Estar en un lío.

In der Klemme sein.
Essere nei guai.

GUN

To stick to one's guns.
Tenir bon.
Estar a pie firme / Calzarse los pantalones.
Festbleiben / Nicht nachgeben.
Tenere duro.

Son of a gun.
Voyou / Salaud.
Delincuente / Desgraciado.
Schurke.
Mascalzone.

GUTS

A man with plenty of guts.
Un homme de poigne.
Un hombre con agallas.
Ein Mann mit viel Mut (Mumm, Courage).
Un uomo di fegato.

GUTTER

To rise from the gutter.
Venir de rien.
Venir de la nada.
Sich aus dem Nichts emporarbeiten.
Farsi dal nulla.

HABIT

Habit is second nature. (prov.)
L'habitude est une seconde nature.
La costumbre es una segunda naturaleza.
Gewohnheiten werden zur zweiten Natur / Gewohnheiten
gehen in Fleisch und Blut über.
L'abitudine è una seconda natura.

To do out of habit.
Faire les choses par habitude (par routine).

Hacer algo por costumbre.
Aus Gewohnheit tun.
Fare per abitudine.

To fall into bad habits.
Prendre de mauvaises habitudes.
Adquirir malas costumbres.
In schlechte Gewohnheiten verfallen.
Prendere cattive abitudini.

HAIR (♦)

Hair raising.
Horrible.
Horripilante / Que le hace erizar a uno el pelo.
Haarsträubend.
Orrendo / Che fa rizzare i capelli.

(♦) My hair stood on end! (p. 253)
Mes cheveux se dressèrent!
Se me erizó el pelo.
Mir sträubten sich die Haare.
Mi si rizzarono i capelli!

He came within a hair's breadth of being killed.
Il s'en est fallu de peu qu'il ne fut tué.
Faltó un pelo para que se matase.
Um Haaresbreite wurde er getötet / Um Haaresbreite entkam
er dem Tod.
Poco mancò che rimanesse ucciso.

(♦) Keep your hair on! (p. 254)
Ne vous mettez pas en colère! / Ne vous excitez pas!
¡No se enoje! / ¡No se excíte!
Ruhig Blut!
Non adiratevi! / Non eccitarti!

HALF

A good beginning is half the battle. (prov.)
A moitié fait qui bien commence.
Quien tiene un buen principio, ha ganado mitad de la batalla.
Gut begonnen ist halb getan / Guter Anfang ist halbe Arbeit.
Chi ben comincia è a metà dell'opera.

Half a word to the wise.
A bon entendeur, salut!
A buen entendedor pocas palabras.
Dem Klugen (Erfahrenen) genügen wenige Worte.
A buon intenditor poche parole.

A half-wit.
Un imbécile.
Imbécil / Zonzo.
Ein Halbverrückter.
Un cretino.

To be half seas over.
Etre gai.
Estar borracho.
Angesäuselt (Angeheitert / Blau) sein.
Essere brillo.

To be half-hearted.
Avoir peu envie de réussir.
Tener pocas ganas de triunfar.
Lustlos sein.
Aver poca voglia di riuscire.

He's not half a bad fellow.
C'est un brave garçon.
Es un buen tipo.
Er ist durch und durch ein guter Junge.
E' un bravo ragazzo.

HALLOO
Don't halloo until you are out of the wood.
Ne chante pas victoire trop vite.
No hay que cantar victoria antes del tiempo.
Freue dich nicht zu früh; / Lobe den Tag nicht vor dem Abend!
Non cantar vittoria prima del tempo / Non dir quattro se non l'hai nel sacco.

HALVES (♦)
(♦) To do a thing by halves. (p. 256)
Faire une chose à moitié.
Hacer una cosa a mitad.
Etwas nur halb (nicht gründlich) tun.
Fare una cosa in maniera incompleta / Fare una cosa a metà.

HAMMER

To go at it hammer and tongs.
Y aller des pieds et des mains / Faire quelque chose avec
fougue.
Hacer algo con ganas / Hacer algo con mucho empeño.
Etwas mit aller Kraft tun / Alles dransetzen.
Mettercela tutta / Fare qualcosa con foga.

HAND (♦)

(♦) To eat out of somebody's hand. (p. 258)
Etre prêt à obéir.
Estar dispuesto a obedecer.
Jemandem aus der Hand fressen.
Essere pronto a obbedire.

To be hand and glove with someone.
Etre intimement lié à quelqu'un / Etre cul et chemise avec
quelqu'un.
Estar en confianza con una persona / Ser como hermanos con
alguien.
Mit jemandem sehr vertraut sein / Mit jemandem unter einer
Decke stecken.
Avere grande intimità con qualcuno / Essere culo e camicia con
qualcuno.

Not to lift a hand.
Ne pas lever le petit doigt.
No levantar ni siquiera un dedo.
Keinen Finger rühren für . . .
Non muovere un dito (in favore di . . .).

To show one's hand.
Découvrir son jeu.
Descubrir las propias cartas.
Seine Karten aufdecken.
Scoprire il proprio gioco.

To live from hand to mouth.
Vivre au jour le jour.
Vivir al día.
Von der Hand in den Mund leben.
Vivere alla giornata.

On the other hand.
D'autre part.
Por otra parte.
Auf der anderen Seite.
D'altra parte.

To get out of hand.
Devenir indiscipliné.
Volverse indisciplinado.
Ausser Kontrolle geraten / Die Kontrolle verlieren.
Diventare indisciplinato.

To be an old hand.
Etre un bon connaisseur.
Ser un buen entendedor.
Ein alter Fachmann / Ein alter Hase.
Essere un buon conoscitore.

(♦) To give someone a big hand. (p. 260)
Applaudir chaleureusement quelqu'un.
Aplaudir a alguien calurosamente.
Jemandem stürmischem Beifall geben.
Applaudire qualcuno calorosamente.

(♦) To get the upper hand. (p. 261)
Avoir le dessus.
Tener la ventaja.
Die Überhand gewinnen.
Avere la meglio su qualcuno.

HANDSOME

Handsome is as handsome does. (prov.)
Ce n'est pas la beauté qui compte mais la bonté.
Lo que cuenta no es la belleza sino la bontad.
Edel ist, wer edel handelt.
Ciò che conta è la bontà, non la bellezza.

A handsome fortune.
Un grand patrimoine.
Una gran fortuna.
Ein stattliches (beträchtliches) Vermögen.
Un gran patrimonio.

261

HANDY

To come in handy.
S'avérer utile.
Demostrarse útil.
Gelegen kommen.
Rivelarsi utile.

HANG

To hang about.
Flâner / Traîner.
Callejear / Holgazanear.
Herumlungern / Sich herumtreiben.
Bighellonare.

HANGER

A hanger-on.
Un escroc.
Un arrimado / Un gorrón.
Ein Mitläufer / Ein Anhänger / Eine Klette / Ein Schmarotzer.
Uno scroccone.

HAPPENED

A man happened to pass there.
Quelqu'un passa par hasard / Quelqu'un vint à passer.
Un hombre pasaba por casualidad por ahí.
Ein Mann kam zufällig dort vorbei.
Un uomo passava di là per caso.

HAPPY

As happy as a king. (comp.)
Heureux comme un roi.
Felíz como un rey.
Sich königlich freuen.
Felicissimo / Felice come una pasqua.

To be happy-go-lucky.
Etre sans soucis.
Atenerse a la suerte / Tomar las cosas así como vienen.
Das Leben nehmen, wie es kommt.
Prendere il mondo come viene / Essere spensierato.

HARD

Hard cash.
Argent comptant.
Dinero en efectivo / Dinero contante y sonante.
Bargeld / Klingende Münze / Hartgeld.
Denaro in contanti.

A hard nut to crack.
Tomber sur un os / Un problème difficile.
Un problema difícil.
Eine harte Nuss zu knacken / Ein schwieriges Problem zu lösen.
Un osso duro / Un problema difficile da risolvere.

To be as hard as nails. (comp.)
Avoir le cœur dur / Etre dur comme la pierre.
Ser muy recio.
Eisern sein / Ein hartes Herz haben.
Essere molto forte / Essere duro di cuore.

To be hard up.
Etre fauché.
No tener dinero / Estar pelado (de dinero).
Kein Geld haben / Blank sein.
Essere in bolletta (al verde).

To be hard on a person.
Etre très sévère avec quelqu'un.
Ser muy severo con una persona / Ser muy rígido con una persona.
Mit jemandem streng sein.
Essere molto severo con una persona.

Hard-fisted.
Avare.
Avariento.
Geizig.
Avaro.

As hard as a stone. (comp.)
Etre dur comme la pierre.
Durísimo.
Steinhart.
Durissimo / Duro come una pietra.

263

HARDLY

I hardly knew him.
Je le connaissais peu.
Le conocía poco.
Ich kannte ihn kaum.
Lo conoscevo appena.

HARE

As mad as a March hare. (comp.)
Fou à lier.
Loco de remate / Loco rematado.
Total übergeschnappt.
Matto da legare.

To run with the hare and hunt with the hounds.
Ménager la chèvre et le chou / Faire le double jeu.
Hacer un doble juego / Pretender quedar bien con Dios y con el diablo.
Es mit beiden Seiten halten / Ein doppeltes Spiel spielen.
Tenere il piede in due staffe / Fare il doppio gioco.

First catch your hare then cook it. (prov.)
Il ne faut pas vendre la peau de l'ours avant de l'avoir tué.
No hay que vender la piel del oso antes de cazarlo.
Du kannst die Bärenhaut nicht verkaufen, bevor du den Bären erlegt hast.
Non vendere la pelle dell'orso prima d'averlo ucciso.

HARM

To be out of harm's way.
Etre en sécurité / Etre à l'abri.
No correr peligro alguno.
In Sicherheit sein.
Essere al sicuro.

HARMLESS

As harmless as a dove. (comp.)
Innoffensif.
Inócuo como un cordero.
Harmlos (Unschädlich / Unschuldig).
Molto innocuo.

264

HARP

To harp on a subject.
Insister lourdement sur quelque chose.
Porfiar en un argumento.
Auf einem Thema herumreiten / Dauernd von einer Sache reden.
Insistere tediosamente su un argomento.

HASH

To make a hash of something.
Faire un méli-mélo.
Hacer una chambonada.
Etwas vermasseln / Ein Mischmasch machen.
Fare un pasticcio.

HASTE

More haste less speed. (prov.)
Qui veut aller loin ménage sa monture.
Quien se apresura, nada asegura.
Eile mit Weile.
Chi va piano va sano e va lontano.

To make haste.
Hâter le pas / Se dépêcher.
Darse prisa / Apresurarse.
Sich beeilen.
Affrettarsi.

HAT (♦)

(♦) Keep it under your hat! (p. 681)
Motus! / Bouche cousue!
¡No lo digas a nadie!
Behaltes es für Dich! / Sprich nicht darüber!
Acqua in bocca!

To talk through one's hat.
Se vanter.
Decir panzanadas.
Übertreiben / Aufschneiden / Faseln / Kohl reden.
Spararle grosse / Vantarsi.

(♦) At the drop of a hat. (p. 267)
Sur le champ! / Pour un rien.
¡De inmediato! / Por una inecia.
Beim geringsten Anlass / Sofort.
Subito! / Per un nonnulla.

HATCH

Don't count your chickens before they're hatched. (prov.)
Il ne faut pas vendre la peau de l'ours avant de l'avoir tué.
No cuentes tus gallinas antes que metan los huevos.
Du kannst das Fell des Bärens nicht verkaufen, bevor du ihn
hast / Zähle deine Küken nicht, bevor sie ausgeschlüpft sind.
Non dire quattro se non l'hai nel sacco.

HATCHET (♦)

(♦) To bury the hatchet. (p. 78)
Faire la paix.
Hacer las paces.
Das Kriegsbeil begraben / Frieden schliessen.
Fare la pace.

To dig up the hatchet.
Commencer les hostilités.
Iniciar hostilidades.
Den Krieg erklären / Feindschaft ansagen.
Iniziare le ostilità.

HATTER

To be as mad as a hatter. (comp.)
Etre fou à lier.
Ser tan loco como una cabra.
Fuchsteufelswild / Total übergeschnappt.
Essere matto da legare.

HAVE

I won't have it.
Je ne le permettrai pas.
No lo permitiré / No lo toleraré.

266

Ich will es nicht haben / Ich wünsche es nicht / Ich werde es nicht gestatten.
Non lo permetterò.

I want to have it out with you.
Je veux m'expliquer avec vous.
Necesito explicarme con Usted.
Ich möchte die Sache mit Ihnen bereinigen.
Voglio chiarire la cosa con voi.

HAVES

The haves and the have-nots.
Les riches et les pauvres.
Los ricos y los desposeidos.
Die Besitzenden und die Habenichtse / Die Reichen und die Armen.
I ricchi ed i poveri.

HAY

To make hay while the sun shines.
Battre le fer tant qu'il est encore chaud.
Hacer las cosas antes que no haya remedio.
Das Eisen schmieden, solange es heiss ist.
Battere il ferro finchè è caldo.

To look for a needle in a hay stack.
Chercher une aiguille dans une meule de foin.
Buscar una aguja en un pajár.
Eine Nadel im Heuschober (Strohhaufen) suchen.
Cercare un ago in un pagliaio.

HEAD (♦)

To have a good head upon one's shoulders.
Etre sensé / Avoir la tête sur les épaules.
Tener sentido común / Tener la cabeza en su lugar.
Einen gesunden Menschenverstand haben.
Aver buon senso / Aver la testa sulle spalle.

I could do it on my head.
Je saurais le faire les yeux fermés.
Podría hacerlo con los ojos tapados.

Das könnte ich im Schlaf (machen).
Io saprei farlo a occhi chiusi.
I can't make out head or tail of it.
Je n'y comprends rien.
No puedo encontrarle ni pies ni cabeza.
Ich kann daraus nicht schlau werden.
Non ci capisco un'acca (un tubo).
To have a poor head for figures.
Etre peu doué pour le calcul.
No tener cabeza para los calculos.
Ein schlechter Rechner sein / Ein schlechtes Gedächtnis für
Zahlen haben.
Essere poco abile nei calcoli.
To be head over heels in love.
Etre amoureux fou.
Estar enamorado locamente / Estar enamorado perdido.
Hals über Kopf verliebt sein.
Essere innamorato cotto.
To keep one's head above water.
Faire la planche / Tenir à la surface.
Tenerse a flote / Mantenerse a flote.
Sich über Wasser halten / Seinen Kopf über Wasser halten.
Tenersi a galla.
(♦) To lose one's head. (p. 270) (p. 353)
Perdre la tête.
Perder la cabeza.
Seinen Kopf verlieren.
Perdere la testa.

HEADED
To be hot-headed.
Etre impulsif / Avoir la tête chaude.
Ser impulsivo.
Hitzköpfig sein.
Essere impulsivo / Essere una testa calda.

HEADS
Two heads are better than one. (prov.)
Deux précautions valent mieux qu'une.

Dos cabezas valen más que una.
Zwei Köpfe sind besser als einer.
Due teste valgono più di una.

HEADY

A heady wine.
Un vin qui monte à la tête.
Un vino que se sube a la cabeza.
Ein berauschender Wein / Ein zu Kopf steigender Wein.
Un vino che dà alla testa.

HEAPS

To feel heaps better.
Etre beaucoup mieux.
Estar mucho mejor.
Sich sehr viel besser fühlen.
Stare molto meglio.

HEART

To heart's content.
A votre gré.
Al gusto.
Nach Herzenslust.
A proprio piacimento.

To be down at heart.
Etre découragé.
Estar descorazonado.
Mutlos sein / Entmutigt sein.
Essere depresso / Essere giù di corda.

At heart he's not bad.
Dans le fond il n'est pas méchant.
En el fondo no es malo.
Er hat kein schlechtes Herz / Im Grunde ist er nicht schlecht.
In fondo non è cattivo.

To learn by heart.
Apprendre par cœur.
Aprender de memoria.

Auswendig lernen.
Imparare a memoria.

To have one's heart in one's boots.
Avoir peur.
Tener miedo.
Das Herz in der Hose haben.
Aver paura.

To cry one's heart out.
Pleurer à chaudes larmes.
Llorar a mares.
Sich die Augen ausweinen.
Piangere a calde lacrime / Consumarsi dal pianto.

To set one's heart on something.
Désirer ardemment une chose.
Desear ardientemente alguna cosa.
Etwas aus vollem Herzen wünschen.
Desiderare ardentemente una cosa.

Take heart!
Courage!
¡Cobren ánimo!
Fassen Sie Mut!
Fatevi coraggio!

To wear one's heart upon one's sleeve.
Parler le cœur sur la main.
Hablar con el corazón en la mano.
Das Herz auf der Zunge haben.
Parlare col cuore in mano.

HEARTBURN

Heartburn.
Brûlures d'estomac.
Ardor de estomago.
Sodbrennen.
Bruciore di stomaco.

HEARTY

A hearty laugh.
Un rire de bon cœur.

272

Una profunda carcajada.
Ein herzliches Lachen.
Una risata di cuore (di gusto).

HEAVEN

To move heaven and earth.
Remuer les montagnes.
Remover cielo y tierra.
Himmel und Hölle in Bewegung setzen.
Muovere mari e monti.

HEAVY

As heavy as lead. (comp.)
Lourd comme le plomb.
Pesado como el plomo.
Schwer wie Blei / Sehr schwer.
Molto pesante / Pesante come il piombo.

Heavy-handed.
Maladroit.
Torpe.
Plump / Ungeschickt.
Maldestro.

HEELS

To take to one's heels.
Prendre ses jambes à son cou.
Huir / Escapar.
Die Beine in die Hand nehmen.
Darsela a gambe (levate).

To kick one's heels.
Devoir attendre.
Ser dejado esperando.
Ungeduldig warten.
Essere lasciato ad aspettare.

HEIGHT

The height of perfection.
Le sommet de la perfection.

Lo máximo de la perfección.
Der Gipfel an Perfektion.
L'apice della perfezione.

The height of folly.
Le comble de la folie.
El colmo de la locura.
Der Gipfel an Torheit / Gipfel der Torheit.
Il colmo della follia.

HELL

To suffer hell on earth.
Souffrir les peines de l'enfer.
Sufrir las penas del infierno.
Höllenqualen leiden (auf der Erde).
Soffrire molto / Patire le pene dell'inferno.

HELP

Help yourself, please!
Servez-vous, je vous en prie!
¡Sírvase por favor!
Bitte, bedienen Sie sich! / Bedienen Sie sich bitte!
Si serva, prego!

I don't see him more than I can help.
Je ne le vois que le strict nécessaire.
No le veo más de lo necesario.
?! Ich sehe keine Notwendigkeit mehr, ihm zu helfen.
Lo vedo il meno possibile.

HELPED

It can't be helped.
Il n'y a pas de remède.
No hay más remedio.
Es lässt sich nichts machen (ändern).
Non c'è rimedio / E' inevitabile.

HEN

A hen-pecked husband.
Un mari qui se laisse commander par sa femme.

274

Un marido que es mandado por la mujer.
Ein Pantoffelheld.
Un marito tiranneggiato dalla moglie.

A hen-party.
Réunion seulement de femmes.
Reunión exclusiva para mujeres.
Damengesellschaft / Kaffeekränzchen.
Una riunione di sole donne.

HERE

Here and there.
Ici et là.
Por aquí y por allá / Aquí y allá.
Hier und dort / Hierhin und dorthin / Hier und da.
Qua e là.

Here, there and everywhere.
Partout.
Por donde sea.
Überall.
Dappertutto.

That is neither here nor there.
Cela ne concerne pas ce problème.
Esto no tiene nada que ver.
Das gehört nicht zur Sache / Das besagt nichts.
Non rientra nell'argomento.

HIDE

To save one's hide.
Sauver sa peau.
Salvar el cuero.
Die eigene Haut retten.
Salvare la pelle.

To hide one's head.
Se cacher à cause de la honte.
Esconderse por la vergüenza.
Sich vor Scham verbergen (verstecken).
Nascondersi per la vergogna.

HIGH (♥)

To have high jinks.
Faire bombance.
Echar una cana al áire.
Übermütige Laune haben / Ausgelassen sein.
Fare baldoria.

High and mighty.
Arrogant.
Arrogante.
Erhaben / Arrogant / Hochmütig.
Arrogante.

(♦) To like the high life. (p. 277)
Aimer mener grand train.
Amar el lujo.
Das Leben im Luzus lieben / Ein luxuriöses Leben lieben.
Amare la vita lussuosa.

High-handed.
Autoritaire / Exigeant.
Arbitrario / Despótico.
Anmassend.
Prepotente.

To search high and low.
Chercher partout.
Buscar por doquiér / Buscar por todas partes.
Überall suchen.
Cercare dappertutto / Cercare per mare e per terra.

HIGHBROW

A highbrow.
Un intellectuel.
Un intelectual / Un sabihondo.
Eine Intellektuelle / Ein Intellektueller.
Un intellettuale.

HIGHLY (♥)

(♦) To be highly - strung. (p. 278)
Avoir un tempérament nerveux.

276

277

Tener un carácter nervioso.
Reizbar / Überempfindlich.
Avere un temperamento nervoso.

HINGE

Everything hinges on what he decides.
Tout dépend de sa décision.
Todo depende de lo que decida él.
Alles hängt von seiner Entscheidung ab.
Tutto dipende dalla sua decisione.

HINT

To hint at something.
Faire allusion à quelque chose.
Aludir a algo.
Etwas andeuten / Auf etwas anspielen.
Fare allusione a qualcosa.

HIT

To hit the nail on the head.
Faire mouche / Tomber juste.
Acertar / Atinar / Dar en el blanco.
Den Nagel auf den Kopf treffen / Ins Schwarze treffen / Den Kern der Sache treffen.
Azzeccare / Colpire nel segno.

To make a hit.
Frapper.
Caer en gracia / Impresionar favorablemente.
Einen Treffer erzielen / Erfolg haben.
Far colpo.

HITCH

Everything went off without a hitch.
Tout alla à merveille.
Todo ha ido sin tropiezos.
Alles lief reibungslos (glatt) ab.
Tutto andò liscio.

HOARSE

As hoarse as a crow. (comp.)
Très rauque.
Muy ronco.
Heiser / Rauh / Wie ein Rabe krächzen.
Molto rauco / Rauco come una rana.

HOLD

To hold out.
Tenir bon.
Mantenerse firme.
Aushalten / Durchhalten / Standhalten.
Tener duro.

Hold your tongue!
Taisez-vous!
¡Cierre la boca!
Haltet den Mund! / Seid still! / Seien Sie still!
State zitto!

To hold one's own.
Etre sur ses gardes.
Mantenerse firme sobre lo que uno piensa.
Sich nicht einmischen.
Stare sulle proprie.

Not to hold water.
Ne pas être valable.
No ser válido.
Nicht stichhaltig sein.
Non essere valido.

HOLE

A square peg in a round hole.
Un poisson hors de l'eau.
Un pez fuera del agua.
Ein Mensch am falschen Platz / Ein Fisch ausserhalb des Wassers.
Un pesce fuor d'acqua.

To put someone in a hole.
Mettre quelqu'un dans les ennuis.
Meter en líos a alguien.

Jemandem Schwierigkeiten machen / Jemanden in Verlegenheit bringen.
Mettere qualcuno nei pasticci.

HOLLOW

Hollow promises.
Fausses promesses.
Promesas de marinero.
Leere Versprechungen.
False promesse / Promesse da marinaio.

Hollow words.
Mots qui sonnent faux.
Palabras huecas.
Hohle (Leere, Nichtssagende, Nichtige) Worte.
Parole false.

HOME

I look upon Paris as my home.
Je considère Paris comme ma patrie.
Considéro París mi tierra adoptiva.
Ich betrachte Paris als meine Heimat.
Considero Parigi la mia patria / A Parigi mi sento a casa mia.

HOMELY

A homely girl.
Une fille moche.
Una muchacha muy simple (de apariencia).
Ein hausbackenes Mädchen.
Una ragazza bruttina.

A homely old lady.
Une vieille dame sans façons.
Una señora anciana muy a la mano.
Eine gemütliche alte Dame.
Una vecchia signora alla mano.

HONEST

To earn an honest penny.
Gagner honnêtement sa vie.

Ganarse honradamente la vida.
Sich sein Geld ehrlich (redlich) verdienen.
Guadagnarsi onestamente la vita.

HONEY

As sweet as honey. (comp.)
Doux comme le miel.
Dulce como la miel.
Süss wie Honig.
Dolce come il miele.

HOOK

Hook, line, and sinker.
Tout à fait.
Del todo.
Vollständig.
Del tutto.

By hook or by crook.
De gré ou de force.
Por las buenas o por la malas / Por angas o por mangas.
Unter allen Umstanden / So oder so.
Di riffa o di raffa.

HOOT

I don't care a hoot!
Cela ne me touche pas!
¡No me importa un comino!
Das ist mir schnuppe (egal, gleich)!
Non me ne importa un fico secco!

It's not worth two hoots!
Ça ne vaut rien!
¡No vale un comino! / ¡No vale nada!
Es ist keinen Pfifferling wert!
Non vale un fico.

HOP (♦)

(♦) Hop it! (p. 284)
Fiche le camp!
¡Véte! / ¡Desaparece!
Verzieh dich! / Verdufte! / Verschwinden Sie!
Sparisci!

HOPE

While there is life there is hope. (prov.)
Tant qu'il y a de la vie il y a de l'espoir.
Mientras haya vida hay esperanza.
Solange es Leben gibt, gibt es Hoffnung.
Finchè c'è vita c'è speranza.

HORNS

To draw in one's horns.
Reculer.
Hacerse para atrás.
Die Hörner einziehen / Sich zurückziehen.
Tirarsi indietro.

HORSE (♦)

(♦) To get something straight from the horse's mouth. (p. 285)
Obtenir un tuyau.
Obtener de fuente fidedigna una información.
Etwas aus erster Hand (Quelle) erhalten.
Ottenere una informazione di prima mano.

You may take a horse to water, but you can't make him drink.
On ne saurait faire boire un âne qui n'a pas soif.
Se puede llevar el caballo al agua, pero no se le puede hacer beber.
Das ist verlorene (vergebliche) Liebesmüh / Man kann niemanden zu etwas zwingen.
Non si può far bere l'asino per forza.

One shouldn't look a gift horse in the mouth. (prov.)
A cheval donné on ne regarde pas à la dent.

A caballo regalado no se le mira el diente.
Einem geschenkten Gaul schaut man nicht ins Maul.
A caval donato non si guarda in bocca.

To eat like a horse.
Manger comme un loup.
Comer como lobo.
Fressen wie ein Wolf.
Mangiare come un lupo.

HORSES
To hold one's horses.
Réprimer son impatience.
Refrenar la propria impaciencia.
Seine Ungeduld zügeln.
Frenare la propria impazienza.

HOT (♦)
As hot as fire. (comp.)
Brûlant.
Caliente como el fuego / Ardiente como las brasas.
Glühend heiss.
Molto caldo.

As hot as pepper. (comp.)
Très piquant.
Muy picante / Qué pica mucho.
Sehr scharf / Brennend scharf.
Molto piccante.

Hot foot.
En vitesse / A la hâte.
Muy deprisa.
Schnellen Fusses / In grosser Eile.
In gran fretta.

Give it him hot!
Passe-lui un bon savon!
¡Dále una buena regañada!
Gib es ihm tüchtig! / Zeig es ihm! / Heiz ihm ein!
Dagli una bella strigliata!

286

(♦) **To get into hot water.** (p. 287)
Se mettre dans de mauvais draps.
Meterse en líos.
In des Teufels Küche geraten.
Mettersi nei guai.

HOUND

To hound out.
Chasser.
Sacar afuera.
Davon jagen / Fortjagen / Wegjagen.
Cacciar via.

HOUSE (♥)

To get on like a house on fire.
Faire de grands progrès.
Hacer grandes progresos / Adelantarse mucho en algo.
Blitzschnell vorankommen / Grosse Fortschritte machen.
Fare grandi progressi.

(♦) **To bring the house down.** (p. 289)
Faire s'écrouler le théâtre sous les applaudissements.
Hacer venir abajo.el teatro por los aplausos.
Stürmischen Beifall auslösen.
Far crollare il teatro per gli applausi.

To keep open house.
Garder sa porte ouverte.
Ser disponible.
Offenes Haus halten / Gastfrei sein.
Tenere la porta di casa sempre aperta.

House-warming.
Pendaison de crémaillère.
Fiesta de estreno de la nueva casa.
Einzugsfest.
Festa per inaugurare una casa nuova.

HOWL

To howl with laughter.
Se tordre de rire / Se bidonner.

Ahogarse de la risa.
Sich halb tot lachen.
Sbellicarsi dalle risa.

HUDDLE

To go into a huddle with somebody.
Avoir un entretien secret avec quelqu'un.
Reunirse con alguien para aconsejarse o planear algo secreto.
Sich mit jemandem beraten / Die Köpfe zusammenstecken.
Avere un abboccamento segreto con qualcuno.

HUFF

To be in a huff.
Etre irrité.
Estar enojado.
Ärgerlich (Wütend) sein / Gekränkt sein.
Essere adirato.

HUM

To hum and haw.
Hésiter.
Titubear al hablar / Tropezarse con las palabras.
Herumdrucksen / Unschlüssig sein.
Titubare / Esitare nel parlare.

To make things hum.
Faire aller les choses avec succès.
Hacer que las cosas vayan de manera expédita.
Die Sache in Schwung bringen.
Far andare le cose con brio.

HUMBLE

To eat humble pie.
S'humilier.
Humillarse / Tragar amargo.
Sich demütigen / Abbitte tun / Zu Kreuze kriechen.
Umiliarsi.

290

HUMDRUM

To live a humdrum life.
Mener une vie monotone.
Hacer una vida rutinaria.
Ein eintöniges (fades, langweiliges) Leben führen.
Fare una vita monotona.

HUMOUR

To be in humour for . . .
Etre en veine de . . .
Tener ganas de . . .
Aufgelegt sein zu . . . / Laune haben zu . . .
Essere in vena di . . .

HUNCH

To have a hunch.
Avoir un soupçon.
Tener una sospecha.
Eine (Vor)Ahnung haben / Einen Verdacht haben.
Avere un sospetto.

HUNGRY

To be as hungry as a hunter. (comp.)
Avoir une faim de loup.
Tener un hambre de lobos.
Hungrig sein wie ein Tiger.
Avere una fame da lupo.

HUNT

To hunt for a lost pen.
Etre à la recherche d'un stylo égaré.
Buscar una pluma que se ha perdido.
Eifrig nach einer verlorenen Feder suchen.
Cercare una penna smarrita.

HUSH

To hush up a scandal.
Etouffer un scandale.

Encubrir un escándalo.
Einen Skandal vertuschen.
Soffocare uno scandalo.

HUSTLE

Hustle and bustle.
Activité grouillante.
Vaivén / Actividad febríl.
Gehetze.
Piena attività.

ICE (♦)

To break the ice. (p. 69)
Briser la glace.
Romper el hielo.
Das Eis brechen.
Rompere il ghiaccio.

To cut no ice.
Ne pas avoir d'importance.
No tener la menor importancia.
Keinen Eindruck machen / Nichts zu sagen haben.
Non avere importanza.

To be on thin ice.
Aborder un sujet délicat / Mettre le doigt sur la plaie.
Tocar un punto delicado.
An eine delikate Sache rühren.
Toccare un tasto delicato.

ICEBERG

She's an iceberg.
C'est un glaçon.
Ella es un pedazo de hielo.
Sie ist wie ein Eisberg / Sie ist eine kalte Person / Sie ist wie
ein Stück Eis / Sie ist eiskalt.
E' una persona fredda / E' un iceberg / E' un pezzo di ghiaccio.

IDEA

I haven't an idea.
Je ne sais vraiment pas.

No sé / No tengo idea.
Ich habe keine Ahnung.
Non so proprio.

IDEAS

A man of ideas.
Un homme ingégneux.
Un hombre de ingenio.
Ein Mann voller Ideen.
Un uomo ingegnoso.

IDLE

Idle talk.
Discussions inutiles.
Charlas inútiles / Babosadas.
Leeres Gerede / Gewäsch.
Chiacchiere inutili.

IGNORANT

I am quite ignorant of the fact.
J'ignore complètement le fait.
No estoy enterado de los hechos.
Ich weiss absolut nichts von der Sache / Ich kenne die Tatsache nicht.
Sono completamente all'oscuro del fatto.

IGNORED

He ignored my offer.
Il ne tint pas compte de mon offre.
Ignoró mi oferta.
Er ignorierte mein Angebot / Er nahm keine Notiz von meinem Angebot.
Non tenne conto della mia offerta.

ILL

It's an ill wind that blows no good. (prov.)
A quelque chose malheur est bon.
No hay mal que por bien no venga.

Etwas Gutes ist an allem.
Tutto il male non viene per nuocere.

III weeds grow apace. (prov.)
Les choses maléfiques se répandent rapidement.
Mala hierba nunca muere.
Unkraut verdirbt nicht.
La mala erba non si spegne mai / Le cose malefiche si diffondono rapidamente.

I was taken ill.
Je suis tombé malade.
Me puse enfermo.
Ich erkrankte.
Caddi ammalato.

III-natured.
Mauvais caractère.
De mala indole / De mal carácter.
Unfreundlich / Bösartig.
Di cattivo carattere.

An ill-timed remark.
Une observation déplacée.
Una observación inoportuna.
Eine unpassende Bemerkung.
Un'osservazione inopportuna (fatta a sproposito).

IMAGE
John's the very image of his father.
John est tout le portrait de son père.
John es el mero retrato de su padre.
John ist ganz der Vater / John ist das Abbild seines Vaters.
John è proprio il ritratto di suo padre.

IMITATION
Imitation is the sincerest form of flattery.
L'imitation est la manifestation la plus sincère de l'adulation.
La imitación es la manifestación más sincera de adulación.
Nachahmung ist die reinste Form von Schmeichelei.
La manifestazione più sincera dell'adulazione è l'imitazione.

IMMATERIAL

It is immaterial to me whether you are early or late.
Ça m'est égal si tu arrives en avance ou si tu arrives en retard.
No me interesa si llegas tarde o puntual.
Es ist unwesentlich (belanglos) für mich, ob du früh oder spät ankommst / Es ist mir gleich, ob du früh oder spät kommst.
Mi è del tutto indifferente se arrivi in anticipo o se arrivi in ritardo.

IMMERSED

He was immersed in the music.
Il était plongé dans la musique.
Estaba ensimismado en la música.
Er war in Musik versunken.
Era immerso nella musica.

IMPERATIVE

It is imperative that you do your homework.
Il est indispensable que tu fasses tes devoirs.
¡Es indispensable que tu hagas los deberes!
Es ist unumgänglich (dringend nötig / unbedingt erforderlich), dass du deine Hausaufgaben machst.
E' essenziale che tu faccia il compito.

IMPLY

Silence implies consent. (prov.)
Qui ne dit mot consent.
El silencio implíca aconsentimiento.
Stillschweigen bedeutet Zustimmung.
Chi tace acconsente.

IMPOSE

To impose upon.
Profiter.
Abusar de . . .
Jemanden ausnützen / Jemanden missbrauchen.
Approfittare.

IN

To be in on something.
Etre au courant de quelque chose.
Estar al día con algo.
In einer Sache auf dem laufenden sein.
Essere al corrente di qualcosa.

In fashion.
A la mode.
De moda.
Nach der Mode.
Di moda.

INCH (♦)

He came within an inch of being hit by the car.
Il s'en est fallu de peu qu'il ne soit renversé par la voiture.
Por un pelo no he sido arrollado por un coche.
Um ein Haar wurde er von dem Auto überfahren.
Per un pelo non fu investito dalla macchina.

Every inch an Italian.
Il est Italien de la tête aux pieds.
Es un Italiano de los pies a la cabeza.
Von Kopf bis Fuss Italiener / Durch und durch Italiener.
E' un Italiano da capo a piedi.

Within an inch of ...
A un poil de ...
Estar a punto de ...
Um ein Haar / Fast.
A un pelo da ...

(♦) Give him an inch and he'll take a mile. (p. 297)
Tu lui donnes un doigt et il te prend tout le bras.
Si le das la mano te toma el brazo.
Gibt man ihm den kleinen Finger, so nimmt er die ganze Hand.
Se gli dai un dito, si prenderà tutto il braccio.

Not to yield an inch.
Ne céder en rien.
No hay que ceder de una pulgada.
Nicht einen Zoll weichen / Nicht im geringsten nachgeben.
Non cedere d'un millimetro.

INDIFFERENT

His French is very indifferent.
Son français est vraiment désastreux.
Su Francés deja a que desear / Su Francés es chueco.
Sein Französisch ist sehr mittelmässig.
Il suo francese è assai scadente.

INFRINGE

To infringe upon someone's rights.
Violer les droits de quelqu'un.
Violar los derechos de alguien.
Die Rechte von jemandem verletzen
Violare i diritti di qualcuno.

INNOCENT

As innocent as a dove. (comp.)
Innocent / Ingénu.
Inocente como un cordero.
Völlig unschuldig.
Innocente come una colomba.

INQUIRE

To inquire about somebody.
Prendre des renseignements sur quelqu'un.
Informarse de alguien.
Sich über jemanden informieren (erkundigen).
Informarsi di qualcuno.

INQUIRING

An inquiring mind.
Un esprit avide de connaissances.
Una mente aguda / Una mente ávida de saber.
Ein forschender Geist / Wissbegierig sein.
Una mente avida di sapere.

INROADS

To make inroads upon one's health.
Ruiner sa santé.

Mermarse la salud.
Seiner Gesundheit schaden / Seine Gesundheit überbeanspru-
chen / Mit seiner Gesundheit spielen.
Danneggiare la propria salute.

INS

To know all the ins and outs of English grammar.
Connaître à fond la grammaire anglaise / Connaître les tenants
et les aboutissants de la grammaire anglaise.
Conocer todos los pormenores de la gramática inglesa.
Die englische Grammatik bis ins Kleinste kennen / Die englische
Grammatik in- und auswendig kennen.
Conoscere a fondo la grammatica inglese.

INSIDE

Your jersey is inside out.
Ton pull-over est à l'envers.
Tu suéter está al revés.
Du hast deinen Pullover falsch herum an / Dein Pullover ist
links / Die Innenseite deines Pullovers ist aussen.
Il tuo maglione è alla rovescia.

Inside a month.
Moins d'un mois.
En menos de un més.
Innerhalb eines Monats / In weniger als einem Monat.
Tra meno d'un mese.

INSTANCE

For instance.
Par exemple.
Po ejemplo.
Zum Beispiel.
Per esempio.

INTENT

To be intent upon one's work.
Etre absorbé par son travail.

Estar ocupado con el propio trabajo.
Mit seiner Arbeit eifrig beschäftigt sein.
Essere intento al proprio lavoro.

INVENTION

Necessity is the mother of invention. (prov.)
Nécessité est mère d'industrie.
La necesidad es la madre de las invenciones.
Not macht erfinderisch.
Il bisogno aguzza l'ingegno / Necessità è madre dell'invenzione
(delle arti).

IRON (♦)

To iron out any troubles.
Eliminer les difficultés.
Eliminar cualquier dificultad.
Alle Schwierigkeiten ausbügeln (ausgleichen; beseitigen).
Eliminare le difficoltà.

(♦) To strike while the iron is hot. (prov.) (p. 301)
Battre le fer tant qu'il est encore chaud.
Darle al hierro mientras esté caliente.
Das Eisen schmieden, solange es heiss ist.
Battere il ferro finché è caldo.

To rule with an iron hand.
Commander avec une poigne de fer.
Gobernar con mano de hierro.
Mit eiserner Hand regieren.
Governare con mano di ferro.

To have too many irons in the fire.
Avoir trop de choses en main.
Querer abarcar demasiadas cosas.
Zu viele Eisen im Feuer haben.
Avere troppe cose per le mani / Avere troppa carne al fuoco.

IT

Keep at it!
Ne (le) lâche pas!

301

¡Persiste! / ¡Sigue dandole!
Nicht nachlassen! / Mach weiter! / Nicht aufgeben!
Non mollare!

JACK

Before you can say Jack Robinson.
En un clin d'œil.
En menos que no se diga.
Im Nu / Ehe man sich's versieht.
In un batter d'occhio / In men che non si dica.

Jack of all trades.
Homme à tout faire.
Aprendíz de todo pero oficial de nada / Un hacelotodo.
Ein Mann für alles / Alleskönner / Allerweltskerl / Handsdampt
in allen Gassen.
Tuttofare.

Jack-in-office.
Fonctionnaire qui veut se donner de l'importance.
Un personaje que pretende darse mucha importancia.
Wichtigtuerischer Beamter.
Funzionario che vuol darsi importanza.

Every man Jack.
« Tutti quanti » / Et tous les autres.
Todo el mundo.
Jedermann / Hin und Kunz.
Tutti quanti.

JERICHO

Go to Jericho!
Va au diable!
¡Véte al diablo!
Scher Dich zum Teufel!
Va a farti benedire!

JIFFY

In a jiffy.
En un clin d'œil.

302

En menos que no se diga / En un abrir y cerrar de ojos.
Im Nu / In einem Augenblick.
In un batter d'occhio.

JINGO

By jingo!
Parbleu!
¡Caramba! / ¡Diablos! / ¡Por Dios!
Alle Wetter! / Potztausend! / Donnerwetter!
Perbacco!

JOCKEY

To jockey for position.
Manœuvrer avec habileté pour acquérir une position.
Maniobrar para sacar ventaja o ganar un puesto.
Sich geschickt in eine Position (Stellung) hineinmanövrieren /
Sich durch Protektion eine Stellung verschaffen wollen.
Manovrare abilmente per raggiungere una posizione.

JOKE

It's no joke.
C'est une affaire sérieuse / C'est sérieux!
Esto es en serio.
Es ist kein Scherz (Witz).
E' un affare serio / Non è uno scherzo.

JOT

To jot down something.
Prendre des notes.
Tomar apuntes.
Etwas schnell notieren (aufschreiben).
Buttare giù appunti.

JUGGLE

To juggle with words.
Jouer avec les mots / Jongler avec les mots.
Jugar con las palabras / Hacer un juego de palabras.
Mit Worten spielen.
Giocare con le parole.

JUMP (♦)

To jump at an offer.
Se dépêcher d'accepter une offre / Sauter sur l'occasion.
Aprovechar con rapidez de una oferta.
Auf ein Angebot eingehen.
Affrettarsi ad accettare un'offerta.

(♦) To jump on someone. (p. 305)
Se lancer contre quelqu'un.
Abalanzarse contra de alguien.
Sich auf jemanden stürzen / Jemandem aufs Dach steigen.
Scagliarsi / Lanciarsi contro qualcuno.

To jump down a person's throat.
Interrompre quelqu'un brusquement.
Interrumpir a alguien con brusquedad.
Eine Person anschnauzen (anfahren) / Auf eine Person losgehen.
Interrompere qualcuno bruscamente.

(♦) To jump the queue. (p. 306)
Passer devant quelqu'un / Resquiller.
Colarse en una cola.
Sich vordrängen / Aus der Reihe tanzen.
Passare avanti agli altri che sono in fila.

To jump out of one's skin.
Avoir une peur bleue.
Tener mucho miedo.
Grosse Angst haben.
Avere molta paura.

JUST

I was just about to go.
J'étais sur le point de sortir.
Estaba a punto de salir / Estaba apenas saliendo.
Ich war gerade dabei zu gehen.
Ero sul punto di uscire / Stavo per uscire.

I just managed to catch the train.
J'ai juste réussi à prendre le train à temps.
He podido apenas tomar el tren.
Ich schaffte es gerade noch, den Zug zu nehmen / Ich erwischte den Zug gerade noch.
Sono riuscito a stento a prendere il treno.

306

That's just like her!
Ça c'est bien d'elle!
¡Esta es precisamente ella!
Das sieht ihr ganz ähnlich!
Questo è proprio da lei!

Just now.
Il y a un instant.
Desde hace poco.
Jetzt / Jetzt gleich / Soeben.
Poco fa.

JUSTICE
To do oneself justice.
Se faire honneur.
Salir con honra.
Sich Ehre machen.
Farsi onore.

JUSTIFIED
To feel justified in doing something.
Se sentir en droit de faire quelque chose.
Sentirse en derecho de hacer algo.
Sich berechtigt fühlen, etwas zu tun.
Sentirsi in diritto di fare qualcosa.

KEEL
To keel over.
Tomber comme foudroyé.
Volcarse / Caer patas arriba / Desplomarse.
Umfallen / Kentern.
Cadere di schianto.

KEEN
A keen appetite.
Un bon appétit.
Un buen apetito.
Einen guten Appetit / Einen Heisshunger.
Un buon appetito.

As keen as mustard. (comp.)
Très enthousiaste.
Muy entusiasta.
Versessen(auf) . . . / Feuer und Flamme(für) . . .
Molto entusiasta.

To be keen on . . .
Etre passionné de . . .
Ser apasionado de . . . / Ser aficionado de . . .
Begeistert sein von . . . / Lust haben zu . . . / Erpicht sein auf . . .
Essere appassionato di . . .

KEEP (♦)

To keep open house.
Etre hospitalier / Laisser sa porte ouverte.
Ser disponible / Ser hospital.
Gastfreundlich sein / Offenes Haus haben.
Essere ospitale / Tenere la porta di casa sempre aperta.

To keep the ball rolling.
Saisir la balle au bond / Faire avancer les choses.
Hacer que las cosas marchen.
Etwas in Gang halten.
Fare andare avanti la cosa.

To keep one's head.
Ne pas perdre la tête / Garder la tête sur les épaules.
No perder la cabeza.
Seinen Verstand behalten / Nicht den Kopf verlieren.
Non perdere la testa.

To keep one's temper.
Garder son calme.
Contenerse / Refrenarse.
Die Ruhe bewahren.
Mantenere la calma.

To keep good hours.
Aller au lit tôt / Se coucher comme les poules.
Ir a la cama temprano.
Zeitig ins Bett gehen.
Andare a letto presto.

To keep in with someone.
Rester en rapport avec quelqu'un.
Sostener relaciones con alguien.
Gut Freund bleiben mit jemandem / Mit jemandem zusammen-
halten.
Mantenere rapporti con qualcuno.

To keep oneself to oneself.
Rester dans son coin / Ne pas être sociable.
Ser poco sociable / Ser huraño.
Sich zurückhalten / Für sich bleiben / Ungesellig sein.
Tenersi in disparte / Non essere socievole.

To have just enough to keep body and soul together.
Avoir juste de quoi vivre.
Tener apenas de que vivir.
Eben genug haben, um Leib und Seele zusammenzuhalten.
Avere appena abbastanza di che vivere.

(♦) To keep on one's toes. (p. 310)
Rester sur la pointe des pieds / Etre circonspect.
Ser cauteloso.
Jemandem auf die Hühneraugen (Zehen) treten.
Stare guardingo.

That will keep!
Ça peut attendre!
¡Eso puede esperar!
Das eilt nicht.
Quello può aspettare!

Keep off the grass!
Ne plaisante pas!
¡Mantén las distancias! / ¡No hagas así!
Bitte nicht! / Halte dich zurück!
Non scherzare! / Non fare così!

KEEPING
Out of keeping with ...
En désaccord avec ...
Estar en desacuerdo con ...
Nicht im Einklang mit ... / Nicht in Übereinstimmung mit ...
In disaccordo con ...

KEEPS

For keeps.
Pour toujours.
Para siempre.
Auf (Für) immer / Endgültig.
Per sempre.

KETTLE (♦)

(♦) A pretty kettle of fish. (p. 196)
Une belle salade / Un beau gâchis!
Un buen lío.
Eine schöne Bescherung.
Un bel pasticcio.

KEYED

I felt all keyed up.
Je me sentais très excité.
Estaba muy excitado.
Ich fühlte mich völlig überreizt (überspannt).
Mi sentivo in uno stato di grande eccitazione.

KICK (♦)

He gets a kick out of sailing.
Ça lui plaît énormément de faire de la voile.
Goza llendo en bote de vela.
Er hat am Segeln mächtigen Spass.
Se la gode un mondo ad andare in barca a vela.

To kick up a fuss.
Faire du vacarme (du tapage).
Hacer un relajo.
Aufsehen erregen / Wirbel machen.
Fare una scenata.

(♦) To kick the bucket. (p. 312)
Mourir / Passer de vie à trépas.
Morir / Pasar a mejor vida.
Draufgehen / Abkratzen / Sterben.
Morire / Tirare le cuoia.

KID

To handle with kid gloves.
Traiter avec beaucoup d'égards / Prendre avec des pincettes.
Tratar con guantes de seda.
Mit Glacéhandschuhen anfassen.
Trattare coi guanti di velluto / Prendere con le pinze.

KILL (♦)

To kill two birds with one stone.
Faire d'une pierre deux coups.
Matar dos pájaros de un tiro.
Zwei Fliegen mit einem Schlag töten.
Prendere due piccioni con una fava.

To kill time.
Tuer le temps.
Matar el tiempo.
Die Zeit totschlagen.
Ammazzare il tempo.

(♦) It's killing me! (p. 314)
Ça me fait mal!
¡Me duele! / ¡Me está matando!
Das bringt mich (noch) um!
Mi fa un male terribile!

To be dressed to kill.
Etre habillé de façon extravagante.
Estar vestido de manera llamativa.
Todschick gekleidet sein.
Essere vestito in modo da far colpo.

KIND

Nothing of the kind!
Absolument pas!
¡Para nada!
Keineswegs!
Niente affatto!

We had a coffee of a kind.
Nous avons bu une espèce de café.

Tomamos algo que parecía café.
Wir tranken so etwas wie Kaffee (etwas Kaffeeartiges).
Bevemmo una specie di caffè.

I kind of expected it.
Je m'y attendais presque.
Me lo esperaba.
Ich erwartete es fast.
Quasi me l'aspettavo.

KINGDOM

Kingdom come.
L'autre monde / L'au-delà.
El otro mundo / El más allá.
Jenseits.
L'altro mondo / L'aldilà.

KINK

To have a kink.
Avoir des lubies.
Tener la cabeza a pájaros.
Einen Tick (Klaps) haben.
Avere grilli per la testa.

KIP

To have a kip.
Faire un somme.
Hacer una siesta.
Ein Schläfchen (Nickerchen) machen / Etwas pennen.
Fare un pisolino.

KITE

Go and fly a kite!
Va au diable!
¡Véte al diablo!
Geh zum Teufel!
Va a farti benedire!

KNACK

To have a knack for something.
Il est fait pour cela.
Estar hecho para algo.
Etwas loshaben / Etwas gut verstehen / Für etwas ein besonderes Geschick besitzen.
Essere tagliato per qualcosa.

KNIFE

War to the knife.
Guerre féroce.
Lucha encarnizada.
Krieg bis aufs Messer.
Guerra accanita / Guerra fino all'ultimo sangue.

KNOCK

To knock down a price.
Obtenir un rabais sur un prix.
Lograr una rebaja de precio.
Einen Preis drücken.
Ottenere una riduzione su un prezzo (uno sconto).

To knock off work.
S'arrêter de travailler / Cesser de travailler.
Parar de trabajar.
Die Arbeit einstellen / Feierabend machen.
Smettere di lavorare.

KNOT

To tie oneself up in knots.
Se mettre dans de beaux draps.
Meterse en líos.
Sich selber die Schlinge knüpfen / Sich in Schwierigkeiten bringen.
Mettersi nei guai.

KNOTTY

A knotty problem.
Un problème embrouillé.

316

Un asunto enredado.
Ein verwickeltes (verzicktes / schwieriges) Problem.
Una questione intricata.

KNOW

To know about . . .
Avoir connaissance de . . .
Estar enterado de . . .
In Kenntnis sein von . . . / Bescheid wissen über . . .
Essere a conoscenza di . . .

To know something by heart.
Savoir quelque chose par cœur.
Saber algo a memoria / Saber algo al dedillo.
Etwas aus dem Kopf wissen / Auswendig können.
Sapere qualcosa a memoria.

To know one's own mind.
Savoir ce qu'on veut.
Saber lo que se quiere / Saber lo de uno.
Wissen, was man will.
Sapere quel che si vuole.

To know what's what.
Savoir le pourquoi et le comment.
Estar bien informado sobre una cosa.
Genau Bescheid wissen.
Essere preparato (di una persona che sa il fatto suo).

I don't know him from Adam.
Je ne le connais ni d'Eve ni d'Adam.
No le conozco para nada.
Ich kenne ihn überhaupt nicht.
Non lo conosco affatto.

To know the ropes.
En savoir long.
Saber todas las tretas de un asunto o negocio.
Sich auskennen / Die Schliche kennen.
Saperla lunga.

A know-all.
Un puits de science.
Un sabihondo.

Ein Besserwisser / Ein Schlaumeier.
Un sapientone.

A know-nothing.
Un ignare.
Un ignorante.
Ein Unwissender / Eine Unwissende.
Un ignorantone.

To be in the know.
Etre au courant.
Estar al corriente.
Bescheid wissen / Eigeweiht sein / Im Bilde sein.
Essere al corrente.

KNOWLEDGE
Without my knowledge.
A mon insue.
Sin que yo estuviese enterado.
Ohne mein Wissen.
A mia insaputa.

KNUCKLE
To knuckle down to work.
Se mettre au travail avec entrain.
Aplicarse con tesón al trabajo.
Mit Eifer an die Arbeit gehen.
Mettersi al lavoro di buona lena.

LABOUR
To labour under many difficulties.
Se heurter à beaucoup de difficultés.
Trabajar con dificultad.
Unter vielen Schwierigkeiten zu leiden haben / Mit vielen
Schwierigkeiten zu kämpfen haben.
Affaticarsi contro molte difficoltà.

LADDER
The ladder of success.
Le chemin pour atteindre le succès.

El camino del éxito.
Die Erfolgsleiter.
La strada che porta al successo.

LADY

A lady-killer.
Un Don Juan / Un tombeur de dames.
Un donjuán / Un mujerero.
Ein Herzensbrecher.
Un dongiovanni.

LAMB

One may as well be hanged for a sheep as for a lamb. (prov.)
Autant vaut-il faire les choses à fond.
Es lo mismo tomar el toro por los cuernos que por la cóla / Es
mejor realizar algo hasta lo último.
Wenn schon, denn schon.
Tanto vale fare le cose fino in fondo / Chi ha fatto trenta
può fare trentuno.

LANDED

I was landed with the bill.
Le compte me fut confié / Je dus payer l'addition.
Me zamparon la cuenta / Tuve que pagar la cuenta.
Mir wurde die Rechnung aufgehalst / Die Rechnung landete
bei mir.
Il conto fu affibbiato a me.

LANE

It's a long lane that has no turning. (prov.)
Même les plus belles choses ont une fin / Tout a une fin.
Nada es eterno.
Nichts währt ewig.
Niente dura in eterno.

LAP

He just lapped it up.
Cela lui a beaucoup plu.

Se ha relamido del gusto.
Er verschlang es geradezu.
Gli è piaciuto molto.

LARGE

As large as life. (comp.)
En chair et en os.
De carne y hueso.
In Lebensgrösse.
In persona / In carne ed ossa.

LARK

If the sky falls, we shall catch larks. (prov.)
A quelque chose malheur est bon.
No hay mal que por bien no venga.
Das Böse kommt niemals alleine / Jedes Unglück hat auch
sein Gutes.
Tutto il male non viene per nuocere.

What a lark!
Quelle rigolade!
¡Qué divertido!
Wie lustig! / Welch ein Spass!
Che spasso!

I only did it for a lark.
Je l'ai fait seulement pour rire.
Lo hice por broma.
Ich habe es nur aus Spass gemacht.
L'ho fatto solo per scherzo.

LASH

To lash out.
Réprimander durement.
Censurar / Regañar.
Um sich schlagen / Ausschlagen / Ausfallend werden.
Rimproverare aspramente.

LAST (♦)

(♦) The last straw! (p. 575)
Le comble!

¡Lo máximo!
Der Gipfel! / Das fehlte gerade noch! / Jetzt reicht's!
Il colmo!

LATE

Of late.
Récemment.
Desde hace poco / Ultimamente.
Neuerdings / In letzter Zeit.
Di recente.

Better late than never.
Mieux vaut tard que jamais.
Mejor tarde que nunca.
Lieber spät als gar nicht.
Meglio tardi che mai.

LATER

Later on.
Plus tard.
Luego.
Später.
Più tardi.

Sooner or later.
Tôt ou tard.
Tarde o temprano.
Früher oder später.
Prima o poi.

LATEST

Have you heard the latest?
Tu connais la dernière?
¿Has oído la última novedad?
Hast du das Neueste gehört? / Hast du die letzten Neuigkeiten
gehört?
Hai sentito l'ultima?

LAUGH

He who laughs last laughs best. (prov.)
Rira bien qui rira le dernier.

El que rie por último rie mejor.
Wer zuletzt lacht, lacht am besten.
Ride bene chi ride l'ultimo.

To split one's sides with laughter.
Se tordre de rire / Se bidonner.
Matarse de la risa.
Sich kaputtlachen / Sich halb tot lachen.
Sbellicarsi dalle risa.

To laugh up one's sleeve.
Rire sous cape.
Reirse adentro.
Sich ins Fäustchen lachen.
Ridere sotto i baffi.

To laugh on the wrong side of one's mouth.
Passer du rire aux larmes / Rire jaune.
Pasar de la felicidad al pesar.
Jemandem vergeht das Lachen.
Passare dalla gioia al disappunto.

LAUGHING

He's a laughing stock.
Il est objet de dérision.
Está sujeto al ridículo.
Er ist die Zielscheibe des Spottes / Er ist Gegenstand des Gelächters.
E' oggetto di derisione.

LAW (♦)

Necessity knows no law. (prov.)
Nécessité ne connaît pas de loi.
La necesidad hace al hombre lobo.
Not kennt kein Gebot.
Necessità non ha legge.

(♦) To take the law into one's own hands. (p. 323)
Faire justice soi-même / Faire sa justice soi-même.
Hacer justicia por sí mismo.
Sich selber Gerechtigkeit verschaffen.
Farsi giustizia da sè.

LAY

Lay off!
Arrête!
¡Acábale ya! / ¡Aléjate!
Hör auf (damit)!
Smettila!

LAZY

Lazy-bones!
Paresseux!
¡Haragán! / ¡Perezoso!
Faulpelz!
Pigrone!

LEAD (♦)

(♦) To lead someone up the garden path. (p. 221)
Tromper quelqu'un.
Engañar a alguien.
Jemanden an der Nase herumführen.
Ingannare qualcuno.

To lead astray.
Dévier.
Llevar por mal camino / Descarriar.
In die Irre führen.
Sviare / Portare fuori strada.

LEAF

To turn over a new leaf.
Repartir à zéro / Commencer une nouvelle vie.
Comenzar una nueva vida / Hacer borrón y cuenta nueva.
Ein neues Leben beginnen.
Cominciare una vita nuova / Ricominciare da capo / Voltar
pagina.

LEAK

To spring a leak.
Présenter un défaut.
Mostrar un punto débil.

Ein Leck bekommen.
Presentare un errore / Far acqua.

The news leaked out.
La nouvelle a transpiré.
La noticia se ha filtrado.
Die Neuigkeiten (Nachrichten) sickerten durch.
La notizia trapelò.

LEARN

To learn something by heart.
Apprendre quelque chose par cœur.
Aprender de memoria.
Etwas auswendig lernen.
Imparare qualcosa a memoria.

LEAST

Least said, soonest mended. (prov.)
Les choses s'arrangent sans besoin de tant de discours.
Con menos palabras las cosas se arreglan mejor.
Je weniger Worte desto besser.
Meno se ne parla, prima si aggiustano le cose.

I'm not in the least tired.
Je ne suis pas du tout fatigué.
No estoy para nada cansado.
Ich bin nicht im geringsten müde.
Non sono affatto stanco.

LEAVE (♦)

To be on leave.
Etre en permission.
Estar de franco / Estar de permiso.
Beurlaubt sein.
Essere in licenza.

To leave no stone unturned.
Ne rien laisser au hasard.
No dejar nada de intentado / Intentarlo todo.
Nichts unversucht lassen.
Non lasciar nulla di intentato.

By your leave.
Avec votre permission.
Con vuestro permiso.
Mit Ihrer Erlaubnis (Genehmigung) / Mit Verlaub.
Col vostro permesso.

Leave it at that!
Laisse tomber!
¡Déjalo! / ¡Olvidate!
Belass es dabei! / Lass es dabei bewenden!
Lascia perdere!

(♦) To leave someone holding the baby. (p. 22)
Laisser quelqu'un dans de beaux draps.
Dejar a alguien en un lío.
Jemanden in Schwierigkeiten lassen / Jemandem die Sache
am Hals lassen / Jemandem etwas aufhalsen.
Lasciar qualcuno nei guai.

To leave someone in the lurch.
Laisser quelqu'un dans de beaux draps.
Dejar a alguien en un lío.
Jemanden im Stich lassen.
Lasciar qualcuno nei guai.

To take French leave.
Filer à l'anglaise.
Irse sin pagar.
Sich auf französisch verabschieden.
Svignarsela all'inglese.

You should leave off drinking.
Vous devriez cesser de boire.
Debería dejar de beber / Debería dejar de tomar.
Sie sollten das Trinken aufgeben.
Dovreste smettere di bere.

LEECH

To stick like a leech.
Etre pot de colle.
Estar pegado como una sanguijuela.
Wie eine Klette an jemandem hängen.
Stare attaccato (appiccicato) come una sanguisuga.

LEFT

What is left.
Ce qui est resté.
Lo que ha quedado.
Was übrig geblieben ist.
Ciò che è rimasto.

A left-handed compliment.
Un compliment ambigu.
Un cumplido de doble sentido / Una alabanza maliciosa.
Ein zweifelhaftes Kompliment.
Un complimento ambiguo.

LEG (♦)

(♦) Not to have a leg to stand on. (p. 680)
Ne pas avoir la moindre chance de réussir / Etre coincé.
No tener ni donde caerse muerto.
Keinen festen Boden unter den Füssen haben.
Non avere la minima speranza di riuscita / Essere fregato.

He's on his last leg.
Il n'a plus qu'un souffle de vie.
Está en las últimas.
Er pfeift aus dem letzten Loch.
E' al lumicino.

(♦) To find one's legs. (p. 328)
S'habituer / S'acclimater.
Adaptarse.
Seine Beine gebrauchen lernen.
Ambientarsi.

(♦) To pull someone's leg. (p. 450)
Mener quelqu'un par le bout du nez.
Burlarse de alguien.
Jemanden auf den Arm nehmen / Jemanden aufziehen.
Prendere qualcuno per il naso / Prendere qualcuno in giro /
Prendere qualcuno per il sedere.

LEGS

To take to one's legs.
Prendre ses jambes à son cou.

Escapar / Huir / Poner pies en polvorosa.
Seine Beine unter die Arme nehmen / Sich beeilen.
Darsela a gambe.

LEND

To lend a hand.
Prêter main-forte.
Dar una mano.
Mit zugreifen / Helfen.
Dare una mano.

LENGTH

To keep someone at arm's length.
Tenir quelqu'un à la distance nécessaire.
Tener alguien a distancia.
Sich jemanden vom Leibe halten / Jemanden auf Distanz halten.
Tenere qualcuno a debita distanza.

He would go to any length.
Il ferait n'importe quoi.
Haría cualquier cosa.
Er würde alles Erdenkliche tun.
Farebbe qualunque cosa.

LENGTHS

I'm ready to go to all lengths.
Je suis prêt à faire l'impossible.
Haré lo imposible / Haré cuanto esté de mi parte.
Ich bin bereit, aufs Ganze zu gehen / Ich werde vor nichts
zurückschrecken.
Sono pronto a fare l'impossibile.

LEOPARD

A leopard can't change his spots. (prov.)
Le caractère ne se change pas / Chassez le naturel, il revient
au galop!
El lobo aunque vista de oveja, lobo se queda.
Man kann nicht aus seiner Haut.
Il carattere non si cambia / Il lupo perde il pelo ma non il vizio.

329

LESS

The less said the better. (prov.)
Moins il parle, mieux ça vaut.
¡Lo menos habla, mejor!
Je weniger Worte desto besser / Reden ist Silber, Schweigen ist Gold.
Meno se ne parla, meglio è.

In less than no time.
En moins de temps qu'il ne faut pour le dire / En un clin d'œil.
En menos que no se diga.
In allerkürzester Zeit.
In meno che non si dica.

LET

To let fly at a person.
Lui en dire des vertes et des pas mûres.
Lanzarse verbalmente contra de una persona / Sacarle a una persona los paños al sol.
Über jemanden herfallen / Jemanden mit Schimpfworten überfallen.
Dirne di cotte e di crude a una persona.

LETTER

A red-letter day.
Une journée très importante.
Un día de gran importancia.
Festtag / Freudentag / Glückstag.
Una giornata molto importante.

LEVEL

On the level.
Sur de bonnes bases.
Obrar rectamente / Ser o decir la pura verdad.
Ehrlich / Fair.
Su giuste basi.

To keep a level head.
Garder son calme.
Mantener la calma / Mantenerse bien equilibrado.
Einen vernünftigen (klaren) Kopf behalten / Die Ruhe bewahren.
Restare calmo.

LEVY
To levy taxes.
Encaisser les taxes / Encaisser les impôts.
Recaudar los impuestos.
Steuern eintreiben.
Riscuotere le tasse.

LICK
To lick one's lips.
Se lécher les babines.
Lamerse los bigotes / Lamerse de gusto.
Sich den Mund lecken / Gelüste haben.
Leccarsi i baffi.

To lick someone's shoes.
Lécher les bottes de quelqu'un.
Adular con servilismo / Sobar la leva.
Vor jemandem kriechen.
Leccare i piedi a qualcuno.

LID
That puts the lid on it!
Ça c'est le comble!
¡Esto es el colmo!
Das setzt der Sache die Krone auf! / Das ist der Gipfel!
Questo è il colmo!

LIE
Let sleeping dogs lie.
Ne réveillez pas le chat qui dort.
No muevas las aguas revueltas.
Schlafende Hunde soll man nicht aufwecken.
Non svegliare il can che dorme.

To lie in wait.
Etre aux aguets.
Acechar.
Auf der Lauer liegen.
Stare in agguato.

To lie oneself out of trouble.
S'en sortir au moyen d'un mensonge.
Sacarse de apuros con una mentira.
Sich aus Schwierigkeiten herauslügen.
Cavarsi dai guai con una bugia.

LIFE

She was the life and soul of the party.
Elle était le boute-en-train de la soirée.
Ella era el alma de la fiesta.
Sie war die Seele der Party / Die Party stand und fiel mit ihr.
Era l'anima della festa.

To have the time of one's life.
S'amuser follement.
Divertirse como nunca.
Sich grossartig amüsieren.
Divertirsi un mondo.

To give one's life blood for ...
Risquer sa vie pour ...
Arriesgar la vida por ...
Sein Herzblut geben für ... / Sein Leben geben für ...
Arrischiare la vita per ...

LIFT (♦)

Not to lift a hand to help somebody.
Ne pas lever le petit doigt.
No alzar un dedo para ayudar a alguien.
Nicht einen Finger rühren, um jemandem zu helfen.
Non muovere un dito per aiutare qualcuno.

(♦) To give someone a lift. (p. 333)
Prendre quelqu'un en voiture.
Dar un jalón a alguien / Dar un pasaje.

332

Jemanden im Auto mitnehmen.
Dare un passaggio a qualcuno / Dare uno strappo a qualcuno.

LIGHT

As light as air. (comp.)
Léger comme une plume.
Ligero como el áire.
Leicht wie Luft / Leicht wie eine Feder.
Leggerissimo / Leggero come una piuma.

To make light of . . .
Prendre à la légère.
Tomar a la ligera . . .
Auf die leichte Schulter nehmen.
Prendere alla leggera.

As light as a feather. (comp.)
Très légère.
Ligera como una pluma.
Leicht wie eine Feder.
Molto leggero / Leggero come una piuma.

Light-fingered.
Agile.
De mano ligera.
Geschickt / Langfingerig / Diebisch.
Agile / Svelto di mano.

Light-handed.
Qui a du tact / Diplomate.
Que tiene tacto.
Gefühlvoll / Taktvoll.
Che ha tatto.

Light-headedness.
Etourderie.
Frívolo / Ligero de cascos.
Leichtsinnigkeit / Leichtfertigkeit.
Sventatezza.

To throw light upon a matter.
Eclaircir quelque chose / Elucider.

Aclarar un asunto.
Eine Sache erhellen (aufklären).
Chiarire una cosa / Far luce su una cosa.

LIKE (♥)

As like as two peas in a pod. (comp.)
Se ressembler comme deux gouttes d'eau.
Iguales como dos gotas de agua.
Sich gleichen wie ein Ei dem anderen.
Simili come due gocce d'acqua.

As like as two drops of water. (comp.)
Se ressembler comme deux gouttes d'eau.
Iguales como dos gotas de agua.
Sich gleichen wie ein Ei dem anderen.
Simili come due gocce d'acqua.

As like as two beans. (comp.)
Très ressemblant.
Muy parecidos.
Sich gleichen wie ein Ei dem anderen.
Molto simili / Simili come due gocce d'acqua.

What's he like?
Comment est-il? / A quoi ressemble-t-il?
¿Que te parece?
Wie sieht er aus? / Wie ist er?
Com'è?

I like the look of him.
J'aime son aspect.
Me gusta su aspecto / Me gusta su apariencia.
Ich mag sein Aussehen / Er gefällt mir.
Mi piace il suo aspetto.

(♦) Like father, like son. (prov.) (p. 336)
Tel père, tel fils.
Tal el padre, tal el hijo.
Wie der Vater, so der Sohn.
Tale il padre, tale il figlio.

To smoke like a chimney.
Fumer comme un pompier.
Fumar como una chimenea.

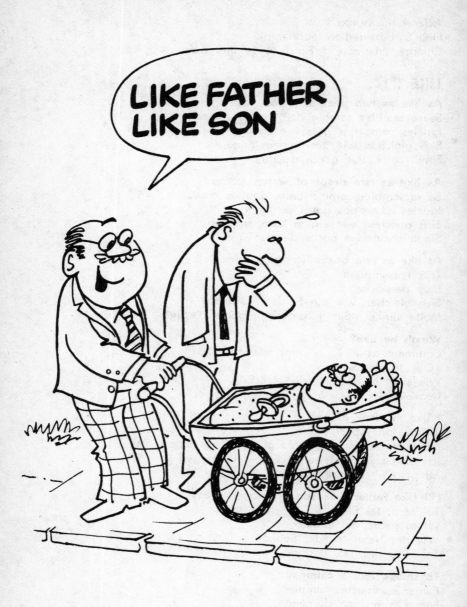

Rauchen wie ein Schlot.
Fumare come un turco / Fumare come una ciminiera.

To drink like a fish.
Boire comme un trou / Boire comme un Polonais.
Tomar como una esponja.
Trinken wie ein Säufer / Trinken wie ein Bierkutscher.
Bere come una spugna.

To fit like a glove.
Aller comme un gant.
Sentarle a uno bien (un traje).
Wie angegossen passen (sitzen).
Stare a pennello.

To hate like poison.
Haïr fortement.
Odiar ferozmente.
Wie die Pest hassen.
Odiare fortemente.

Like a shot.
En un éclair.
Como un rayo.
Wie der Blitz / Sofort.
In un lampo.

It looks like rain.
On dirait qu'il va pleuvoir.
Parece que va a llover.
Es sieht nach Regen aus.
Sembra che voglia piovere.

To swim like a duck.
Nager comme un poisson.
Nadar como un pez.
Schwimmen wie ein Fisch.
Nuotare benissimo / Nuotare come un pesce.

To swear like a trooper.
Jurer comme un charretier.
Blasfemar / Jurar como turco.
Wie ein Landsknecht fluchen.
Bestemmiare come un turco.

To spread like wildfire.
Se répandre en un clin d'œil.
Esparcerse con rapidez.
Sich wie Feuer ausbreiten (verbreiten).
Spargersi molto rapidamente / Dilagare.

I've never seen the like of it!
Je n'ai jamais vu une chose pareille!
¡Nunca he visto algo parecido!
Ich habe noch niemals Derartiges (Dergleichen / Ähnliches) gesehen!
Non ho mai visto una cosa simile!

Like blazes (like mad, like crazy).
En toute vitesse / A la va vite / En un éclair.
De toda prisa.
Wie Feuer / Wie verrückt / Wie toll.
In fretta e furia.

LIKING

To take a liking to someone.
Prendre quelqu'un en sympathie.
Tomar simpatía por una persona.
Zu jemandem eine Zuneigung fassen / An jemandem Gefallen finden.
Prendere qualcuno in simpatia.

It is to my liking.
Ça me va / Ça me va comme un gant.
Es de mi gusto.
Es ist nach meinem Geschmack / Es gefällt mir / Es sagt mir zu / Es passt mir gut.
Mi va a genio / Mi va a pennello.

LIMELIGHT

To be in the limelight.
Etre sous les feux de la rampe / Etre en vue.
Estar en vista.
Im Rampenlicht sein / Im Mittelpunkt stehen.
Essere alla ribalta / Essere molto in vista.

To be fond of the limelight.
Aimer la notoriété.
Ser amante de la celebridad.
Das Licht der Öffentlichkeit lieben / Sich gerne in den Mittel-
punkt stellen.
Essere amante della notorietà.

LIMIT
That's the limit!
Ça c'est le comble!
¡Esto es el colmo!
Das ist (doch) die Höhe! / Das ist der Gipfel!
Questo è il colmo!

LINE
To toe the line.
Etre aux ordres de . . .
Estar a las ordenes.
Sich der Disziplin beugen / Spuren.
Stare agli ordini.

LINES
Hard lines!
Dommage!
¡Que lástima!
Pech! / Schade!
Peccato!

LINGER
To linger.
Perdre du temps.
Demorarse.
Verweilen / Sich aufhalten / Zögern / Trödeln / Versäumen.
Perdere tempo.

LINING
Every cloud has a silver lining. (prov.)
A quelque chose malheur est bon.

No hay mal que por bien no venga.
Jedes Unglück hat auch sein Gutes / In jeder Finsternis ist
auch ein Lichtblick.
Non tutto il male viene per nuocere.

LION

The lion's share.
La part du lion.
La parte del león.
Der Löwenanteil.
La parte più grossa / La parte del leone.

LIP

To keep a stiff upper lip.
Tenir bon.
Empecinarse / No soltar.
Die Ohren steif halten.
Tener duro.

LIT

To be lit up.
Etre ivre / Etre gai.
Estar algo borracho.
Betrunken sein / Blau sein.
Essere ubriaco.

LITTLE (♦)

(♦) A little bird told me . . . (p. 341)
J'ai su indirectement . . . / Mon petit doigt m'a dit . . .
Un pajarito me ha dicho que . . .
Mein kleiner Finger hat es mir gesagt.
Ho saputo indirettamente . . . / Mi ha detto l'uccellino . . .

LIVE

Live and let live!
Vis et laisse vivre!
Vive y deja vivir.
Leben und leben lassen! / Leb und lass leben!
Vivi e lascia vivere!

To live up to something.
Garder foi à quelque chose / Etre cohérent.
Vivir en conformidad con algo.
In etwas Vertrauen haben / Einer Sache vertrauen.
Tener fede a qualcosa.

To live from hand to mouth.
Vivre au jour le jour.
Vivir al día.
Von der Hand in den Mund leben.
Vivere alla giornata.

LIVEN

To liven up a party.
Donner du mordant à une fête.
Animar una fiesta.
In eine Party Leben bringen / Eine Party beleben.
Dare vita ad una festa.

LOAD

To have loads of fun.
S'amuser follement.
Divertirse un montón.
Eine Menge Spass haben.
Divertirsi un mondo.

LOAF

Half a loaf is better than none.
Il vaut mieux tenir que courir / Un tiens vaut mieux que deux
tu l'auras.
Mitad pollo hoy es mejor que uno entero mañana.
Etwas ist besser als gar nichts.
Meglio un uovo oggi che una gallina domani.

LOAFER

He's a loafer.
Il gaspille son temps dans l'oisiveté.
Desperdicia el tiempo sin hacer nada.
Er ist ein Faulenzer (Müssiggänger / Taugenichts).
Sciupa il tempo nell'ozio.

LOCK

Lock, stock and barrel.
Avec armes et bagages.
Con todos sus pertrechos.
Mit Stumpf und Stil / Mit Sack und Pack / Mit allem Drum und Dran.
Con armi e bagagli.

Under lock and key.
Sous clef.
Bajo llave.
Hinter Schloss und Riegel / Unter Verschluss.
Sotto-chiave.

Lock the stable door after the horse is stolen. (prov.)
Fermer l'écurie quand les chevaux sont dehors.
Cerrar el corrál después que el ganado se ha escapado.
Eine Gegenmassnahme zu spät ergreifen / Eine Gegenmassnahme ergreifen, wenn das Unglück bereits geschehen ist.
Chiudere la stalla dopo che i buoi sono fuggiti.

LOG

Roll my log and I'll roll yours.
Une main lave l'autre.
Una mano ayuda a la otra.
Eine Hand wäscht die andere.
Una mano lava l'altra.

To sleep like a log.
Dormir comme un loir.
Dormir como piedra.
Schlafen wie ein Klot (Sack / Bär).
Dormire come un ghiro.

To fall like a log.
Tomber comme une masse.
Caerse estruendosamente.
Hinfallen (umfallen) wie ein Klotz.
Cadere come un sasso.

LOGGERHEADS

To be at loggerheads with someone.
Etre à couteaux tirés avec quelqu'un.

Estar a las últimas con alguien.
Sich in den Haaren liegen.
Essere ai ferri corti con qualcuno.

LONG

In the long run.
A la longue.
A la larga.
Auf die Dauer.
A lungo andare.

So long!
Au revoir! / A bientôt!
¡Hasta la vista!
Bis dann!
Arrivederci!

Of long standing.
De longue date.
Que ha prevalecido largo tiempo / Muy antiguo.
Seit langer Zeit bestehend / Alten Datums / Alt.
Di vecchia data.

LONGER (♦)

(♦) To take longer. (p. 345)
En avoir encore pour longtemps / Tarder.
Atrasarse.
Länger brauchen.
Averne ancora per molto.

LOOK (♦)

Look before you leap! (prov.)
Réfléchis avant d'agir!
¡Piensa antes de actuar!
Erst wägen, dann wagen!
Medita prima di agire!

To look blue.
Etre triste.
Estar triste.
Traurig aussehen.
Essere triste.

344

To look forward to . . .
Il me tarde de . . .
No ver la hora de . . .
Sich freuen auf . . . / Erwartungsvoll entgegensehen.
Non veder l'ora di . . .

To be on the look out.
Se tenir sur le qui-vive.
Estar en guardia.
Ausschau halten.
Stare all'erta.

(♦) To look down on someone. (p. 347)
Mépriser quelqu'un.
Considerar a alguien con desprecio.
Auf jemanden herabschauen (heruntersehen).
Disprezzare qualcuno.

To look hard at . . .
Avoir le regard fixe / Regarder fixement.
Mirar fijamente a . . .
Starren auf . . . / Anstarren / Mit den Augen fixieren.
Guardare fissamente . . .

By the look of things.
A ce qu'il paraît.
Por lo que parece.
Wie die Dinge aussehen.
A quanto pare.

To look over something.
Examiner quelque chose.
Examinar algo / Dar un vistazo a algo.
Etwas durchsehen / Etwas (über)prüfen.
Esaminare qualcosa.

(♦) To look like nothing on earth. (p. 348)
Avoir mauvaise mine.
Tener mala facha.
Schlecht aussehen.
Avere un brutto aspetto / Avere una brutta cera.

Look here!
Ecoute un peu!
¡Oye!

Schau mal (her)! / Hör mal (zu)!
Senti un po'!

Look out!
Attention!
¡Cuidado!
Pass auf! / Vorsicht!
Attenzione!

LOOSE (♦)

As loose as a rope of sand. (comp.)
Très incohérent.
Sin ninguna coherencia.
Sehr unlogisch.
Molto incoerente.

(♦) To have a screw loose. (p. 350)
Manquer d'un boulon (d'une case).
Faltarle a uno un tornillo.
Eine Schraube locker haben.
Mancare di una rotella / Mancare di un venerdì.

(♦) He is at a loose end! (p. 351)
Il ne sait pas quoi faire!
¡No sabe que hacer!
Er weiss nicht, was er tun soll!
Non sa che fare! / Non sa dove sbattere la testa!

LORD

To live like a lord.
Vivre en grand seigneur.
Vivir como un rey.
Wie ein König leben.
Vivere da gran signore; da re.

As drunk as a lord. (comp.)
Saoûl comme un Polonais.
Borracho como el aguardiente.
Stockbetrunken.
Ubriaco fradicio.

To swear like a lord.
Jurer comme un charretier.

Blasfemar / Jurar como un turco.
Fluchen wie ein Landsknecht.
Bestemmiàre come un turco.

LOSE (♦)

(♦) To lose one's head. (p. 353)
Perdre la tête.
Perder la cabeza.
Seinen Kopf verlieren.
Perdere la testa.

To lose ground.
Perdre du terrain.
Perder terreno.
(An) Boden verlieren.
Perdere terreno.

LOSER

He's a bad loser.
Il est mauvais perdant / Il est mauvais joueur.
Es un mal perdedor.
Er ist ein schlechter Verlierer.
Non sa perdere.

LOT

A bad lot.
Une personne malhonnête.
Una persona deshonesta.
Ein übler Genosse.
Una persona disonesta.

To throw in one's lot with somebody.
Partager le sort de quelqu'un.
Compartir la propia suerte con alguien / Compartir el propio destino con alguien.
Das Los mit jemandem teilen / Sich auf Gedeih und Verderb mit jemandem verbinden.
Condividere la sorte di qualcuno.

LOUD

As loud as thunder. (comp.)
Bruit très fort (assourdissant).
Muy recio.
So laut wie ein Donnerschlag / Laut wie Donner.
Molto forte (di suono, rumore ecc.).

LOUSY

Lousy with money.
Cousu d'or.
Pudriendose de dinero / Lleno de dinero.
Geld wie Flöhe haben / Vor Geld stinken / Stinkreich sein /
Geld wie Heu haben.
Pieno di quattrini.

LOVE (♦)

(♦) Love me, love my dog. (prov.) (p. 355)
Si tu m'aimes tu dois aimer aussi mon chien.
Quien me ama, me acepta tal y como soy yo y son mis
amigos.
Liebst du mich, so musst du auch meinen Hund lieben /
Liebst du mich, so musst du auch meine Freunde akzeptieren.
Chi ama me, ama il mio cane / Devi accettare i miei
amici anche se ti sono sgraditi.

I should love to come . . .
Je serais très heureux de venir.
Me gustaría mucho venir / Estaría muy contento de venir /
Me encantaría venir.
Ich würde gerne kommen . . .
Sarei felicissimo di venire . . .

To play for love.
Jouer par passion.
Jugar por pasión.
Aus Leidenschaft spielen.
Giocare per passione.

To fall in love with . . .
Tomber amoureux de . . .

354

355

Enamorarse de ...
Sich verlieben in ...
Innamorarsi di ...

LOW

To be in low waters.
Etre sur la paille / Etre fauché.
Estar escaso de dinero.
Kein Geld haben / Blank sein.
Essere al verde; in bolletta.

To be in low spirits.
Etre abattu.
Estar abatido / Estar desanimado.
Niedergeschlagen sein / Bedrückt sein.
Essere abbattuto.

LUCK

Bad luck to him!
Qu'il aille au diable!
¡Que le parta un rayo! / ¡Malhaya a él!
Der Teufel hole ihn! / Der Schlag soll ihn treffen!
Accidenti a lui!

LUCKY

You lucky beggar!
Tu as de la chance!
¡Dichoso tú!
Du Glückspilz! / Du Glücklicher!
Beato te!

You're a lucky dog!
Vous avez vraiment de la chance!
¡Tiene Usted mucha suerte!
Sie sind ein Glückspilz! / Sie haben wirklich Glück!
Siete davvero fortunato!

LUMP

You will have to lump it.
Vous devrez vous arranger tant bien que mal.

Arreglense como puedan.
Sie werden sich damit abfinden müssen.
Dovrete arrangiarvi.

LUNGS

She cried her lungs out.
Il a crié de toutes ses forces.
Ha gritado con todo su aliento.
Sie schrie sich die Lunge heraus.
Ha gridato con quanto fiato aveva in corpo.

LURCH

To leave someone in the lurch.
Plaquer quelqu'un.
Dejar plantada a una persona.
Jemanden im Stich lassen.
Piantare in asso qualcuno.

LURK

To be on the lurk.
Epier / Etre aux aguets.
Estar en acecho / Estar atizbando.
Auf der Lauer sein.
Stare a spiare.

MAD

As mad as a hatter. (comp.)
Fou à lier.
Loco de atar.
Fuchsteufelswild / Total übergeschnappt.
Matto da legare.

As mad as a March hare. (comp.)
Fou à lier.
Loco como una cabra.
Total übergeschnappt.
Matto da legare.

To drive mad.
Faire devenir fou.

Hacer enloquecer.
Verrückt machen.
Far impazzire.

MADE

(♦) A self-made man. (p. 359)
Un autodidacte.
Un hombre hecho por sí mismo.
Selfmademan / Ein Mann, der durch eigene Kraft hochgekommen ist.
Un uomo che s'è fatto da sè.

MAKE

Make hay while the sun shines. (prov.)
Il faut battre le fer tant qu'il est encore chaud.
Las cosas hay que hacerlas mientras estén calientes / La ocasión la pintan calva.
Schmiede das Eisen, solange es heiss ist.
Batti il ferro finchè è caldo / Bisogna macinare fin che piove.

One swallow does not make a summer. (prov.)
Une hirondelle ne fait pas le printemps.
Una golondrina no hace verano.
Eine Schwalbe macht noch keinen Sommer.
Una rondine non fa primavera.

To make up one's mind.
Se décider.
Resolverse / Decidirse.
Seine Meinung bilden / Sich entscheiden.
Decidersi.

(♦) To make a meal of something. (p. 360)
Exagérer.
Exagerar.
Übertreiben.
Esagerare.

To make merry.
Faire bombance / Faire la noce.
Ir de juerga / Divertirse.
Spass machen / Lustig sein.
Far baldoria.

To make the most of something.
Exploiter une chose au maximum.
Explotar algo a lo máximo.
Das Beste aus etwas herausholen.
Sfruttare al massimo qualcosa.

To be on the make.
Chercher son avantage.
Buscar ventaja.
Auf einen Vorteil bedacht sein.
Cercare il proprio vantaggio.

I can't make anything of it!
Je n'arrive pas à le déchiffrer.
No logro figurarmelo / No puedo descifrarlo.
Ich kann nichts damit anfangen! / Ich kann es nicht entziffern.
Non riesco a decifrarlo!

I can't make him out.
Je ne sais pas le comprendre.
No logro entenderle.
Ich kann ihn nicht verstehen / Ich werde nicht klug aus ihm.
Non lo so capire.

I'll make it worth your while.
Tu auras la récompense que tu mérites.
Te recompensaré apropiadamente.
Ich werde deine Mühe entsprechend lohnen (entlohnen) / Ich
werde dich entsprechend entlohnen.
Ti ricompenserò adeguatamente.

To make fun of . . .
Se moquer de . . .
Burlarse de . . .
Jemanden zum besten haben / Sich über jemanden lustig
machen / Jemanden auf den Arm nehmen.
Prendere in giro / Prendersi gioco di . . .

Make up for lost time!
Rattrape le temps perdu!
¡Recúpera el tiempo perdido!
Hole die verlorene Zeit wieder auf!
Recupera il tempo perduto!

MAN

A man about town.
Un homme influent.
Un hombre influyente.
Ein Lebemann.
Un uomo influente.

To man a ship.
Equiper un navire.
Equipar un barco.
Ein Schiff bemannen.
Equipaggiare una nave.

A lady's man.
Un homme qui aime la compagnie des femmes.
Un personaje de salote.
Ein Frauenheld / Ein Salonlöwe.
Un uomo da salotto.

MANAGE

I don't know how to manage him.
Je ne sais pas comment le prendre.
No sé como manejarlo (a una persona).
Ich weiss ihn nicht zu nehmen.
Non so come prenderlo.

To manage without . . .
Se passer de . . .
Arreglarselas sin . . .
Auskommen ohne . . . / Zu Rande kommen ohne . . . / Es schaffen ohne . . .
Far senza . . . / Fare a meno di . . .

MANGER

A dog in the manger.
Un égoïste stupide / Le chien du jardinier.
Un egoista estúpido / Ser como el perro del hortelano.
Ein Neidhammel.
Uno stupido egoista.

MANNER

In a manner of speaking.
Façon de parler!
Así, como quien dice ...
Sozusagen.
Per modo di dire.

By all manner of means!
Certainement!
¡Claro!
Ganz sicher! / Gewiss!
Certamente!

MANY

Many-sided.
Aux multiples facettes.
De muchos lados / De muchas facetas.
Vielseitig.
Che ha molti lati (molti aspetti).

MARBLE

As cold as marble. (comp.)
Froid comme le marbre.
Frío como el mármol.
Kalt wie Marmor (Stein).
Freddissimo / Freddo come il marmo.

MARK

Mark my words!
Prête attention à ce que je dis!
¡Fíjese en lo que digo! / ¡Advierte lo que te digo!
Merk dir meine Worte!
Fa' attenzione a quel che dico!

A man of mark.
Un homme de valeur.
Un hombre sobresaliente.
Ein Mann von Format / Eine markante Persönlichkeit.
Un uomo di valore.

What you say is beside the mark.
Ce que vous dites est hors de propos.
Lo que Usted dice está fuera de lugar.
Was Sie sagen, ist fehl am Platz.
Ciò che dite è fuor di luogo.

Up to the mark.
Dans de bonnes conditions.
En buenas condiciones / Como Dios manda.
Der Sache gewachsen / Den Erwartungen entsprechend / Auf
der Höhe.
In buone condizioni.

MASK

To throw off the mask.
Jeter le masque.
Quitarse la careta.
Die Maske fallenlassen.
Gettare la maschera.

MASTER

To master the English language.
Maîtriser la langue anglaise.
Dominar el Inglés.
Die englische Sprache meistern.
Impadronirsi della lingua inglese.

MATCH

Nobody can match him in French.
Personne ne peut lui tenir tête en français / Personne ne peut
le battre.
Nadie puede batirle en Francés / No tiene igual en Francés.
Niemand kann ihn in Französisch schlagen / Niemand kann
ihm in Französisch das Wasser reichen.
Nessuno può eguagliarlo in francese.

MATCHWOOD

He smashed it into matchwood.
Il l'a réduit en morceaux.

Lo ha hecho pedazos.
Er machte es zu Kleinholz / Er schlug es kurz und klein.
Lo ha fatto a pezzi.

MATTER

A matter-of-course.
Une chose naturelle.
Algo natural.
Eine Selbstverständlichkeit.
Una cosa naturale.

A matter-of-fact person.
Une personne qui a peu d'imagination / Une personne réaliste.
Una persona con poca imaginación.
Eine sachliche Person / Ein Realist.
Una persona coi piedi per terra.

No matter where!
N'importe où!
¡No importa donde! / ¡Donde sea!
Gleichgültig wo! / Egal wo! / Wo auch immer!
Dove capita!

What's the matter?
Qu'y-a-t-il?
¿Qué pasa? / ¿Qué tiene Usted?
Was ist los? / Wo fehlt's?
Che cosa c'è?

MATTERS

Don't make matters worse!
N'empirez pas la situation!
¡No hagan que las cosas empeoren!
Machen Sie die Sache nicht schlimmer!
Non peggiorate la situazione!

ME

Dear me!
Mon Dieu!

365

¡Dios mío!
Meine Güte! / Mein Gott!
Dio mio!

MEANS

A man of means.
Un homme riche / Un richard.
Un hombre pudiente.
Ein bemittelter Mann.
Un uomo ricco.

He means well.
Il a de bonnes intentions.
Tiene buenas intenciones.
Er meint es gut.
Le sue intenzioni sono buone.

To live within one's means.
Vivre sans faire le pas plus long que la jambe.
Vivir en el ámbito de los propios límites.
Seinen Verhältnissen entsprechend leben.
Fare il passo secondo la gamba.

By all means!
Coûte que coûte! / A tout prix! / Naturellement!
¡De todos modos! / ¡A toda costa! / ¡Sea como sea!
Auf alle Fälle! / Unbedingt!
A tutti i costi! / Naturalmente!

MEASLY

A measly salary.
Un salaire de misère.
Un sueldo de miseria.
Ein lumpiges (schäbiges) Gehalt.
Un misero stipendio.

MEASURE

To measure one's words.
Mesurer ses mots.

Medir las palabras.
Seine Worte abwägen.
Misurare le parole.

MEASURED

Measured language.
Des mots bien pesés.
Palabras bien ponderadas.
Ausgewogene Sprache / Wohl überlegte Worte.
Parole misurate / Parole ben soppesate.

MEAT

One man's meat is another man's poison. (prov.)
Les goûts et les couleurs ne se discutent pas.
Lo qué es razón de gusto para uno, puede ser razón de dis-
gusto para otro.
Des einen Glück ist des anderen Verderben / Des einen Tod
ist des anderen Brot.
Ciò che piace ad uno non piace ad un altro.

MEDAL

The reverse of the medal.
Le revers de la médaille.
El revéz de la medalla.
Die Kehrseite der Medaille.
Il rovescio della medaglia.

MEEK

As meek as a lamb. (comp.)
Très doux / Doux comme un agneau.
Manso como una oveja.
Fromm wie ein Lamm / Lammfromm.
Mite come un agnello.

MEET

To meet an expense.
Supporter les frais.
Sufragar un gasto.

Die Unkosten bestreiten / Die Kosten tragen.
Sostenere una spesa.

To make both ends meet.
Joindre les deux bouts.
Hacer que las cuentas salgan.
Mit seinem Einkommen auskommen / Sich nach der Decke strecken.
Sbarcare il lunario.

MEND

Least said soonest mended. (prov.)
Le silence est d'or.
El silencio es oro.
Je weniger geredet wird, desto rascher wird alles wieder gut / Schweigen ist Gold, Reden ist Silber.
Il silenzio è d'oro.

To be on the mend.
Etre en voie d'amélioration.
Ir mejorando.
Auf dem Wege der Besserung sein.
Essere in via di miglioramento.

Mend your manners!
Corrige-toi! / Sois plus élevé!
¡Cuida tus modales!
Besser deine Manieren! / Benimm dich besser!
Sii più educato!

MENTION

Don't mention it!
Il n'y a pas de quoi!
¡De nada!
Nicht der Rede wert! / Gern geschehen!
Non c'è di che!

MERRY

As merry as a cricket. (comp.)
Gai comme un pinson.
Alégre como un pájaro.

Kreuzfidel / Sehr fröhlich.
Molto allegro / Allegro come un grillo.

To make merry.
Faire bombance / Faire la noce.
Ir de juerga / Divertirse.
Lustig sein / Feiern / Scherzen.
Far baldoria.

MESS

You've made a mess of it!
Tu as tout gâché!
¡Has echado todo a perder!
Du hast es verpfuscht (verhunzt)!
Hai sciupato tutto! / Hai combinato un pasticcio!

To get into a mess.
Se fourrer dans un beau guêpier!
Meterse en un lío.
In die Klemme (Patsche) geraten.
Cacciarsi nei guai.

METHOD

There's a method in his madness.
Cela semble une folie mais ça ne l'est pas.
Hay un cierto método en su locura.
Was er tut, ist nicht so verrückt, wie es aussieht.
Sembra una pazzia ma non lo è.

METTLE

To show one's mettle.
Montrer sa constitution.
Demostrar el ánimo que uno tiene.
Seine wahre Natur zeigen / Sein wahres Gesicht zeigen.
Mostrare la propria fibra.

To be on one's mettle.
Se sentir enclin à faire de son mieux.
Estar de ánimo para . . .
Sein Bestes tun wollen.
Sentirsi incitato a fare del proprio meglio.

A man of mettle.
Un homme courageux.
Un hombre valiente.
Ein mutiger Mann.
Un uomo di fegato.

MIDDLE

To take a middle course.
Prendre le juste milieu.
Tomar un camino de en medio.
Einen Mittelweg wählen.
Prendere una via di mezzo.

MIDNIGHT

To burn the midnight oil.
Travailler jusque tard dans la nuit.
Trabajar hasta muy tarde por la noche.
Bis spät in die Nacht arbeiten (aufbleiben).
Lavorare fino a tarda notte.

MIGHT

Might is right. (prov.)
La raison du plus fort est toujours la meilleure / La raison est toujours celle du plus fort.
La razón está de parte del más fuerte.
Gewalt geht vor Recht.
La ragione è del più forte.

With might and main.
Avec toute l'énergie possible.
Con toda energía.
Aus Leibeskräften.
Con tutta l'energia.

MIGHTY

That's mighty nice!
C'est splendide!
¡Esto es espléndido!
Ungeheuer schön!
E' splendido!

370

He's very high and mighty.
Il est très orgueilleux.
Es muy orgulloso.
Er ist sehr erhaben (arrogant / hochmütig).
E' molto orgoglioso.

MILDLY

To put it mildly.
Sans exagérer.
Sin exagerar.
Sich gelinde ausdrücken / Gelinde sagen.
Senza esagerare.

MILK (♦)

(♦) It's no use crying over spilt milk. (prov.) (p. 124)
La page est tournée.
No hay que lamentarse por lo que ya ha pasado.
Was geschehen ist, ist geschehen / Geschehen ist geschehen /
Hin ist hin.
Non serve piangere sul latte versato.

MILL

The mills of God grind slowly. (prov.)
La justice est boîteuse, elle vient à pas lents mais elle vient.
Las vías del Señor son muchas y llenas de obstáculos.
Gottes Mühlen mahlen langsam.
Dio non paga il sabato.

To go through the mill.
Apprendre à fond un métier / Subir une série d'épreuves.
Aprender un trabajo de la « a » a la « zeta ».
Eine harte Schule durchmachen.
Imparare a fondo un mestiere / Superare una serie di prove.

To put someone through the mill.
Soumettre quelqu'un à de dures épreuves.
Someter alguien a pruebas muy difíciles.
Jemanden durch eine harte Schule schicken.
Sottoporre qualcuno a dure prove.

To bring grist to the mill.
Faire venir l'eau au moulin.
Arrimar el ascua a su sardina.
Gewinn bringen.
Essere vantaggioso / Portar acqua al mulino.

MINCE

Not to mince matters.
Dire les choses comme elles sont.
Presentar las cosas tal y como son en realidad.
Kein Blatt vor den Mund nehmen.
Dire le cose come stanno.

MINCEMEAT (♦)

(♦) To make mincemeat of . . . (p. 373)
Réduire en morceaux.
Hacer picadillo de . . .
Aus jemandem Hackfleisch machen.
Fare a pezzi.

MIND (♦)

To mind one's P's and Q's.
Mesurer ses mots.
Curar las propias palabras.
Auf seine Worte achten / Seine Worte mit Bedacht auswählen.
Fare attenzione alle proprie parole.

(♦) To give someone a piece of one's mind. (p. 374)
Sermoner quelqu'un / Passer un savon à quelqu'un.
Regañar a alguien.
Jemandem gründlich die Meinung sagen / Jemandem den
Kopf waschen.
Sgridare qualcuno.

(♦) To change one's mind. (p. 375)
Changer d'idée.
Cambiar de parecer.
Sich anders besinnen.
Cambiare idea.

372

I feel in a better frame of mind.
Je me sens soulagé.
Me siento más animado.
Ich bin in besserer (Gemüts) Verfassung / Ich habe bessere Stimmung (Laune).
Mi sento lo spirito sollevato.

She doesn't know her own mind.
Elle ne sait pas elle-même ce qu'elle veut.
No sabe ni siquiera lo que quiere.
Sie weiss nicht, was sie will.
Non sa neanche lei che cosa vuole.

Out of sight, out of mind. (prov.)
Loin des yeux, loin du cœur.
Lejos de los ojos, lejos del corazón.
Aus den Augen, aus dem Sinn.
Lontano dagli occhi, lontano dal cuore.

He's not in his right mind!
Il lui manque un boulon! (une case).
¡Le falta un tornillo!
Er ist nicht ganz bei Verstand!
Gli manca una rotella!

Make up your mind!
Décide-toi!
¡Decídase! / ¡Resuélvase!
Entschliesse (Entscheide) dich!
Deciditi!

I've a good mind to slap him.
J'ai bien envie de le gifler.
Tengo tantas ganas de abofetearlo.
Ich habe grosse Lust ihn zu ohrfeigen (verhauen).
Ho una gran voglia di prenderlo a schiaffi.

Never mind!
Ça n'a pas d'importance!
¡No importa! / ¡No se preocupe! / ¡No se moleste!
Macht nichts! / Mach dir nichts draus!
Non importa!

Mind your own business!
Occupe-toi de tes affaires!

¡Atiende a lo tuyo!
Kümmere dich um deine eigenen Dinge!
Bada ai fatti tuoi!

I don't mind caviar.
Le caviar ne me déplaît pas.
El caviár no me desagrada.
Ich bin kein Verächter von Kaviar.
Non mi dispiace affatto il caviale.

MINUTE
I won't be a minute.
Je serai vite de retour.
Regresaré en un minuto / Regreso pronto.
Ich bin sofort zurück.
Sarò di ritorno subito.

MISCHIEF
To be up to mischief.
Tramer quelque chose / Comploter.
Hurdir algo malo.
Schaden anrichten / Unheil stiften.
Tramare qualcosa di male (qualche misfatto).

To make mischief between two people.
Semer la discorde entre deux personnes.
Meter cizaña entre dos personas.
Zwietracht zwischen zwei Personen säen.
Mettere la discordia fra due persone.

MISERABLE
To feel miserable.
Se sentir déprimé / Ne pas avoir le moral.
Sentirse desdichado.
Sich miserabel (jämmerlich / elend / erbärmlich) fühlen.
Sentirsi molto depresso.

He made my life miserable.
Il m'a rendu la vie impossible.
Ha hecho de mi vida un infierno.
Er machte mein Leben unerträglich (unglücklich).
Mi ha reso insopportabile la vita.

MISS

A miss is as good as a mile. (prov.)
Un coup manqué même de peu est toujours un coup manqué.
Una oportunidad fallida, aunque pequeña, es siempre un fracaso.
Haarscharf daneben ist auch daneben / Mit knapper Not entrinnen, ist immerhin entrinnen.
Un colpo mancato, anche se per poco, è sempre un colpo mancato.

It was a lucky miss!
Je m'en suis tiré de justesse!
¡Me he salvado por un pelo!
Mit einem blauen Auge davon kommen / Ich karn mit einem blauen Auge davon.
Me la cavai per il rotto della cuffia!

I miss her so much. .
Elle me manque beaucoup.
Me hace mucha falta.
Sie fehlt mir sehr / Ich vermisse sie.
Sento molto la sua mancanza.

MIX

What a mix-up!
Quelle salade! / Quel gâchis!
¡Que confusión! / ¡Que lío!
Welch ein Durcheinander!
Che pasticcio!

MIXED

He's a mixed-up lad.
C'est un garçon un peu brouillon.
Se trata de un muchacho un poco confuso.
Er ist ein verwirrter (konfuser) Junge.
E' un ragazzo un po' confuso.

MOLE

As blind as a mole. (comp.)
Aveugle comme une taupe.

378

Ciego como un topo.
Blind wie eine Eule (Schlange).
Cieco come una talpa.

MOLEHILL

To make a mountain out of a molehill.
Faire une montagne de quelque chose.
Hacer de un grano de arena una montaña.
Aus einer Mücke einen Elefanten machen.
Fare di un granello di sabbia una montagna.

MOLLY-CODDLE

To be molly-coddled.
Etre choyé (gâté).
Ser mimado.
Verzogen sein.
Essere coccolato, viziato.

MOMENT

Not for a moment!
Jamais de la vie!
¡Jamás!
Nicht für einen Augenblick! / Niemals!
Giammai!

MONEY

He's a money-bags.
C'est une personne riche et avare.
Es un rico avariento.
Er ist ein geiziger Geldsack / Er sitzt auf seinem Geld.
E' una persona ricca e avara.

Time is money. (prov.)
Le temps c'est de l'argent.
El tiempo es oro.
Zeit ist Geld.
Il tempo è denaro.

Money makes the mare to go. (prov.)
Avec l'argent on peut tout faire.

El dinero lo hace todo.
Geld macht alles möglich.
Con il denaro si fa tutto.

To get money for jam.
Obtenir quelque chose sans trop se fatiguer.
Obtener algo sin mucho trabajo.
Etwas für ein Butterbrot erhalten / Etwas für einen Apfel und ein Ei bekommen.
Ottenere qualcosa con poca fatica.

It isn't every man's money.
Ce n'est pas la même chose pour tout le monde.
No tiene el mismo valor para todos.
Was für den einen Gold ist, ist für den anderen Silber / Es ist nicht gleichwertig für alle.
Non ha lo stesso valore per tutti.

MONKEY

To monkey around.
Gaspiller son temps / Faire l'imbécile.
Holgazanear / Hacer el fresco.
Herumalbern.
Perdere il tempo in schiocchezze / Fare lo stupido.

Monkey business.
Une affaire louche.
Una estafa.
Krumme Tour / Fauler Zauber.
Un imbroglio.

MONTH

It will take a month of Sundays!
Il faudra une éternité!
Será necesario un siglo para hacerlo.
Es wird eine Ewigkeit dauern!
Ci vorrà un'eternità!

MOOD

To be in a good mood.
Etre de bonne humeur / S'être levé du bon pied.

Estar de buen humor.
In guter Stimmung (Laune) sein / Gut aufgelegt sein.
Essere di buon umore.

MOON

Once in a blue moon.
Une fois tous les trente-six du mois.
En cada muerte de obispo / Muy rara vez.
Alle Jubeljahre einmal / Höchst selten.
Una volta ogni morte di papa.

To moon about.
Flâner.
Holgazanear.
Umherlungern / Bummeln.
Bighellonare.

MOONSHINE

It's all moonshine!
Ce ne sont que des sornettes! / Ce ne sont que des balivernes!
¡Son patrañas!
Es ist alles fauler Zauber! / Es ist alles Unsinn (Geschwafel)!
Sono tutte frottole!

MOOT

It's a moot-point.
C'est un point discutable.
Es una cuestión discutible.
Es ist ein strittiger Punkt.
E' un punto discutibile.

MORE

More and more.
Toujours plus.
Más y más.
Mehr und mehr / Immer mehr.
Sempre più.

MOSS

A rolling stone gathers no moss. (prov.)
Pierre qui roule n'amasse pas mousse.
Un tiro al áire no encuentra blanco.
Ein rollender Stein setzt kein Moos an.
Chi cambia sempre dimora (o occupazione) non fa fortuna.

MOTH

To be like a moth round a candle flame.
Jouer avec le feu / Se brûler les ailes.
Jugar con fuego / Ser como una mariposa, que volando alrededor de una vela, se quema las alas.
Mit dem Feuer spielen.
Scherzare col fuoco.

MOTHER

Necessity is the mother of invention. (prov.)
Nécessité est mère d'industrie.
La necesidad es la madre de las invenciones.
Not macht erfinderisch.
Il bisogno aguzza l'ingegno.

MOTION

To go through the motions.
Faire voir que l'on est actif.
Dar señas de actividad.
Vorgeben, dass man etwas tut.
Far finta di fare qualcosa.

MOUNTAINS

To make mountains out of molehills.
Grossir les difficultés.
Exagerar sobre las dificultades existentes.
Aus einer Mücke einen Elefanten machen.
Esagerare le difficoltà.

To move mountains.
Remuer les montagnes / Faire des miracles.

Remover cielo y tierra.
Berge versetzen / Wunder wirken.
Far miracoli.

MOUSE

As poor as a church mouse. (comp.)
Pauvre comme Job.
Muy pobre / Pelado.
Arm wie eine Kirchenmaus.
Povero in canna.

MOUTH (♦)

My mouth watered.
J'en eus l'eau à la bouche.
Se me hizo agua la boca.
Mir lief das Wasser im Mund zusammen.
Mi venne l'acquolina in bocca.

(♦) Down in the mouth. (p. 384)
Ne pas avoir le moral.
Estar triste.
Niedergeschlagen sein / Bedrückt sein.
Esser depresso / Esser giù di morale.

MOVE

To move heaven and earth.
Déplacer les montagnes.
Remover cielo y tierra.
Himmel und Erde in Bewegung setzen / Himmel und Hölle
in Bewegung setzen.
Muovere mari e monti.

Get a move on!
Dépêche-toi!
¡Date prisa!
Spute dich! / Drück auf die Tube! / Beeil dich!
Affrettati!

MUCH

Too much breaks the bag. (prov.)
Trop c'est trop.

Lo mucho rompe el morral.
Zuviel des Guten schadet nur.
Il troppo stroppia.

Too much is as bad as none at all. (prov.)
Trop c'est trop / Il y a une limite à tout.
Lo excesivo perjudíca.
Zu viel ist ebenso schlecht wie gar nichts / Zu viel des Guten
schadet nur.
Il troppo stroppia.

It's much of a muchness.
C'est à peu près la même chose.
Es más o menos igual.
Praktisch dasselbe / Ziemlich dasselbe.
E' pressappoco uguale.

MUCK

Where there's muck there's money. (prov.)
L'argent n'a pas d'odeur.
Donde hay dinero hay suciedad.
Wo Geld ist, ist Schmutz.
Dove c'è danaro, c'è sporcizia.

To muck about.
Jouer / S'amuser / Lambiner / Lanterner.
Entretenerse.
Herumlungern.
Gingillarsi.

MULE

As stubborn as a mule. (comp.)
Têtu comme un âne.
Necio como una mula.
Störrisch wie ein Esel.
Ostinato come un mulo.

MUM

Mum's the word!
Motus, bouche cousue!

¡No digas nada! / ¡Tápate la boca!
Kein Wort darüber! / Schwamm darüber!
Acqua in bocca!

MURDER

Murder will out. (prov.)
Tout finit par se savoir.
Tarde o temprano todo se sabe.
Die Sonne bringt es an den Tag / Alles kommt ans Licht.
Tutto si viene a sapere / Tutti i nodi vengono al pettine / Il
diavolo fa le pentole ma non i coperchi.

To cry blue murder.
Crier: « au loup! »
Gritar como loco.
Zetermordio schreien / Wie am Spiess schreien.
Gridare: « Al lupo! ».

MUSIC (♦)

(♦) To face the music. (p. 178)
Affronter la critique.
Darle la cara a las críticas.
Sich der Kritik stellen.
Affrontare la critica.

MUST

It's a must!
C'est une chose à faire!
¡Es imprescindible! / ¡Se tiene que hacer!
Es ist ein Muss! / Es ist unerlässlich!
E' una cosa che si deve fare!

MUTE

As mute as a fish. (comp.)
Taciturne / Sombre / Muet comme une carpe.
Mudo como un pez.
Stumm wie ein Fisch.
Muto come un pesce.

386

As mute as a mouse. (comp.)
Très silencieux.
Muy callado.
Mausestill / Mäuschenstill.
Muto come un pesce.

MUTTON

As dead as mutton. (comp.)
Raide mort.
Bien muerto.
Mausetot.
Morto stecchito.

Mutton-head.
Niais / Idiot / Simplet.
Tonto de capirote.
Schafskopf / Blödian.
Zuccone / Stupido.

MY

Oh, my!
Mon Dieu!
¡Dios mio!
Meine Güte! / Mein Gott!
Dio mio!

My eye!
Zut! / Punaise!
¡Caramba! / ¡Diántres!
Ach, du liebe Zeit! / Ach, du lieber Gott!
Frottole! / Porca miseria!

MYSELF

I don't feel quite myself today.
Aujourd'hui je ne me sens pas bien.
Hoy no me siento bien.
Ich bin heute nicht ganz da / Ich fühle mich nicht ganz gut heute.
Non mi sento bene oggi.

387

By myself.
Moi-même.
A solas.
Ich selbst / Allein.
Da solo.

NAGGING

My wife is always nagging.
Ma femme rouspète toujours.
Mi mujer es muy regañona.
Meine Frau nörgelt immer.
Mia moglie brontola sempre.

NAIL

Nail him!
Prends-le! / Attrape!
¡Atrápalo!
Nagel ihn fest!
Prendilo!

To hit the nail on the head.
Frapper juste / Faire mouche.
Dar en el clavo.
Den Nagel auf den Kopf treffen.
Colpire nel segno.

They fought tooth and nail.
Ils se sont battus griffes dehors.
Se batieron ferozmente.
Sie kämpften verbissen.
Si sono battuti con le unghie e coi denti.

NAILED

His eyes were nailed to the painting.
Ses yeux étaient rivés (cloués) sur le tableau.
Sus ojos estaban clavados sobre el cuádro.
Seine Augen waren auf das Gemälde geheftet.
I suoi occhi erano fissi sul quadro.

NAME

Give a dog an ill name and hang him. (prov.)
La calomnie tue / Calomniez, il en restera quelque chose!
Calumnia, calumnia que algo quedará.
Jemanden wegen seines schlechten Rufs oder auf Grund von
Gerüchten verurteilen.
La calunnia uccide.

Name your own price!
Fais ton prix!
Fije su precio.
Nennen Sie Ihren Preis!
Fissa il prezzo!

NAPPING

To catch someone napping.
Prendre quelqu'un au dépourvu.
Agarrar a alquien dormido o desproveído.
Jemanden überrumpeln.
Prendere qualcuno alla sprovvista.

NARROW

He had a narrow escape!
Il s'est sauvé de peu!
¡Se salvó por un pelo!
Er ist mit knapper Not (um Haaresbreite) entkommen!
Si è salvato per un pelo! (per miracolo!).

To narrow down something.
Réduire quelque chose.
Reducir algo.
Etwas einschränken (begrenzen / verringern).
Ridurre qualcosa.

NATURE

The debt of nature.
La mort.
El precio de la vida (la muerte).
Der Tod (Der Tribut der Natur).
La morte.

NEAT

I like my whisky neat.
J'aime le whisky sec.
Me gusta que mi wisky sea puro.
Ich mag meinen Whisky pur.
Mi piace il whisky liscio.

NECESSITY

Necessity is the mother of invention. (prov.)
Nécessité est mère d'industrie.
La necesidad hace al hombre lobo.
Not macht erfinderisch.
Il bisogno aguzza l'ingegno.

Necessity knows no law.
Nécessité ne connaît pas de loi.
La necesidad no tiene leyes.
Not kennt kein Gebot.
Si fa qualsiasi cosa per bisogno.

To make a virtue of necessity.
Faire de nécessité vertu.
Hacer de tripas, corazón.
Aus der Not eine Tugend machen.
Fare di necessità virtù.

NECK (♦)

To get it in the neck.
Etre grondé (réprimandé).
Ser regañado.
Eins aufs Dach bekommen (kriegen).
Essere rimproverato.

To risk one's neck.
Risquer sa peau.
Arriesgar el pellejo.
Kopf und Kragen riskieren.
Rischiare la pelle.

(♦) To give someone a pain in the neck. (p. 391)
Ennuyer quelqu'un.

391

Fastidiar a alguien.
Jemandem Unglück an den Hals wünschen / Jemandem Kummer machen.
Dare fastidio a qualcuno.

NEED

A friend in need is a friend indeed. (prov.)
C'est dans le besoin qu'on reconnaît un véritable ami.
Un amigo en la necesidad es un amigo para siempre.
Ein wahrer Freund bleibt auch in der Not treu.
Il vero amico si conosce nel bisogno.

To be in need of . . .
Avoir besoin de . . .
Tener necesidad de . . .
Etwas dringend brauchen / Etwas sehr nötig haben.
Aver bisogno di . . .

NEEDLE

Don't needle me!
Ne me taquine pas!
¡No me molestes!
Stachle mich nicht auf! / Reiz mich nicht!
Non punzecchiarmi!

To look for a needle in a haystack.
Chercher une aiguille dans une meule de foin.
Buscar un alfiler en el pajár.
Eine Nadel im Heustall suchen.
Cercare un ago in un pagliaio.

To have the needle.
Avoir les nerfs en boule.
Estar nervioso.
Eine Wut haben.
Avere i « nervi ».

As sharp as a needle. (comp.)
Très intelligent / Perspicace.
Muy perspicáz.
Äusserst intelligent / Auf Draht / Auf Zack.
Molto intelligente / Perspicace / Acuto.

NEEDLES

To be on pins and needles.
Etre sur des charbons ardents.
Estar en ascuas.
Auf Kohlen sitzen.
Essere sulle spine.

I've got pins and needles.
J'ai des fourmis . . .
Tengo un hormigueo.
Ich habe das Kribbeln / Es kribbelt mich.
Ho il formicolio.

NEEDLESS

Needless to say!
Inutile à dire.
Inútil decirlo.
Selbstredend! / Selbstverständlich!
Inutile a dirsi!

NEITHER

That's neither here nor there!
Ça n'a rien à voir.
Esto no viene al caso.
Das gehört nicht zur Sache.
Questo non c'entra!

NERVE

What a nerve!
Quel culot! / Quel toupet!
¡Que descarado!
Welche Frechheit! / Welche Nerven!
Che faccia tosta!

It's nerve-racking.
C'est très exaspérant.
Es un quebradero de cabeza / Es una exasperación.
Es ist nervenaufreibend.
E' molto esasperante.

To lose one's nerve.
Perdre son sang-froid.
Perderse de ánimo.
Die Nerven verlieren.
Perdersi di coraggio.

NERVES

To get on someone's nerves.
Taper sur les nerfs.
Molestar a alguien.
Jemandem auf die Nerven gehen (fallen).
Dare sui nervi a qualcuno.

NERVOUS

A nervous breakdown.
Une dépression nerveuse.
Un colapso nervioso.
Ein Nervenzusammenbruch.
Un collasso nervoso / Un esaurimento.

NEST

It's an ill bird that fouls its own nest. (prov.)
Le linge sale se lave en famille.
La ropa sucia se lava en la casa de uno.
Sein eigenes Nest beschmutzen.
I panni sporchi si lavano in casa.

To feather one's nest.
S'enrichir sur le dos des autres.
Enriquecerse deshonestamente.
Sich unehrlich bereichern.
Arricchirsi (in modo disonesto).

NETTLED

To be nettled.
Etre irrité.
Estar enfadado.
Aufgebracht sein (über).
Essere irritato.

NEVER

Never is a long day. (prov.)
Le futur est loin.
El futuro es un nunca acabar.
Die Zukunft ist lang.
Il futuro è lungo.

It's never too late to mend. (prov.)
Il n'est jamais trop tard pour bien faire.
Nunca es demasiado tarde para enmendarse.
Es ist niemals zu spät, um sich zu entschuldigen (um etwas wieder gutzumachen).
Non è mai troppo tardi (per redimersi).

Well I never!
Ça alors!
¡Quien iba a saberlo!
Nein, so was! / Das ist ja unerhört!
Questa poi!

NEWS (♦)

Ill news flies apace.
Les mauvaises nouvelles arrivent vite.
Las malas noticias viajan velozmente.
Schlechte Nachrichten verbreiten sich schnell (kommen schnell herum).
Le cattive notizie arrivano subito.

(♦) No news is good news. (prov.) (p. 396)
Pas de nouvelles, bonnes nouvelles.
Una noticia no recibida es ya una buena noticia.
Nichts Neues bedeutet Gutes.
Nessuna nuova, buona nuova.

No news is staler than yesterday's news.
Il n'y a pas de nouvelles plus vieilles que celles d'hier.
No hay noticia más vieja que aquella de ayer.
Nichts ist fader (langweiliger) als alte Nachrichten.
Non c'è niente di più vecchio delle notizie di ieri.

To break the news to somebody.
Donner une nouvelle à quelqu'un.
Dar noticia de algo a alguien.

Jemandem eine Nachricht überbrigen / Eine Nachricht an jemanden weitergeben / Jemandem eine Nachricht übermitteln.
Dare una notizia a qualcuno.

NEXT

It's next to impossible!
C'est presque impossible!
¡Es casi imposible!
Es ist fast (beinahe) unmöglich!
E' quasi impossibile!

It costs next to nothing!
Ça ne coûte presque rien!
¡No cuesta casi nada!
Es kostet fast nichts!
Non costa quasi nulla!

What next?
Et après?
¿Y luego?
Was (kommt) noch?
E poi?

NICE

A nice mess!
Une belle salade! / Un beau gâchis!
¡Un buen enredo!
Eine schöne Bescherung!
Un bel pasticcio!

NICK

In the nick of time.
Au bon moment.
En el momento crítico.
Zur rechten Zeit / Im richtigen Augenblick / Wie gerufen.
Proprio al momento giusto.

NIGHTCAP

I usually have a nightcap.
D'habitude je bois un petit verre avant d'aller au lit.

Usualmente tomo una copa antes de acostarme.
Gewöhnlich nehme ich einen Schlummertrunk zu mir, bevor ich schlafen gehe.
Di solito prendo un bicchierino (cicchetto) prima d'andare a letto.

NINE

A nine day's wonder.
Une nouveauté qui dure peu.
Una novedad que llama la atención por poco tiempo.
Ein Tagesgespräch / Ein sensationelles Ereignis.
Una novità che attira l'attenzione per poco tempo.

NINES

Dressed up to the nines.
Habillé de façon très recherchée.
Vestido con mucha afectación / Estar muy catrín.
Pikfein gekleidet / Aufgedonnert.
Vestito con grande ricercatezza; da fare colpo.

NINETEEN

To talk nineteen to the dozen.
Parler à toute vitesse.
Hablar con mucha rapidez / Hablar demasiado pronto.
Das Blaue vom Himmel herunterschwatzen.
Parlare velocemente.

NIP (♦)

To nip in the bud.
Tuer dans l'œuf.
Cortar en germen / Destruir al nacer.
Im Keim ersticken.
Soffocare sul nascere.

(♦) There's a nip in the air. (p. 399)
L'air est froid.
El áire se siente helado.
Es ist eine schneidende Kälte / Es geht ein schneidender Wind / Die Luft ist beissend kalt.
L'aria è fredda.

To nip in and out.
Entrer et sortir aussitôt / Zigzaguer.
Entrar y salir de prisa / Zizaguear.
Hinein- und hinausflitzen.
Entrare e uscire in fretta / Zigzagare.

NO

No sooner said than done.
Aussitôt dit aussitôt fait.
Dicho y hecho.
Schneller getan als gesagt / Gesagt, getan.
Detto, fatto.

I did my homework in no time.
Je fis mes devoirs en un rien de temps.
Hice mis deberes muy pronto.
Ich habe meine Hausarbeiten im Nu gemacht.
Feci i compiti prestissimo.

He won't take no for an answer.
Il n'acceptera pas un « non » pour réponse.
No aceptará una respuesta negativa.
Er wird kein « nein » als Antwort akzeptieren.
Non accetterà un« no » in risposta.

NOD

I nodded to him.
Je l'ai salué d'un signe de la tête.
Le saludé con una seña.
Ich nickte ihm zu.
Lo salutai (con un cenno del capo).

NOISE

A big noise.
Une grosse légume.
Un hombre importante / Un pájaro gordo.
Ein hohes (grosses) Tier.
Un pezzo grosso / Un pezzo da novanta.

NONE

None of that!
Arrête!
¡Acába! / ¡Nada de eso!
Nichts dergleichen!
Smettila!

None of your cheek!
Arrête de faire l'insolent!
¡Deja ya de hacer el impertinente!
Lass Deine Frechheiten!
Smettila di fare l'impertinente!

NOSE (♦)

To turn up one's nose.
Froncer le nez / Faire la moue.
Arrugar la naríz.
Die Nase rümpfen.
Arricciare il naso.

(♦) To poke one's nose in somebody else's business. (p. 402)
Fourrer le nez dans les affaires des autres.
No meter las narices en los asuntos ajénos.
Seine Nase in jemandes Angelegenheiten stecken.
Ficcare il naso negli affari altrui.

To pay through the nose.
Payer très cher.
Pagar generosamente.
Übermassig bezahlen müssen / Blechen.
Pagare profumatamente / Pagare salato.

To follow one's nose.
Aller toujours tout droit.
Seguir el proprio olfato.
Immer der Nase nach gehen / Seinem Instinkt folgen.
Andare sempre dritto.

To cut off one's nose to spite one's face.
Donner des verges pour se faire fouetter.
No hay que alborotar los zanates.

402

Sich ins eigene Fleisch schneiden.
Tirar sassate in piccionaia / Danneggiare se stessi (per vendetta verso altri).

(♦) **To keep one's nose to the grindstone.** (p. 404)
Ne pas lever le nez du livre / Travailler sans arrêt.
Trabajar con ahínco.
Jemanden schwer arbeiten lassen / Jemanden schinden.
Lavorare incessantemente.

It's as plain as the nose on your face! (comp.)
C'est bien évident!
¡Es claro como el agua!
Es ist sonnenklar!
E' molto evidente! / E' chiaro come il sole!

NOSY

What a Nosy Parker!
Quel fouinard!
¡Que entremetido!
Welch neugierige Person!
Che ficcanaso!

NOT

Not at all!
Absolument pas!
¡Para nada!
Nichts zu danken! / Gern geschehen!
Niente affatto!

NOTE

To strike the right note.
Faire résonner la note juste.
Tocar el punto justo.
Den richtigen Ton treffen (finden).
Toccare il tasto giusto.

NOTHING

Nothing ventured nothing gained. (prov.)
Qui ne risque rien n'a rien.

Quien no arriesga no gana.
Wer nicht wagt, gewinnt nicht / Ohne Einsatz kein Preis.
Chi non risica non rosica.

Nothing doing!
Rien à faire!
¡Nada que hacer!
Nichts zu machen! / Kommt gar nicht in Frage!
Niente da fare!

NOTICE

Take no notice of ...
Fais semblant de ne pas voir ...
No hacer caso de ...
Nimm keine Notiz von ...
Fai finta di non vedere ...

NOW

Every now and then.
De temps à autre.
De vez en cuando.
Von Zeit zu Zeit / Hier und da / Dann und wann / Gelegentlich.
Di tanto in tanto.

NOWHERE

To get nowhere.
N'aboutir à rien.
No concluir nada.
Zu nichts kommen / Es zu nichts bringen.
Non approdare a nulla.

NUISANCE

You're a regular nuisance!
Vous êtes une vraie plaie!
¡Eres una verdadera lata!
Sie sind wirklich eine Plage (Pest)! / Sie sind ein richtiger
Quälgeist! / Sie sind eine Nervensäge!
Siete una vera peste! / Siete un rompiscatole!

NUMBERED

His days are numbered.
Ses jours sont comptés.
Sus días están contados.
Seine Tage sind gezählt.
I suoi giorni sono contati.

NURSE

To nurse one's grievances.
Se consoler de ses propres ennuis.
Consolarse de los problemas personales.
Sich an einem Unglück weiden / Sich in seinem Unglück bedauern / Sein Unglück fördern.
Consolarsi dei propri guai.

NUT

He's a hard nut to crack!
C'est un os!
Es una cosa un hueso.
Er ist eine harte Nuss / Er ist nicht leicht zu nehmen.
E' un osso duro!

He's off his nut!
Il lui manque un boulon! (une case)
¡Le falta un tornillo!
Er ist verrückt! / Er ist übergeschnappt!
Gli manca una rotella!

NUTSHELL (♦)

(♦) In a nutshell (p. 407)
En deux mots / En bref.
En resumidas cuentas.
In knapper Form / In aller Kürze.
In sunto / In due parole.

NUTTY

He's as nutty as a fruitcake. (comp.)
Il est fou à lier.

Está loco como una cabra.
Er ist verrückt / Er ist bekloppt.
E' matto da legare.

OATH

He was put upon his oath.
Ils le firent jurer.
Hicieron que jurara.
Ihm wurde der Eid abgenommen / Er musste schwören.
Lo fecero giurare.

OATS

To sow one's wild oats.
Mener une vie de bâton de chaise.
Holgazanear.
Sich austoben / Sich die Hörner ablaufen (abstossen).
Correre la cavallina.

OBJECT

He gained his object.
Atteindre le but.
Ha alcanzado su objeto.
Er erreichte sein Ziel.
Ha raggiunto lo scopo.

OBLIGING

Obliging friends.
Des amis serviables.
Amigos serviciales.
Gefällige Freunde / Hilfsbereite Freunde.
Amici servizievoli.

OBSTINATE

As obstinate as a mule. (comp.)
Têtu comme une mule (comme un âne).
Necio como una mula.
Eigensinnig wie ein Esel.
Ostinato come un mulo.

OCCASION

There is no occasion to be angry.
Il n'y a pas de raison de se mettre en colère.
No hay por que enojarse.
Es gibt keinen Grund sich zu ärgern (sich aufzuregen).
Non c'è motivo di arrabbiarsi.

OCCURRED

It occurred to me that ...
Il me vint à l'esprit que ...
Se me vino a la cabeza que ...
Es fiel mir ein, dass ... / Es kam mir der Gedanke, dass ...
Mi venne in mente che ...

ODD

He's an odd chap.
C'est un homme très bizarre.
Es un tipo muy raro.
Er ist ein sonderbarer Kauz / Er ist eine merkwürdige Person.
E' un tipo assai bizzarro.

How odd!
Comme c'est étrange!
¡Que raro!
Wie seltsam! / Wie komisch! / Kurios!
Che strano!

ODDLY

Oddly enough.
Etrange à dire.
Es extraño decirlo.
Seltsamerweise / Sonderbarerweise.
Strano a dirsi.

ODDS

Odds and ends.
Un méli-mélo.
Baratijas / De todo un poco.
Allerlei Kleinigkeiten / Krimskrams / Von allem etwas.
Cianfrusaglie / Un po' di tutto.

To be at odds.
Etre en désaccord.
No estar de acuerdo.
Nicht gut auskommen.
Essere in disaccordo.

OFF

He's off drink.
Il s'est arrêté de boire.
Ha dejado te tomar.
Er hat das Trinken aufgegeben.
Ha smesso di bere.

I'm off!
Je m'en vais!
¡Me marcho!
Ich gehe! / Ich bin schon weg!
Vado!

OFFICIAL

Official red tape.
Les lenteurs de la bureaucratie.
Lerdeces burocráticas.
Bürokratische Langsamkeit / Weg der Bürokratie.
Lungaggini burocratiche.

OIL

To pour oil on the flames.
Jeter de l'huile sur le feu.
Dar leña al fuego.
Öl ins Feuer giessen.
Gettar olio sul fuoco.

To pour oil on troubled waters.
Réapaiser les âmes.
Apaciguar los ánimos.
Die Gemüter beruhigen.
Rappacificare gli animi.

To oil someone's palm.
Graisser la patte à quelqu'un.

Corromper a alguien / Sobornar.
Jemanden schmieren / Jemanden bestechen.
Corrompere qualcuno / Ungere le ruote a qualcuno.

OLD

An old bird.
Un vieux renard.
Un viejo zorro.
Eine alte Schnepfe.
Una vecchia volpe.

Any old thing.
N'importe quoi.
Cualquier cosa.
Irgendetwas Altes / Irgendetwas.
Qualunque cosa.

As old as the hills. (comp.)
Très vieux / Vieux comme Hérode / Vieux comme l'an qua-
rante.
Viejo como Matusalém.
Uralt / Steinalt.
Molto vecchio / Vecchio come Matusalemme / Vecchio come
il cucco.

OLIVE

To hold out the olive-branch.
Offrir la paix.
Presentarse con bandera blanca.
Seinen Friedenswillen zeigen.
Porgere il ramoscello di ulivo.

OMELETTE

You can't make an omelette without breaking eggs.
On ne peut pas faire d'omelette sans casser les œufs / La
fin justifie les moyens.
El fín justifíca los medios.
Wo. gehobelt wird, da fallen Späne.
Non si puó avere la botte piena e la moglie ubriaca.

ON

On the house.
Cadeau de la Maison.
Ofrece la casa (comercial) / Regalo de la casa.
Angebot des Hauses.
Offerto dalla ditta / Omaggio della ditta.

ONCE

Once in a while.
De temps en temps.
De vez en cuando.
Zuweilen / Hin und wieder.
Una volta ogni tanto.

Once bitten twice shy. (prov.)
Chat échaudé craint l'eau froide.
Quien se ha lastimado con un martillo teme también el clavo.
Gebranntes Kind scheut das Feuer.
Chi è stato scottato dall'acqua calda teme anche la fredda.

ONE

One and all.
Et tous les autres.
Todo el mundo.
Alle miteinander.
Tutti quanti.

A one-track mind.
Un esprit étroit.
Una persona cuadrada.
Ein beschränkter Geist / Engstirnig.
Una mente ristretta.

ONLY

I'm only too pleased to see you again.
Je suis vraiment content de te revoir.
Estoy encantado de verte nuevamente.
Ich bin nur zu glücklich, dich wiederzusehen / Ich bin wirklich glücklich, dich wiederzusehen.
Sono proprio contento di rivederti.

OPEN

To come into the open.
Mettre cartes sur table.
Descubrir el juego.
Sich erklären / Offen reden / Farbe bekennen.
Metter le carte in tavola.

To force an open door.
Enfoncer une porte ouverte.
Forzar una puerta abierta.
Freien Zugang erzwingen.
Sfondare una porta aperta.

To be open-handed.
Etre généreux.
Ser generoso.
Freigebig sein.
Essere generoso.

My dad is always open with me.
Mon père est toujours sincère (ouvert) avec moi.
Papá es siempre muy sincero conmigo.
Mein Papa ist immer ehrlich mit mir / Mein Papa spricht immer offen mit mir.
Il babbo è sempre sincero con me.

OPENINGS

There are many openings in your firm.
Il y a beaucoup de postes vacants dans votre entreprise.
En vuestro negocio hay muchas plazas vacantes.
Ihre Firma hat viele freie Arbeitsplätze (offene Stellen).
Ci sono molti posti vacanti nella vostra ditta.

OPPOSITE

The most extreme opposites have some qualities in common.
(prov.)
Les extrêmes se touchent.
Los extremos tienen siempre algo en común.
Gegensätze haben Gemeinsames / Gegensätze ziehen sich an
Gli estremi si toccano.

OPTION

I had no other option.
Je n'avais pas le choix.
No tuve otro remedio / No tuve otra alternativa.
Ich hatte keine andere Wahl.
Non potei fare altro / Non avevo alternativa (scelta).

ORDER

The lift is out of order.
L'ascenseur est en panne.
El elevador está descompuesto.
Der Aufzug ist ausser Betrieb.
L'ascensore è guasto (fuori servizio).

A tall order.
Une tâche ardue.
Una taréa difícil.
Eine zu grosse Aufgabe / Ein bisschen viel verlangt.
Un compito arduo.

OTHER

Every other day.
Tous les deux jours.
Cada dos días.
Jeden zweiten Tag.
Ogni due giorni.

OUNCE

An ounce of common sense is worth a pound of theory.
La pratique vaut mieux que la théorie.
Una onza de sentido común vale una libra de teoría.
Ein Körnchen gesunder Menschenverstand wiegt mehr als ein
Haufen Theorie.
Meglio un po' di buon senso che molta teoria / Val più la
pratica che la grammatica.

OUT

I feel down and out.
Je suis exténué.

414

Me siento muerto de cansancio.
Ich bin erledigt / Ich bin kaputt / Ich fühle mich todmüde
Mi sento stanco morto.

Out of sight, out of mind. (prov.)
Loin des yeux, loin du cœur.
Lejos de los ojos, lejos del corazón.
Aus den Augen, aus dem Sinn.
Lontano dagli occhi, lontano dal cuore.

Murder will out. (prov.)
Tout se paie / Tout finit par se savoir.
Todo mal se descubre a sí mismo / Tarde o temprano todo se sabe.
Die Sonne bringt es an den Tag / Alles kommt ans Licht.
Tutti i nodi vengono al pettine / Tutto si viene a sapere.

It's out.
Il est éteint.
Está apagado.
Es ist aus! / Es ist zuende! / Es kommt nicht in Frage!
E' spento.

We're out of tea.
Nous avons fini le thé.
Hemos terminado el té.
Der Tee ist aus (alle).
Siamo sprovvisti di tè.

She cried her heart out.
Il a pleuré toutes les larmes de son corps / Il a pleuré à chaudes larmes / Il a pleuré tout son saoul.
Lloró con todo su corazón.
Sie weinte sich die Augen aus.
Ha pianto tutte le sue lacrime.

OUTRIGHT

An outright lie.
Un mensonge flagrant.
Una mentira evidente.
Eine glatte Lüge.
Una bugia madornale.

OVER

I've nothing over.
Je n'ai pas d'avance / Il ne m'est rien resté.
No me sobra nada.
Ich habe nichts übrig.
Non mi è avanzato nulla.

It's all over!
Tout est fini!
¡Ya se acabó! / Se ha acabado!
Es ist aus und vorbei!
E' tutto finito!

To be over head and ears in debt.
Etre couvert de dettes.
Estar endeudado hasta el cuello.
Bis zum Kragen (über die Ohren) in Schulden stecken.
Esser indebitato fin sopra i capelli.

OVERLEAP

Ambition often overleaps itself. (prov.)
Qui trop embrasse mal étreint.
Quien todo lo quiere, todo lo pierde.
Ehrgeiz verfehlt leicht sein Ziel / Wer immer mehr will, wird nichts haben.
Chi troppo vuole nulla stringe.

OVERSHOOT

To overshoot the mark.
Exagérer.
Exagerar / Pasarse de la raya.
Übers Ziel hinausschiessen / Übertreiben.
Esagerare / Passare il segno.

OWE

I owe it to you.
Je le dois à toi.
Te lo debo a tí.
Ich habe es dir zu verdanken / Ich bin es dir schuldig.
Lo devo a te.

OWN

To own up.
Confesser / Avouer.
Confesar.
Offen zugeben.
Confessare.

PACK (♦)

To pack someone off.
Expédier quelqu'un sans trop d'histoires.
Despedir a alguien sin muchas ceremonias.
Jemanden fortjagen.
Spedire via qualcuno senza troppi complimenti.

To pack.
Faire son baluchon.
Hacer las maletas.
Packen.
Fare le valigie.

(♦) To pack in something. (p. 418)
S'arrêter de faire quelque chose.
Parar de hacer una cosa.
Aufgeben etwas zu tun.
Smettere di fare qualcosa.

PAINS

To take pains.
Se fatiguer / S'appliquer à faire quelque chose.
Esmerarse.
Sich Mühe geben / Sich anstrengen.
Affaticarsi / Fare qualcosa con cura.

PAINT (♦)

(♦) To paint the town red. (p. 419)
Faire bombance / Faire la noce.
Ir de juerga / Hacer jolgorio.
Die Gegend unsicher machen.
Far baldoria.

PAINTED

The devil is not so black as he is painted. (prov.)
Le diable n'est pas si noir qu'on le dit.
El diablo no es como lo pintan.
Es ist alles weniger schlimm, als man meint / Es ist alles halb
so schlimm / Eine Sache nicht schwärzer machen, als sie ist.
Il diavolo non è poi così brutto come si dipinge.

PALE

As pale as death. (comp.)
Pâle comme la mort.
Pálido como si estuviera muerto.
Totenblass / Leichenblass.
Pallido come la morte.

As pale as a ghost.
Très pâle / Pâle comme la mort.
Pálido como una sábana.
Käsebleich / Kreidebleich / Aschfahl / Weiss wie ein Gespenst.
Pallido come un fantasma.

PALM

To grease someone's palm.
Graisser la patte à quelqu'un.
Sobornar a alguien.
Jemanden bestechen.
Ungere le ruote a qualcuno.

To have an itching palm.
Etre avide d'argent.
Ser codicioso.
Gierig nach Geld sein.
Essere avido di danaro.

To palm something off on someone.
Rouler quelqu'un.
Vender o dar algo indeseable a una persona (sin que se dé
cuenta de ello).
Jemandem etwas aufhängen (andrehen).
Vendere qualcosa a qualcuno con inganno / Rifilare qualcosa
a qualcuno.

PANCAKE

As flat as a pancake. (comp.)
Plat comme une planche / Etre fatigué / Etre à plat.
Muy aplanado / Muy cansado.
Flach wie ein Pfannkuchen / Sehr müde sein.
Completamente piatto / Essere molto stanco.

PANGS

The pangs of hunger.
Les crampes de la faim.
La garra del hambre.
Magenknurren (vor Hunger).
I morsi della fame.

PAPER

To put pen to paper.
Commencer à écrire.
Principiar a escribir.
Die Feder ansetzen.
Incominciare a scrivere.

PART

To part from ...
Se séparer de ...
Separarse de ... / Despedirse de ...
Sich trennen von ... / Sich lösen von ... / Teilen von ... /
Trennen von ...
Separarsi da ...

PASS

To make a pass at a girl.
Faire des propositions louches à une jeune fille / Importuner
une jeune fille.
Hacer insinuaciones a una muchacha.
Einem Mädchen gegenüber zudringlich werden.
Importunare una ragazza.

PAT

To pat oneself on the back.
Etre content de soi.
Estar contento de uno mismo.
Sich selbst beglückwünschen / Sich selbst auf die Schulter klopfen.
Essere contento di sè.

PATIENT

As patient as Job. (comp.)
Avoir une patience d'ange.
Tener la paciencia de Jób.
Geduldig wie ein Engel / Engelsgeduld.
Paziente come Giobbe.

As patient as an ox. (comp.)
Très patient.
Tener mucha paciencia.
Geduldig wie eine Kuh (ein Ochse).
Molto paziente.

PAUL

To rob Peter to pay Paul.
Voler Pierre pour payer Paul.
Contraer una nueva deuda para pagar una vieja.
Eine neue Schuld auf sich nehmen, um eine alte zu begleichen / Neue Schulden machen, um alte bezahlen zu können.
Fare un debito nuovo per pagarne uno vecchio.

Paul Pry.
Fouinard.
Entremetido.
Neugieriger / Schnüffler.
Ficcanaso.

PAVE

To pave the way for someone.
Faire la route (tracer la route) à quelqu'un.
Preparar o abrir el camino para alguien.
Jemandem den Weg bahnen.
Spianare la strada a qualcuno.

PAY

To pay someone in his own coin.
Dent pour dent.
Pagar a alguien con su propria moneda.
Jemandem mit gleicher Münze heimzahlen.
Rendere pan per focaccia / Pagare qualcuno con la stessa moneta.

To pay through the nose.
Payer les yeux de la tête.
Pagar demasiado.
Übermässig bezahlen müssen / Blechen müssen.
Pagare esageratamente (salato).

PEA

As like as two peas in a pod.
Se ressembler comme deux gouttes d'eau.
Parecerse como dos gotas de agua.
Sich gleichen sich wie ein Ei dem anderen.
Simili come due gocce d'acqua.

PEACOCK

As proud as a peacock.
Très vaniteux / Fier comme un paon.
Vanidoso / Engreído.
Stolz wie ein Pfau (Spanier).
Vanitoso come un pavone.

PEARLS

To cast pearls before swine.
Offrir des choses excellentes à ceux qui ne savent pas les apprécier.
Dar caviár a los cerdos.
Perlen vor die Säue werfen.
Gettar margherite ai porci.

PECKED

A hen pecked husband.
Un mari dominé par sa femme.

Un marido asujetado a la mujer.
Ein Pantoffelheld / Ein Ehemann, der unter dem Pantoffel steht.
Un marito dominato dalla moglie.

PEELED

To keep one's eyes peeled.
Garder les yeux grands-ouverts.
Tener los ojos pelados o bien abiertos.
Seine Augen offen halten.
Tenere gli occhi ben aperti.

PEEP

At peep of dawn.
A la pointe de l'aube.
Por la madrugada / Al salir del sol.
Im ersten Morgengrauen / In der Morgendämmerung / Bei Tagesanbruch.
Allo spuntar dell'alba.

PEEPING

A peeping Tom.
Un voyeur.
Un vuaierista / Un mirón.
Ein neugieriger (lüsterner) Kerl / Ein Voyeur.
Un guardone.

PEG

A square peg in a round hole.
Un poisson hors de l'eau.
Un pez fuera del agua.
Ein Mensch am falschen Platze / Eine Fisch ausserhalb des Wassers.
Un pesce fuor d'acqua.

To take someone down a peg or two.
Humilier quelqu'un.
Rebajar o humillar a alguien.
Jemanden ducken.
Umiliare qualcuno.

To peg away.
Trimer / Bûcher / Bosser.
Atarearse / Trabajar con tesón.
Hart arbeiten.
Sgobbare.

To peg out.
Mourir / Passer de vie à trépas.
Morir / Estirar la pata.
Eingehen / Sterben.
Morire / Tirare le cuoia.

PELT

At full pelt.
A toute vitesse.
A toda velocidad.
In voller Geschwindigkeit.
A tutta velocità.

PENCE

Take care of the pence and the pounds will take care of themselves.
Ce sont les petits ruisseaux qui font les grandes rivières.
El ahorro está hecho de centavos.
Wer den Pfennig nicht ehrt, ist des Talers nicht wert.
Il risparmio incomincia dal centesimo.

PENNY (♦)

It isn't worth a penny!
Ça ne vaut pas un sou!
¡No vale un centavo! / ¡No vale nada!
Es ist keinen Heller wert.
Non vale un fico secco!

In for a penny, in for a pound. (prov.)
Quand on commence quelque chose il faut le terminer.
Cuando uno está llevando a cabo una tarea, hay que terminarla.
Wer A sagt, muss auch B sagen.
Quando si è in ballo, bisogna ballare.

(♦) A penny for your thoughts! (p. 427)
Dis-moi ce que tu penses!
Díme lo que piensas.
Ich gäb was dafür, wenn ich wüsste, woran du jetzt denkst.
Dimmi quello che pensi!

It will cost a pretty penny.
Ça coûtera une belle somme / Ça coûtera les yeux de la tête.
Costará un ojo de la cara.
Es wird ein hübsches Sümmchen kosten.
Costerà una bella sommetta / Costerà un occhio della testa.

PEP

He's full of pep.
Il est plein d'énergie.
Está lleno de energias / Está lleno de pimienta.
Er ist voller Schwung / Er hat Elan (Energie).
E' pieno di energia / E' un peperino.

PERISH

Perish the thought!
Il n'en est absolument pas question!
¡Ní por sueños! / ¡Ní por asomo!
Daran ist nicht zu denken! / Nicht im Traum!
Neanche per sogno!

PET

He's my pet aversion.
J'ai une singulière antipathie pour lui.
Me cae particularmente mal.
Er ist mir ein Greuel.
Ho una particolare antipatia per lui.

PETER

To peter out.
S'exténuer.
Extinguirse / Agotarse.
Zu Ende gehen / Sich verlieren / Sich totlaufen / Versanden / Aussterben.
Estinguersi / Esaurirsi.

427

PICK

What I need is a pick-me-up.
J'ai besoin d'un remontant.
Lo que necesito ahora es una copa.
Was ich brauche, ist ein Schnäpschen zur Stärkung / Ich brauche
eine (Magen) Stärkung.
Ciò di cui ho bisogno è un bicchierino stimolante.

To pick quarrels with . . .
Se prendre de querelle avec quelqu'un.
Entablar un pleito con . . .
Mit jemandem Streit suchen / Mit jemandem anbändeln.
Attaccar lite con . . .

To have a bone to pick with somebody.
Avoir un motif de mésentente avec quelqu'un.
Tener algo pendiente con alguien.
Ein Hühnchen mit jemandem zu rupfen haben.
Avere un motivo di discordia con qualcuno.

To pick one's words.
Parler avec affectation.
Echar cortadillos.
Seine Worte wählen.
Parlare in punta di forchetta.

To pick and choose.
Choisir avec difficulté.
Escoger dificultosamente.
Wählerisch sein / Sorgfältig aussuchen.
Scegliere con difficoltà.

PICKED

I picked up a few words of French.
J'ai appris quelques mots français par hasard.
Aprendí por caso unas cuantas palabras de Francés.
Ich habe ein paar Worte Französisch aufgeschnappt (aufgepickt).
Imparai qualche parola di francese per caso.

PICKLE

I'm in a nice pickle.
Je suis dans de beaux draps.

428

Me hallo en un aprieto.
Ich sitze schön in der Patsche / Ich bin in einer misslichen Lage.
Sono in un bell'impiccio / Sono in un bel pasticcio.

PICTURE

You are the picture of health.
Tu resplendis de santé.
Eres el retrato de la salud.
Du siehst aus wie das blühende Leben.
Sei il ritratto della salute.

That boy is the very picture of his father.
C'est tout le portrait de son père.
Ese muchacho es el retrato de su padre.
Dieser Junge ist das Ebenbild seines Vaters.
Quel ragazzo è proprio il ritratto di suo padre.

PIDGIN

To speak pidgin English.
Parler l'anglais comme un petit nègre.
Hablar Inglés como los chinos.
Pidgin-Englisch sprechen / Schlechtes Englisch sprechen.
Parlare un cattivo inglese.

PIE

To eat humble pie.
S'humilier.
Humillarse / Tragar amargo.
Sich demütigen / Abbitte tun / Zu Kreuze kriechen.
Umiliarsi.

To have a finger in the pie.
Etre dans le bain.
Tener las manos en la masa.
Seine Finger im Spiel haben / An einer Sache beteiligt sein.
Aver le mani in pasta.

PIECE (♦)

(♦) To give somebody a piece of one's mind. (p. 374)
Lui faire sa fête / Lui en dire des vertes et des pas mûres.

Decirle unas cuántas verdades a alguien.
Jemandem gründlich die Meinung sagen.
Dirne quattro a qualcuno.

(♦) **To go to pieces.** (p. 120)
Avoir une dépression nerveuse.
Tener un agotamiento nervioso.
Zusammenbrechen / In Stücke gehen.
Avere un esaurimento nervoso / Essere a pezzi.

Piecework.
Travail à la pièce.
Trabajar a destajo.
Akkordarbeit.
Lavoro a cottimo.

PIECRUST

Promises are like piecrusts, made to be broken.
Les promesses ne sont pas faites pour être tenues.
Las promesas están hechas para romperse.
Versprechen sind zum Brechen gemacht.
Le promesse sono fatte per non essere mantenute.

PIG

To buy a pig in a poke.
Acheter à l'aveuglette.
Comprar a ciegas.
Die Katze im Sack kaufen.
Comprare alla cieca (a scatola chiusa).

PIKESTAFF

As plain as a pikestaff. (comp.)
Clair comme l'eau de roche.
Claro como la luz del sol.
Sonnenklar.
Chiaro come la luce del sole.

PILE

He has a pile of money.
Il est plein aux as / Il ramasse l'argent à la pelle.

Tiene un montón de dinero.
Er hat einen Haufen Geld / Er hat eine Stange Geld.
Ha un sacco di soldi.

Don't pile it on!
N'exagérez pas!
¡No exagéres!
Trag nicht so dick auf! / Tragen Sie nicht so dick auf / Über-
treiben Sie nicht.
Non esagerate!

PILL
To swallow a bitter pill.
Avaler des couleuvres.
Tragar quina / Tragar amargo.
Eine bittere Pille schlucken / In den sauren Apfel beissen.
Mandar giù un boccone amaro / Ingoiare la pillola.

PILLAR
To be sent from pillar to post.
Etre balloté d'un côté et de l'autre.
Ser arrojado de un lugar para otro.
Von Pontius zu Pilatus geschickt werden.
Essere sbattuto da un posto all'altro / Essere mandato da
Erode a Pilato.

PILLOW
To take counsel of one's pillow.
La nuit porte conseil.
Tomar consejo de la almohada.
Eine Sache überschlafen.
Dormirci sopra.

PIN
To pin one's faith on somebody.
Miser ses espoirs sur quelqu'un.
Poner todas las esperanzas en alguien.
Sein Vertrauen auf jemanden setzen.
Appuntare le proprie speranze su qualcuno.

PINCH

To be pinched for money.
Etre à court d'argent.
Estar en aprietos (de dinero).
Knapp bei Kasse sein.
Essere a corto di quattrini.

If it comes to the pinch.
Si on est au pied du mur / Si on est aux abois / Si on est coincé.
Si se llegase al conqué.
Wenn es zum Äussersten kommt.
Se si viene messi alle strette.

PINK (♦)

(♦) To be in the pink. (p. 433)
Etre en parfaite santé.
Estar en la mejor de las condiciones.
In Hochform sein / In bester Verfassung sein.
Essere in perfetta salute.

PINS

Pins and needles.
Avoir des fourmis.
Hormigueo.
Kribbeln.
Formicolio.

To be on pins and needles.
Etre sur des charbons ardents.
Estar en ascuas.
Wie auf Kohlen sitzen.
Essere sulle spine.

PIP

He's got the pip.
Il est de mauvaise humeur.
Está de malhumor.
Er hat miese Laune (bekommen).
E' di malumore.

PIPE (♦)

Pipe down!
Arrêtez de parler!
¡No hablen ya!
Den Mund halten.
Smettete di parlare!

(♦) Put that in your pipe and smoke it! (p. 435)
Fais-toi bien rentrer ça dans la tête et penses-y!
Póntelo bien en la cabeza y reflexióna.
Lass Dir das gesagt sein!
Mettitelo bene in testa e pensaci su!

PIPER

He who pays the piper calls the tune.
Qui paie doit être servi comme il se doit.
El que paga tiene siempre razón.
Derjenige, der die Zeche bezahlt, kann den Ton angeben /
Wer bezahlt hat das Recht, zu bestellen, was er möchte.
Chi paga ha il diritto d'essere servito come vuole.

PIPING

It's piping hot.
C'est bouillant.
Está hirviendo.
Es ist siedend heiss / Es ist brühwarm.
E' bollente.

PIQUE

To pique oneself on . . .
Se vanter de . . .
Jactarse de . . .
Sich etwas einbilden auf . . . / Sich brüsten mit . . .
Vantarsi di . . .

PITCH

As black as pitch. (comp.)
Noir corbeau.
Negro como la noche.

Schwarz wie Pech / Schwarz wie die Nacht.
Nero come la pece (come il carbone).

PLACE

Out of place.
Inopportun / Déplacé.
Fuera de lugar.
Fehl am Platz / Unangebracht.
Inopportuno / Fuor di luogo.

PLAIN

This is the plain truth!
Ça c'est la pure vérité!
¡Esta es la pura verdad! / ¡Esta es la verdad clara y pelada!
Dies ist die nackte (reine / glatte) Wahrheit!
Questa è la pura verità!

Everything was plain sailing.
Tout alla comme sur des roulettes.
Todo ha ido a pedir de boca.
Alles ging glatt / Alles verlief gut.
Tutto andò liscio come l'olio.

PLASTERED

To be plastered.
Etre ivre mort.
Estar borracho.
Besoffen sein.
Essere ubriaco fradicio.

PLAY (♦)

(♦) To play the fool. (p. 206)
Faire le niais.
Hacerse el tonto.
Den Narren spielen / Den Dummen spielen.
Fare lo stupido.

To play the game.
Jouer le jeu.

436

Actuar con lealtad.
Sich an die Spielregeln halten / Fair sein.
Agire lealmente.

To play a joke on somebody.
Jouer un tour à quelqu'un.
Hacer una broma a alguien.
Über jemanden Witze reissen / Sich über jemanden lustig machen / Jemanden auf den Arm nehmen / Jemanden verulken (veräppeln).
Fare uno scherzo a qualcuno.

Fair play.
« Fair play ».
Juego leal.
Faires Spiel / Anständigkeit / Fairness.
Gioco leale.

Foul play.
Jeu déloyal.
Juego desleal.
Ein faules (gemeines) Spiel / Betrug.
Gioco sleale.

It's child's play.
C'est très facile / C'est un jeu.
Es un juego de niños / Es muy fácil.
Es ist ein Kinderspiel / Es ist kinderleicht.
E' un gioco da ragazzi.

To play truant.
Faire l'école buissonnière.
Hacer novillos / Capear la escuela.
Die Schule schwänzen / Bummeln.
Marinare la scuola / Bigiare.

PLAYFUL

As playful as a kitten. (comp.)
Plein de verve / Plein d'entrain.
Muy brioso.
Verspielt wie ein Kätzchen.
Molto brioso.

PLEASED

As pleased as Punch. (comp.)
Heureux comme un pape.
Contento como unas pascuas.
Sich königlich freuen.
Contento come una pasqua.

PLENTIFUL

As plentiful as blackberries. (comp.)
Très abondant.
Muy abundante / Copioso.
Reichlich / Im Überfluss.
Molto abbondante.

PLOUGH

To put one's hand to the plough.
Entreprendre un travail.
Emprender un trabajo.
Eine Arbeit unternehmen.
Intraprendere un lavoro.

PLUCK

He's got lots of pluck.
Il a beaucoup de courage.
Tiene muchas agallas.
Er hat viel Schneid (Mut).
Ha molto fegato.

To pluck up courage.
Se donner du courage.
Hacer de tripas corazón / Darse valor.
Mut fassen.
Farsi coraggio / Prendere il coraggio a quattro mani.

PLUMP

As plump as a partridge. (comp.)
Gras comme une dinde.
Bien rechoncho / Rollizo.

438

Schön mollig / Sehr fett / Drall / Prall / Feist / Schön rund /
Rundlich / Gut beieinander.
Molto grasso.

PLUNGE

To take the plunge.
Faire le plongeon.
Echar por en medio / Partir por en medio.
Den entscheidenden Schritt (Sprung) wagen.
Saltare il fosso.

PLY

To ply someone with gifts.
Couvrir de cadeaux quelqu'un.
Llenar de regalos a alguien.
Jemanden mit Geschenken überhäufen (überschütten).
Riempire qualcuno di doni.

POCKET

To put one's pride in one's pocket.
S'humilier.
Humillarse / Esconder el orgullo.
Seinen Stolz überwinden / Klein beigeben.
Umiliarsi.

POINT

To ask point-blank.
Demander de but en blanc.
Pedir de primas a primeras.
Rundheraus (geradewegs) fragen / Unverblümt (offen) fragen /
Klipp und klar fragen.
Chiedere di punto in bianco.

To make a point of something.
Attribuer une grande importance à quelque chose.
Recalcar sobre alguna cosa / Dar mucha importancia a algo.
Wert (Gewicht) auf etwas legen.
Attribuire grande importanza a qualcosa.

To come to the point.
En venir au fait.
Llegar al quid de la cuestión.
Zur Sache kommen.
Venire al sodo.

It's my strong point!
C'est mon fort!
¡Esto es mi fuerte!
Es ist meine starke Seite! / Es ist meine Stärke!
E' il mio forte!

POISON
To hate somebody like poison.
Haïr profondément quelqu'un.
Odiar a alguien entrañablemente.
Jemanden wie die Pest hassen.
Odiare qualcuno profondamente.

A poison-pen letter.
Une lettre anonyme.
Una carta anónima.
Ein anonymer Brief.
Una lettera anonima.

POKE
To poke fun at somebody.
Se moquer de quelqu'un.
Burlarse de alguien.
Sich über jemanden lustig machen.
Prendere in giro qualcuno.

To buy a pig in a poke.
Acheter à l'aveuglette.
Comprar a ciegas.
Die Katze im Sack kaufen.
Comprare alla cieca (a scatola chiusa).

To poke one's nose into other people's affairs.
Fourrer son nez dans les affaires des autres.
Meter las narices en los asuntos ajénos.
Seine Nase in anderer Leute Angelegenheiten stecken.
Ficcare il naso negli affari altrui.

POKER

As stiff as a poker. (comp.)
Très rigide.
Muy rigido.
Steif wie ein Stock.
Molto rigido.

POLE

He's up the pole.
Il est un peu déboussolé.
Le falta un tornillo.
Er ist verrückt.
E' un po' svitato.

POLISH

To polish off one's work.
Mener à terme un travail.
Despachar el trabajo.
Seine Arbeit schnell erledigen.
Sbrigare il proprio lavoro.

His English needs polishing up.
Son anglais a besoin de s'améliorer.
Su Inglés necesita un perfeccionamiento.
Sein Englisch muss noch aufpoliert werden.
Il suo inglese ha bisogno di una rispolverata.

POOR

As poor as a church mouse. (comp.)
Pauvre comme Job.
Pobre como una rata.
Arm wie eine Kirchenmaus.
Povero in canna.

POORLY

To be poorly off.
Etre à court d'argent.
Estar en un aprieto de dinero.
Armselig (dürftig) dran sein / Sehr schlecht gehen.
Star male (finanziariamente).

To think poorly of . . .
Avoir une triste opinion de . . .
Tener una mala opinión de . . .
Nicht viel halten von . . . / Schlecht denken von . . .
Avere una cattiva opinione di . . .

POP

To pop off.
S'en aller à toute vitesse.
Irse de repente.
Abhauen / Sich aus dem Staub machen / Plötzlich verschwinden.
Andarsene di corsa.

To pop the question.
Faire une proposition de mariage.
Hacer una propuesta de casamiento.
Einen Heiratsantrag machen.
Fare una proposta di matrimonio.

POSSUM

To play possum.
Feindre d'être malade.
Simular de estar enfermo.
Sich krank stellen.
Fingersi malato.

POST

Post-haste.
A la hâte.
Rápidamente.
Eiligst / Schnellstens.
In gran fretta.

Between you, me and the gate-post.
Soit dit entre nous.
Dicho en confianza / Dicho entre nos.
Im Vertrauen / Unter uns gesagt.
Detto in confidenza / A quattrocchi / Detto fra noi.

442

POT

To go to pot.
Aller à la ruine.
Ir en quiebra.
Kaputtgehen / Auf den Hund kommen.
Andare in rovina.

A watched pot never boils. (prov.)
Il ne faut jamais soulever le couvercle de la marmitte.
Olla removida nunca hierve.
Beim Warten wird die Zeit lang.
Pentola guardata non bolle mai.

To make a pot of money.
Gagner un argent fou.
Hacer un montón de dinero.
Geld wie Heu machen / Einen Haufen Geld machen / Eine
Stange Geld machen / Ein Heidengeld machen.
Fare un sacco di quattrini.

The pot calling the kettle black.
L'hôpital qui se moque de la charité.
Mirar la pája en el ojo ajeno sin ver el tronco en el propio /
La olla le dijo al comál que tiznado estás.
Ein Esel schilt den anderen Langohr.
Accusare uno di un difetto che si possiede nella stessa misura /
Il bue che disse « cornuto » all'asino.

To make the pot boil.
Gagner sa vie.
Ganarse la vida.
Das Brot verdienen / Die Sache in Gang bringen.
Guadagnarsi il pane.

POTTER

To potter about.
Travailler sans entrain.
Trabajar poco y mal.
Herumwerkeln / Herumhantieren.
Lavoricchiare.

POTTY

To be potty.
Etre fou.
Estar loco / Estar chiflado.
Verrückt sein.
Essere pazzo.

POUR (♦)

(♦) It never rains but it pours. (prov.) (p. 445)
Un malheur ne vient jamais seul.
Las desgracias nunca vienen solas.
Ein Unglück kommt selten allein.
Le disgrazie non vengono mai sole.

To pour cold water on a plan.
Faire tomber à l'eau un projet.
Desinflar un proyecto.
Einen Plan verübeln vermasseln.
Gettar acqua fredda su un progetto.

To pour oil on troubled waters.
Jeter de l'eau sur le feu.
Echar agua al fuego.
Die Gemüter beruhigen.
Gettar acqua sul fuoco.

PRACTICE

Practice makes perfect. (prov.)
Expérience passe science.
La práctica vale más de la teoría.
Probieren geht über Studiern.
La pratica vale più della grammatica.

PRESENCE

Presence of mind.
Présence d'esprit.
Presencia de ánimo.
Geistesgegenwart.
Presenza di spirito.

445

PRESSING

You are very pressing!
Tu es trop insistant!
¡Eres muy insistente!
Sie sind sehr aufdringlich.
Insisti troppo!

PRICE

Every man has his price. (prov.)
C'est seulement une question de prix.
Cada hombre tiene su precio.
Alles hat seinen Preis.
E' solo questione di prezzo.

Not at any price!
Pour rien au monde!
Por nada al mundo / Ní por todo el oro del mundo.
Um keinen Preis!
Per nulla al mondo!

PRIME

To be in one's prime.
Etre à la fleur de l'âge.
Estar en la flor de la edad.
In der Blüte seiner Jahre sein / Im besten Alter sein.
Essere nel fiore degli anni.

PROMISES

Promises are like piecrust, made to be broken. (prov.)
Les promesses ne sont pas faites pour être tenues.
La promesas están hechas para romperse.
Versprechen sind zum Brechen da.
Le promesse sono fatte per non essere mantenute.

PROOF (♦)

(♦) The proof of the pudding is in the eating. (p. 447)
Ce sont les faits qui comptent et non les paroles.
Lo que cuenta son los hechos y no las palabras / Obras
son amores y no buenas razones.

Tatsachen zählen.
Quello che conta sono i fatti.

PROPOSE

Man proposes, God disposes. (prov.)
L'homme propose et Dieu dispose.
El hombre propone, Dios dispone.
Der Mensch denkt und Gott lenkt.
L'uomo propone e Dio dispone.

PROUD

As proud as a peacock. (comp.)
Fier comme un paon.
Engreído.
Stolz wie ein Pfau (Spanier).
Tronfio come un pavone.

As proud as Lucifer. (comp.)
Fier / Hautain.
Muy altivo / Soberbio.
Sehr prächtig.
Molto altero.

To do someone proud.
Faire honneur à quelqu'un.
Honrar a alguien.
Jemandem grosse Ehre erweisen / Jemanden königlich bewirten.
Fare onore a qualcuno.

PROVE

The exception proves the rule. (prov.)
L'exception confirme la règle.
La excepción confirma la regla.
Die Ausnahme bestätigt die Regel.
L'eccezione conferma la regola.

PRY

A Paul Pry.
Un fouinard.

Un entremetido / Un metido.
Ein Schnüffler / Jemand, der seine Nase in alles steckt / Ein Neugieriger.
Un ficcanaso.

P'S

To mind one's P's and O's.
Mesurer ses mots.
Tener cuidado de lo que uno dice.
Seine Worte abwägen / Auf seine Worte achten.
Badare a quel che si dice.

PUDDING

To get more praise than pudding.
Avoir plus d'éloges que de récompenses.
Tener más elogios que recompensas.
Mehr Lob als Dank erhalten.
Ricevere più elogi che ricompense.

PULL (♦)

(♦) To pull someone's leg. (p. 450)
Se moquer de quelqu'un.
Burlarse de alguien.
Jemanden auf den Arm nehmen / Jemanden aufziehen.
Prendere in giro qualcuno.

To pull the strings.
Manœuvrer.
Maniobrar.
Die Fäden in der Hand haben.
Manovrare.

(♦) Pull yourself together! (p. 451)
Courage!
¡Serénate!
Reiss Dich zusammen!
Fatti coraggio!

To pull something off.
Porter quelque chose à terme.
Terminar algo.

449

Etwas zuwege bringen / Etwas schaukeln / Etwas schaffen.
Portare qualcosa a compimento.

PUMP

I pumped the rules of the game into the boys' heads.
J'ai enfoncé les règles du jeu dans la tête des enfants.
He metido en la cabeza de los muchachos las reglas del juego.
Ich habe den Jungen die Spielregeln eingetrichtert.
Ho ficcato in testa ai ragazzi le regole del gioco.

PUNCH

As pleased as Punch. (comp.)
Etre content comme un pape.
Estar contento como unas pascuas.
Sich königlich freuen.
Contento come una pasqua.

As proud as Punch. (comp.)
Etre fier comme un paon.
Ser engreído.
Aufgeblasen wie ein Pfau.
Tronfio come un pavone.

PUPPY

Puppy-love.
Amour enfantin (puéril).
Amor de niños.
Jugendliebe.
Amore fanciullesco.

PURPOSE

On purpose.
Exprès.
De adrede / De intención / De propósito.
Absichtlich.
Di proposito.

It was to no purpose.
Cela a été fait en vain.
Ha sido para nada.

Es war vergeblich (umsonst).
E' avvenuto invano.

PURSE

Purse proud.
Orgueilleux de sa propre richesse.
Orgulloso de las riquezas de uno.
Geldstolz / Protzig.
Orgoglioso della propria ricchezza.

To hold the purse strings.
Tenir les cordons de la bourse.
Tener el control de la economía familiar.
Den Geldbeutel verwalten.
Avere il controllo dell'economia familiare.

PUSH (♦)

Let's push off!
Allons-y!
¡Vámonos!
Hauen wir ab! / Machen wir uns davon!
Andiamo!

(♦) To get the push. (p. 454)
Se faire mettre à la porte / Se faire renvoyer.
Hacer que le despidan a uno del trabajo.
Rausfliegen / Entlassen werden.
Farsi licenziare.

PUSSY

To pussy-foot.
Etre prudent / Ne pas se compromettre.
Ser prudente / No comprometerse.
Schleichen (wie eine Katze) / Leisetreten / Sich nicht festlegen /
Herumreden / Wie eine Katze um den heissen Brei schleichen.
Essere prudente / Non compromettersi.

PUT (♦)

(♦) To put one's foot down. (p. 208)
S'arc-bouter.

Hacer hincapié.
Energisch werden / Ein Machtwort sprechen / Mit dem Fuss
auftreten.
Puntare i piedi.

(♦) **To put one's best foot forward.** (p. 46)
Allonger le pas.
Caminar .de buen paso.
Sein Bestes tun.
Camminare di buon passo / Allungare il passo.

To put away for a rainy day.
Economiser par prudence.
Guardar dinero para los tiempos difíciles.
Geld für schlechte Zeiten zurücklegen / Einen Notgroschen
zurücklegen / Geld für Notzeiten auf die hohe Kante legen.
Risparmiare in previsione di tempi più duri.

To put off.
Renvoyer / Décourager.
Aplazar / Posponer.
Wegstellen / Ablegen / Verschieben / Vertrösten (mit) / Ab-
sagen / Abbrigen (von).
Rimandare / Scoraggiare.

To put up with.
Supporter.
Aguantar / Tolerar.
Sich abfinden mit ... / Hinnehmen / Ertragen.
Sopportare / Tollerare.

To put someone through his paces.
Mettre à l'épreuve l'habileté de quelqu'un.
Poner alguien a la prueba.
Jemanden auf Herz und Nieren prüfen.
Provare l'abilità di qualcuno.

To put someone up for the night.
Accueillir quelqu'un pour la nuit.
Dar hospitalidad a alguien por la noche.
Jemanden für die Nacht (bei sich) aufnehmen (unterbringen).
Ospitare qualcuno per la notte.

PUTTY
He deserves a putty medal.
Il mérite une médaille en chocolat.
Se merece una medalla de cartón.
Er verdient einen Papierorden.
Merita una medaglia di cartone.

PUZZLE
To puzzle out something.
Résoudre quelque chose.
Desenredar o descifrar algo.
Etwas heraustüfteln (herausknobeln / herausbekommen).
Risolvere qualcosa.

To puzzle over something.
Se creuser la cervelle.
Ponderar algo / Tratar de resolver algo.
Sich den Kopf zerbrechen über . . .
Scervellarsi su qualcosa.

Q
On the q. t.
En cachette / En douce.
De escondidas.
Heimlich / Still und heimlich / Im Verborgenen.
Di nascosto / Alla chetichella.

QUAGMIRE
To be in a quagmire.
Etre dans de beaux draps.
Estar metido en un atascadero.
In der Patsche sein (stecken).
Essere nei pasticci.

QUANDARY
To be in a quandary.
Se trouver en difficulté.
Encontrarse en dificultades.
Sich in einem Dilemma befinden.
Trovarsi in difficoltà.

QUARREL

To pick a quarrel with someone.
Se prendre de querelle avec quelqu'un.
Comenzar a reñir con alguien.
Mit jemandem Streit suchen / Mit jemandem anbändeln.
Attaccar lite con qualcuno.

To quarrel with one's bread and butter.
Se plaindre de son état.
Quejarse de la propia situacion.
Mit seinem Los unzufrieden sein.
Lamentarsi del proprio stato.

QUARTER

To give quarter.
Laisser respirer / Accorder un répit.
Dar cuartel (a un enemigo).
Nachsicht üben.
Dare respiro / Accordare grazia.

QUARTERS

To come to close quarters.
En venir aux mains.
Venir a las manos.
Handgemein werden.
Venire alle mani.

QUEER

To be in Queer street.
Se trouver en difficulté.
Encontrarse en un callejón sin salida.
In der Tinte sitzen.
Trovarsi in difficoltà.

QUENCH

To quench one's thirst.
Se désaltérer.
Apagar la sed / Quitarse la sed.
Seinen Durst löschen.
Dissetarsi / Spegnere la sete.

QUESTION

Out of the question.
Hors de propos.
Imposible / Fuera de toda discusión.
Ausser Frage.
Fuori discussione.

Beyond all question.
Hors de doute.
Fuera de duda.
Ohne Frage / Fraglos.
Fuor di dubbio.

QUICK

As quick as lightning. (comp.)
Rapide comme l'éclair.
Velóz como un relámpago.
Wie der Blitz / Blitzschnell.
Veloce come il fulmine.

QUIET

To live in peace and quiet.
Vivre en paix.
Vivir en paz.
In Ruhe und Frieden leben.
Vivere in santa pace.

As quiet as a lamb. (comp.)
Très tranquille.
Manso como un cordero.
Sehr ruhig / Sehr still / Lammfromm.
Molto tranquillo / Mite come un agnello.

QUIT

Death quits all scores. (prov.)
La mort règle tous les comptes.
La muerte desquita todas las cuentas.
Der Tod begleicht alle Rechnungen / Der Tod tilgt alle Schuld /
Mit dem Tod endet alle Schuld.
La morte salda tutti i conti.

Let's quit!
Finissons-en!
¡Terminemos ya!
Lass uns aufhören (damit)! / Schluss damit!
Finiamola!

QUITS

Now we're quits!
Maintenant nous sommes quites!
¡Ahora estamos empatados!
Jetzt sind wir quitt!
Ora siamo pari!

QUITTANCE

Omittance is no quittance. (prov.)
Ne pas réclamer son dû ne veut pas dire pour autant l'annuler.
La falta de demanda de pago, no cancela la deuda.
Unterlassung bedeutet nicht Erlassung / Eine versäumte Mahnung bedeutet nicht Erlassen der Schuld.
La mancata richiesta di pagamento non annulla il debito.

QUIVER

I've an arrow left in my quiver.
J'ai encore une carte à jouer.
Tengo todavía una carta en mano.
Ich habe noch ein Eisen im Feuer.
Ho ancora una carta da giocare / Ho ancora una freccia al mio arco.

RACK

To rack one's brains.
Se creuser la tête.
Devanarse los sesos / Quebrarse uno la cabeza.
Sich den Kopf zerbrechen.
Lambiccarsi il cervello.

To go to rack and ruin.
Se ruiner / Aller au diable.
Caer en la ruina.

459

Völlig zugrunde gehen.
Andare in malora.

RACKET

To kick up a racket.
Faire du boucan.
Hacer bullicio / Hacer baraúnda.
Auf die Pauke hauen / Ein Spektakel veranstalten / Lärm (Krach) schlagen / Wirbel (Radau) machen.
Fare un baccano d'inferno.

RACKING

A racking pain.
Une douleur vive.
Un dolor desgarrante.
Ein rasender Schmerz.
Un dolore tremendo.

RACY

He has a racy style.
Il a un style enjoué.
Su estílo tiene mucho brío.
Er hat einen rassigen Stil.
Ha uno stile brioso.

RAG

We always rag him.
Nous nous moquons toujours de lui.
Nos burlamos de él continuamente.
Wir nehmen ihn immer auf den Arm / Wir ziehen ihn immer auf.
Lo prendiamo sempre in giro (per il naso).

RAGE (♦)

(♦) These maxi-dresses are all the rage. (p. 13)
Ces maxi-vêtements sont le dernier cri.
Estas maxifaldas están muy en boga.
Diese Maxi-Kleider sind jetzt die grosse Mode.
Questi maxi-vestiti sono di gran moda.

460

To get into a rage.
Se mettre dans une rage folle.
Ponerse furioso / Ponerse como los once mil diablos.
In Wut geraten.
Montare su tutte le furie.

RAILS

To go off the rails.
Dérailler / Ne pas bien aller / Avoir une dépression nerveuse.
No estar muy bien.
Aus dem Geleise kommen / Durcheinander sein.
Non stare bene / Avere un esaurimento.

RAIN (♦)

(♦) It never rains but it pours. (prov.) (p. 445)
Un malheur ne vient jamais seul.
La desgracias nunca vienen solas.
Ein Unglück kommt selten allein.
Le disgrazie non vengono mai sole.

It's raining cats and dogs.
Il pleut des cordes / Il pleut à verse.
Llueve a cántaros.
Es schüttet wie mit Kannen / Es giesst in Strömen.
Piove a catinelle.

RAINY

To put away for a rainy day.
Economiser par prudence.
Ahorrar por aquello de las dudas.
Für schlechte Zeiten sparen / Aus Vorsorge Geld zurücklegen /
Für Notzeiten Geld auf die hohe Kante legen.
Risparmiare in previsione di giorni peggiori.

RAISE

To raise a family.
Elever (maintenir) une famille.
Levantar una familia.
Eine Familie gründen.
Metter su famiglia.

461

RAKE

As thin as a rake. (comp.)
Maigre comme un clou.
Flaco como un macarrón.
Dünn wie eine Latte / Steckendünn.
Magro come un chiodo (come un grissino).

I'll have to rake up some cash.
Je devrai ramasser par-ci par-là un peu d'argent.
Tengo que juntar un poco de dinero.
Ich werde etwas Geld auftreiben müssen / Ich muss ein bisschen
Geld zusammenkratzen.
Dovrò raggranellare un po' di denaro.

RAM

To ram something down somebody's throat.
Faire avaler des couleuvres à quelqu'un.
Hacerle tragar una papa a alguien.
Jemandem etwas aufzwingen.
Far inghiottire un rospo a qualcuno.

RAMROD

As stiff as a ramrod. (comp.)
Très raide / Très rigide.
Muy rígido.
Steif wie ein Stock.
Molto rigido.

RANDOM

At random.
Par hasard.
Por caso.
Aufs Geratewohl / Auf gut Glück / Blindlings / Zufällig.
A casaccio.

RANK

To rise from the rank.
Venir de rien.

Venir de la nada.
Von der Pike auf dienen.
Venire dalla gavetta.

RANSOM

A king's ransom.
Une grosse somme.
Una gran suma de dinero.
Eine Riesensumme / Ein königliches Lösegeld.
Una grossa somma.

RAP

To take the rap.
Endosser la faute.
Atribuirse la culpa.
(Zu einer Strafe) Verdonnert werden.
Addossarsi la colpa.

RAPID

As rapid as lightning. (comp.)
Rapide comme l'éclair.
Velóz como un relampago.
Schnell wie der Blitz / Blitzschnell.
Veloce come un fulmine.

RAT

To smell a rat.
Suspecter un piège / Flairer un piège.
Sospechar una trampa.
Lunte (den Braten) riechen.
Sospettare un tranello.

He looked like a drowned rat.
Il était trempé jusqu'aux os.
Estaba calado hasta los huesos.
Er war pudelnass.
Era bagnato come un pulcino (fino alle ossa).

463

RATTLED

To be rattled.
Etre en colère / Etre effrayé.
Estar enfadado.
Nervös sein / Verärgert sein.
Essere arrabbiato.

RAW

In the raw.
Nu comme un ver.
Desnudo.
Splitternackt.
Nudo.

RAZOR

To be on a razor's edge.
Etre sur la corde raide.
Caminar sobre la cuerda floja.
Auf des Messers Schneide stehen.
Camminare sul filo del rasoio.

RAZZLE

To go on the razzle.
Se laisser aller à la joie.
Gozar de la vida.
Sich toll amüsieren.
Darsi alla pazza gioia.

READ

A well-read man.
Un homme cultivé.
Un hombre culto / Un hombre de letras / Un hombre leído.
Ein sehr belesener Mann / Ein gebildeter (bewanderter) Mann.
Un uomo colto.

REAL

This is the real thing!
C'est vraiment ce qu'il faut!

¡Esto es lo que hace falta!
Das ist das einzig Wahre!
Questo è proprio quello che ci vuole!

REAP

He that sows the wind will reap the whirlwind. (prov.)
Qui sème le vent récolte la tempête.
Quien siembra vientos recoge tempestades.
Wer Wind sät, wird Sturm ernten.
Chi semina vento raccoglie tempesta.

REASON

It stands to reason!
C'est évident!
Es razonable.
Es ist klar! / Es leuchtet ein / Es ist einleuchtend!
E' ovvio!

Without rhyme or reason.
Sans rime ni raison.
Sin ninguna razón.
Ohne Sinn und Verstand / Ohne Grund.
Senza motivo.

RECKONING

Short reckonings make long friends. (prov.)
Les bons comptes font les bons amis.
Entre dos amigos, un notario y dos testigos.
Glatte Rechnung, gute Freunde.
Patti chiari, amicizia lunga.

RECORD

It's off the record.
Ce n'est pas officiel / C'est officieux.
No es oficial.
Es ist inoffiziell.
Non è ufficiale / E' ufficioso.

465

RED (♦)

(♦) To paint the town red. (p. 419)
Faire bombance / Faire la noce.
Ir de juerga.
Auf die Pauke hauen / Die Gegend unsicher machen.
Far baldoria.

(♦) To see red. (p. 467)
Etre très en colère / Voir rouge.
Estar enfurecido.
Rot sehen.
Essere molto arrabbiato / Vedere rosso.

They're in the red.
Ils ont le compte à découvert.
Estar sin blanca / Están sin blanca.
Sie sind im Rot / Sie haben das Konto überzogen.
Hanno il conto scoperto / Sono in rosso.

A red-letter day.
Un jour important.
Un día de importancia.
Ein Festtag / Ein Freudentag / Ein Glückstag.
Un giorno importante.

The burglar was caught red-handed.
Le voleur fut pris en flagrant délit.
El ladrón fué cogido con las manos en la masa.
Der Einbrecher wurde auf frischer Tat ertappt.
Lo scassinatore fu colto in flagrante (fu preso con le mani nel sacco).

To draw a red herring across the path.
Détourner l'attention de quelque chose.
Desviar la atención de un argumento.
Ein Ablenkungsmanöver durchführen.
Distrarre l'attenzione da una cosa.

Red-tape.
Bureaucratie pédante et minutieuse.
Burocracia pedante y obsesiva.
Bürokratisch.
Burocrazia pedante e minuziosa.

As red as blood. (comp.)
Rouge feu.
Rojo como la sangre.
Rot wie Blut / Blutrot.
Molto rosso / Rosso come il sangue.

As red as a cherry. (comp.)
Rouge comme une cerise.
Rojo como una cereza.
Rot wie eine Kirsche / Kirschrot / Feuerrot / Rosenrot.
Rosso come una ciliegia.

As red as fire.
Très rouge.
Rojo encarnado.
Feuerrot.
Rosso come il fuoco.

As red as a rose.
Très rouge.
Muy rojo.
Rosenrot.
Molto rosso.

REEK

He reeks of beer.
Il pue la bière.
Hiede a cerveza.
Er riecht (stinkt) nach Bier.
Puzza di birra.

REFRESHER

A refresher course.
Stage de formation (de perfectionnement; de recyclage).
Un curso para ponerse al día.
Auffrischungskurs / Wiederholungskurs.
Un corso di aggiornamento.

REGULAR

A regular rascal.
Chenapan / Vaurien.

468

Un buen pícaro / Un verdadero pícaro.
Ein richtiger Schuft (Schurke / Halunke) / Ein richtiger Spitzbube (Gauner).
Un vero furfante.

A regular humbug.
Un goujat / Un grand bavard / Un embrouilleur.
Un buen granuja / Un verdadero granuja.
Ein richtiggehender Schwindler (Betrüger).
Un perfetto cialtrone.

As regular as clockwork. (comp.)
Précis comme une horloge.
Lleva una vida muy regular.
Pünktlich wie die Uhr.
Molto regolare / Preciso come un orologio.

REIN

Mrs Brown keeps a tight rein on her son.
Madame Brown tient en bride son fils / Madame Brown fait filer droit son fils.
La señora Brown lleva a su hijo con mano de hierro.
Frau Brown hat ihren Sohn fest an der Kandare (fest in der Hand / fest an den Zügeln) / Frau Brown halt ihren Sohn fest im Zaum.
La signora Brown tiene a freno suo figlio.

To give rein to one's imagination.
Donner libre cours à la fantaisie.
Dar rienda suelta a la imaginación.
Seiner Phantasie freien Lauf lassen.
Dare libero corso alla propria fantasia.

RELIEVE

A thief relieved him of his wallet.
Un voleur lui faucha son portefeuille.
Un ladrón le quitó la cartera.
Ein Dieb stahl ihm seine Brieftasche / Ein Dieb erleichterte ihn um seine Brieftasche.
Un ladro lo alleggerì del portafogli.

I felt relieved.
J'ai éprouvé un soulagement.
He sentido alivio / Sentí algo de alivio.
Ich fühlte mich erleichtert (beruhigt).
Ho provato un senso di sollievo / Mi sentii sollevato.

To relieve one's feelings.
Se défouler / Se confier / Ouvrir son cœur.
Desahogarse.
Seinen Gefühlen Luft machen.
Sfogarsi.

RELISH
I don't relish the idea of going now.
Je ne crois pas que ce soit le bon moment pour y aller.
No me agrada ir en este momento.
Ich bin nicht gerade begeistert davon, jetzt zu gehen.
Non mi alletta l'idea di andare ora.

REPAIR
In bad repair.
En mauvais état.
En mal estado.
In schlechtem Zustand.
In cattivo stato.

In good repair.
En bon état.
En buen estado.
In gutem Zustand.
In buono stato.

REPORTS
Idle reports.
Bruits sans fondements.
Voces infundadas.
Leere Gerüchte.
Voci infondate.

REST

To rest on one's laurels.
Dormir sur ses lauriers.
Dormirse sobre los laureles.
Auf seinen Lorbeeren ausruhen.
Dormire sugli allori.

To lose one's nights rest.
Perdre le sommeil.
Perder el sueño.
Seine Nachtruhe (seinen Schlaf) verlieren / Die Nacht schlaflos verbringen.
Passare la notte in bianco.

RETIRE

To retire from the world.
Entrer au couvent.
Retirarse del mundo / Alejarse del mundo.
Ins Kloster gehen / Sich von der Welt zurückziehen.
Entrare in convento.

To retire into oneself.
Se replier sur soi-même.
Cerrarse en sí mismo.
Sich verschliessen.
Chiudersi in sè.

RETURN

Happy returns of the day!
Tous mes vœux!
¡Muchas felicitaciones! / ¡Enhorabuena!
Herzlichen Glückwunsch zum Geburtstag!
Tanti auguri! / Cento di questi giorni!

RICH

As rich as Croesus. (comp.)
Riche comme Crésus.
Muy rico.
Reich wie ein Krösus / Steinreich.
Ricco come un Creso / Ricco sfondato.

As rich as a Jew. (comp.)
Très riche.
Muy rico.
Reich wie ein Jude / Sehr reich.
Molto ricco.

RID

To get rid of . . .
Se libérer de . . .
Librarse de . . . / Deshacerse de . . .
Sich befreien von . . . / Jemanden (etwas) loswerden.
Liberarsi di . . . / Sbarazzarsi di . . .

RIDDANCE

Good riddance to bad rubbish.
Une perte avantageuse.
Ni en fotografía.
Ein vorteilhafter Verlust.
Meglio perderlo che trovarlo.

RIDDLE

To speak in riddles.
Parler de façon énigmatique / Parler à mots couverts.
Hablar enigmáticamente.
In Rätseln sprechen.
Parlare in modo enigmatico.

RIDE

To take somebody for a ride.
Se moquer de quelqu'un / Jouer un tour à quelqu'un.
Burlarse de alguien con el engaño / Joder a alguien.
Jemanden reinlegen / Jemanden auf den Arm nehmen.
Prendere in giro qualcuno / Ingannare qualcuno.

To ride the high horse.
Se donner de grands airs.
Darse ínfulas.
Auf einem hohen Ross reiten.
Darsi grandi arie.

RIGHT

Right-hand man.
Une aide précieuse / Le bras droit.
Un hombre que es el brazo derecho / Un auxiliar muy importante.
Rechte Hand / Rechter Nebenmann.
Aiutante prezioso / Braccio destro.

The right man in the right place. (prov.)
L'homme qu'il faut.
El hombre que hace falta.
Der richtige Mann am richtigen Platz.
L'uomo giusto al giusto posto.

To be in one's right mind.
Etre sain d'esprit.
Estar en sus cabales.
Bei vollem Verstand sein.
Essere sano di mente.

As right as rain! (comp.)
Très juste!
¡Claro! / ¡Justo!
Ganz richtig! / Korrekt! / In Ordnung!
Giustissimo!

Right you are!
Ça va!
¡Está bien! / ¡Muy bien!
Richtig! / Jawohl!
Va bene!

RING (♦)

There was a ring of sincerity in the speech.
Il y avait un accent de sincérité dans ses paroles.
Hay algo de sinceridad en lo que dice.
Da war ein Klang von Aufrichtigkeit in dem Gespräch.
C'era un accento di sincerità nel discorso.

(♦) To give someone a ring. (p. 474)
Passer un coup de fil à quelqu'un.
Llámar por teléfono a una persona.

Jemanden anrufen.
Dare a qualcuno un colpo di telefono.

RINGS

To have rings under one's eyes.
Avoir les yeux cernés / Avoir des poches sous les yeux.
Tener ojeras.
Ringe unter den Augen haben.
Avere gli occhi cerchiati / Avere le borse sotto gli occhi.

RIPE

As ripe as a cherry. (comp.)
Très mûr.
Está maduro / Está listo para . . .
Reif (wie eine rote Kirsche) / Ausgereift.
Molto maturo.

RIPPING

To have a ripping good time.
S'amuser follement.
Pasar un buen rato.
Sich prima amüsieren.
Divertirsi un mondo.

RISE

To give rise to . . .
Faire naître . . .
Promover algo.
Verursachen / Hervorrufen / Erregen.
Far nascere . . .

To give rise to the occasion.
Etre à la hauteur de la situation.
Estar a la altura de la situación.
Sich der Lage gewachsen zeigen.
Essere all'altezza della situazione.

RIVET

To rivet one's attention upon something.
River son attention sur quelque chose.

Fijarse en algo.
Seine Aufmerksamkeit auf etwas richten.
Fissare la propria attenzione su qualcosa.

ROAR

To roar with laughter.
Se tordre de rire / Se bidonner.
Matarse de la risa.
Vor Lachen brüllen.
Sbellicarsi dalle risa.

ROBBERY

Daylight robbery!
C'est bel et bien un vol!
Un robo a la luz del dia.
Ein guter Raubzug! / Ein Fang, der sich sehen lässt!
Un furto bell'e buono!

ROCK

To reach rock-bottom.
Toucher le fond.
Tocar el fondo.
Einer Sache auf den Grund gehen.
Toccare il fondo.

ROCKER

He's off his rocker!
Il est fou!
¡Está loco!
Er ist übergeschnappt (verrückt).
E' matto da legare!

ROCKS

To run upon the rocks.
Rencontrer de sérieuses difficultés.
Encontrar dificultades muy graves.
Auf eine Serie von Schwierigkeiten stossen.
Incontrare serie difficoltà.

476

To be on the rocks.
Etre sur la paille / Etre fauché.
Estar sin dinero / Estar pelado.
Pleite sein / In Geldnot sein.
Essere al verde.

On the rocks.
Avec des glaçons.
Con hielo.
Mit Eis / On the rocks.
Con ghiaccio.

ROD

Spare the rod and spoil the child. (prov.)
Le médecin qui a pitié ne guérit pas la plaie / Il faut savoir être sévère / La pitié n'est pas le meilleur remède.
En la vida hay que ser severos / La compasión no es siempre el mejor remedio.
Wer die Rute spart, verzieht das Kind.
Il medico pietoso fa la piaga cancrenosa.

To make a rod for one's own back.
Chercher des ennuis.
Buscarse problemas.
Sich die Rute selber flechten / Sich selbst ins Unglück stürzen.
Andare in cerca di guai.

ROLL

To roll up.
Arriver par hasard.
Llegar por casualidad.
Aufkreuzen / Auftauchen.
Capitare per caso (in un luogo).

ROLLING

To be rolling in money.
Rouler sur l'or / Ramasser l'argent à la pelle.
Estar nadando en dinero.
In Geld schwimmen.
Far soldi a palate / Nuotare nell'oro.

A rolling stone gathers no moss. (prov.)
Pierre qui roule n'amasse pas mousse.
Quien mucho abraza nada abarca.
Ein rollender Stein setzt kein Moos an.
Chi tenta troppe vie non raggiunge nessuna meta.

ROLLS

They are going to strike his name off the rolls.
Ils retirent son nom du tableau / Ils le rayent du tableau.
Su nombre va a ser eliminado del colegio profesional.
Sie sind im Begriff seinen Namen von der Liste zu streichen.
Hanno intenzione di cancellare il suo nome dall'albo.

ROME

Rome was not built in a day. (prov.)
Rome ne s'est pas faite en un jour.
Roma no fué construida en un día.
Rom wurde nicht an einem Tag erbaut.
Roma non fu fatta in un giorno.

When in Rome, do as the Romans do. (prov.)
Lorsque tu vas à Rome, fais comme les Romains.
Si vas a Roma, haz como los romanos.
Mit den Wölfen heulen / Sich fremden Sitten anpassen.
Quando a Roma vai, fa' come vedrai.

ROMP

To romp home.
Gagner avec facilité.
Ganar con facilidad.
Leicht gewinnen.
Vincere con facilità.

ROOF

The roof of heaven.
La voûte du ciel.
El techo del cielo.
Himmelsgewölbe / Himmelszelt / Firmament.
La volta del cielo.

To raise the roof.
Faire le diable à quatre.
Hacer un ruído de todos los diablos / Removerlo todo (para conseguir una cosa).
Krach schlagen.
Fare il diavolo a quattro.

ROOM
To make room.
Faire place.
Hacer lugar.
Platz machen.
Fare posto.

There is no room!
Il n'y a pas de place!
¡No hay lugar!
Da ist kein Platz! / Es gibt keinen Platz! / Besetzt!
Non c'è posto!

ROOST
To rule the roost.
Faire la loi.
Mandar / Hacer el mandamás.
Das Regiment (Wort) führen / Herrschen.
Spadroneggiare.

Curses come home to roost.
Les malédictions retombent sur la tête de ceux qui les envoient.
Las maldiciones recaen sobre la cabeza de quien las profiere.
Wer anderen eine Grube gräbt, fällt selbst hinein.
Le maledizioni ricadono sul capo di chi le manda.

ROOT
To get at the root of the matter.
Aller au fond des choses.
Ir hasta el fondo de un asunto.
Den Kern der Sache treffen.
Andare in fondo alla faccenda.

To root out.
Déraciner.
Desarraigar / Arrancar de raíz.
Ausrotten / Ausreissen.
Sradicare.

ROOTED

He was rooted to the ground.
Il était cloué au sol.
Estaba como clavado al suelo.
Er stand wie angewurzelt da / Er war wie angewurzelt.
Era inchiodato al suolo.

ROPE

The rope gave way.
La corde se cassa.
Se rompió la cuerda.
Das Seil gab nach / Das Seil lockerte sich.
La corda si ruppe.

To be at the end of one's rope.
Etre à bout de forces et de ressources.
Haber agotado hasta el último recurso / Estar en las últimas.
Mit seinem Latein (mit seiner Weisheit) am Ende sein.
Essere allo stremo delle forze.

Give him enough rope and he'll hang himself!
Qu'il crée sa propre ruine!
Dále suficiente cuerda y se colgará a sí mismo.
Er richtet sich selbst zugrunde.
Che si rovini con le sue mani!

ROPES (♦)

(♦) To get to know the ropes. (p. 481)
Connaître son métier.
Conocer bien el oficio.
Er beginnt etwas von seiner Arbeit zu verstehen.
Cominciare a conoscere il proprio mestiere.

To teach someone the ropes.
Enseigner les ficelles d'un métier à quelqu'un.

480

481

Enseñarle a alguien el oficio.
Jemandem die Kniffe beibringen.
Insegnare a qualcuno un mestiere.

To learn the ropes.
Apprendre un métier.
Aprender las tretas de un trabajo.
Sich einarbeiten.
Imparare un mestiere.

ROSE

It's no bed of roses!
Ce n'est pas tout rose!
¡No todo es color de rosa!
Es ist kein Honiglecken!
Non sono tutte rose!

There's no rose without a thorn. (prov.)
Il n'y a pas de roses sans épines.
No hay rosas sin espinas.
Es gibt keine Rose ohne Dornen / Ohne Schweiss kein Preis.
Non c'è rosa senza spine.

To see things through rose-coloured spectacles.
Voir tout en rose.
Ver las cosas color de rosa.
Die Dinge durch eine rosarote Brille sehen.
Veder tutto roseo.

ROT

To talk rot.
Dire des bêtises.
Decir tonteras.
Unsinn reden / Quatsch reden.
Dire sciocchezze.

Tommy rot!
Des sottises! Balivernes!
¡Patrañas!
Purer Blödsinn! / Quatsch!
Fesserie!

ROTTEN

What rotten luck!
Quelle malchance!
¡Mala suerte!
So ein Pech!
Che sfortuna!

ROUGH

To rough it.
Vivre mal à l'aise.
Vivir sin lujos ni comodidades / Hacer una vida de cartujo.
Einfach leben.
Vivere in condizioni disagiate.

One must learn to take the rough and the smooth.
Il faut prendre la vie comme elle vient.
Hay que aprender a tragar lo dulce y lo amargo.
Man muss das Leben nehmen, wie es ist (kommt).
Bisogna prendere la vita come viene.

A rough diamond.
Le bourru bienfaisant.
Un diamante en bruto / Un hombre tosco pero bueno.
Ein Mensch mit gutem Kern und rauher Schale.
Un burbero benefico.

A rough customer.
Un rustre.
Un palurdo.
Ein Grobian / Ein grober Kerl.
Uno zoticone.

ROUND (♦)

As round as an apple. (comp.)
Rond comme une pomme.
Bien redondo.
Rund wie ein Ball.
Tondo come una mela.

As round as a ball. (comp.)
Rond comme un ballon.

Redondo como un globo.
Rund wie ein Kugel / Kugelrund.
Tondo come una palla.

As round as a globe.
Très rond.
Muy redondo.
Kugelrund.
Molto rotondo.

To round off something.
Terminer quelque chose.
Terminar una cosa.
Etwas abschliessen.
Finire qualcosa.

(♦) To get round the difficulty. (p. 485)
Tourner la difficulté.
Pasar por encima de una dificultad.
Um Schwierigkeiten herumkommen / Schwierigkeiten um-
gehen.
Aggirare la difficoltà (l'ostacolo).

To sleep round the clock.
Dormir douze heures de suite.
Dormir la mitad del día / Dormir demasiado.
Einmal um die Uhr schlafen / Volle 24 Stunden schlafen.
Dormire dodici ore filate.

ROUNDABOUT

A roundabout phrase.
Un tour de phrase.
Un circunloquio.
Eine weitschweifige (umständliche) Redensart.
Una circonlocuzione / Un giro di frase.

RUB (♦)

The teacher tried to rub in the lesson.
Le maître essaya de faire entrer la leçon dans la tête des élèves.
El profesor trató de imprimir la lección en la cabeza de sus
alumnos.

485

Der Lehrer versuchte (den Schülern) die Lektion einzutrichtern /
Der Lehrer paukte (hämmerte) die Lektion ein.
Il maestro cercò di far entrare la lezione in testa agli studenti.

(♦) To rub somebody up the wrong way. (p. 487)
Irriter quelqu'un.
Llevarle a alguien la contraria.
Jemanden verstimmen (verschnupfen).
Irritare qualcuno.

To rub shoulders with somebody.
Avoir des rapports avec quelqu'un / Etre en rapport avec quelqu'un.
Tener relaciones con alguien.
Mit jemandem verkehren.
Intrattenere rapporti con qualcuno.

There's the rub!
C'est là la difficulté / Voilà le hic!
Allí está la dificultad.
Das ist der wunde Punkt / Da liegt der Hase im Pfeffer.
Qui sta la difficoltà!

RUBBISH

Good riddance to bad rubbish!
Il vaut mieux l'avoir en photo qu'en pension.
Mejor perderlo que encontrarlo / ¡Ni en fotografía!
Sei froh, dass Du ihn los bist!
Meglio perderlo che trovarlo!

RUBY

As red as a ruby. (comp.)
Rouge rubis.
Rojo como un tomáte.
Rubinrot / So rot wie ein Rubin.
Rosso rubino.

RULE

As a rule.
C'est la règle.

Por regla general.
In der Regel.
Di regola.

RUM

A rum fellow.
Un type étrange.
Un tipo extravagante.
Ein ulkiger (drolliger) Kerl.
Un tipo strambo.

RUMMAGE

To rummage about.
Mettre sens dessus - dessous.
Revolverlo todo.
Herumwühlen / Herumstöbern.
Mettere sottosopra.

RUMOUR

Rumour says . . .
Le bruit court que . . .
Hay rumores que . . .
Das Gerücht sagt . . . / Laut Gerücht . . . / Laut Gerede . . .
Corre voce che . . .

RUMPUS

To kick up a rumpus.
Faire le diable à quatre.
Hacer un ruído de todos los diablos.
Krawall (Spektakel) machen / Einen Höllenlärm machen.
Fare il diavolo a quattro.

RUN (♦)

To run to earth.
Trouver après maintes recherches.
Encontrar algo después de mucho buscar.
Etwas mit Mühe herausfinden (aufstöbern, erjagen).
Trovare dopo tante ricerche.

To run up against a brick wall.
Aller à l'encontre d'un inconvénient.
Ir contra de un inconveniente.
Gegen eine Mauer anlaufen / Auf Widerstand stossen.
Andare incontro a un inconveniente.

Things must run their course.
Il faut que les choses suivent leur cours.
Hay que dejar que las cosas sigan su curso.
Man soll den Dingen ihren Lauf lassen.
Bisogna lasciare che le cose seguano il loro corso.

It runs in our family.
C'est une chose héréditaire.
Es una cuestión hereditaria.
Es liegt in der Familie / Es liegt im Blut / Es ist erblich.
E' una cosa ereditaria.

A run of bad luck.
Une période de malchance.
Un período de mala racha / Un período de mala suerte.
Eine Pechsträhne.
Un periodo di sfortuna.

To run riot.
Faire le diable à quatre.
Hacer un ruído de todos los diablos / Removerlo todo (para conseguir una cosa).
Sich austoben / Krawall machen.
Fare il diavolo a quattro.

To run short of . . .
Rester à court de . . .
Estar a cortas de . . .
Knapp sein an . . .
Rimanere sprovvisto di . . .

In the long run.
A la longue.
A la larga.
Auf die Dauer / Am Ende / Schliesslich.
A lungo andare.

My blood ran cold.
Mon sang se glaça.

Se me heló la sangre de las venas.
Das Blut erstarrt mir in den Adern / Das Herz bleibt mir stehen.
Mi si gelò il sangue nelle vene.

To run in a car.
Faire le rodage d'une voiture.
Hacer el rodaje de un carro.
Ein Auto einfahren.
Fare il rodaggio di un'automobile.

(♦) To run into . . . (p. 491)
Tomber sur . . .
Toparse con alguien.
Hineinlaufen / Rennen in . . . / Fahren (rennen) gegen . . . /
Zusammenstossen / Geraten in . . .
Imbattersi in . . .

RUN-DOWN (♦)

(♦) To feel run-down. (p. 492)
Se sentir à terre / Etre abattu.
Sentirse por los suelos.
Ich bin erschöpft / Ich fühle mich abgespannt (abgearbeitet).
Sentirsi a terra.

RUSH

To rush somebody off his feet.
Contraindre quelqu'un à prendre une décision hasardeuse.
Obligar a alguien a tomar una decisión apresurada.
Jemanden zu einer Entscheidung zwingen.
Costringere qualcuno a prendere una decisione avventata.

Rush hour.
Heure de pointe.
Horas de punta.
Hauptverkehrszeit.
Ora di punta.

RUST

Better wear out than rust out. (prov.)
Il vaut mieux être actif.

491

Mejor cansarse que oxidarse.
Es ist besser, sich zu erschöpfen als einzurosten.
E' meglio stancarsi che fare la ruggine.

RUSTY

My Spanish is a little rusty.
Je suis un peu rouillé en espagnol.
En Español estoy un poco fuera de práctica.
Ich bin in Spanisch aus der Übung.
Sono un po' fuori esercizio in spagnolo.

RUT

To get into a rut.
Etre esclave de la routine.
Hacer una cosa por rutina / Ser esclavo de la rutina.
In einen Trott verfallen.
Essere schiavo della routine.

SACK

To get the sack.
Etre licencié.
Ser despedido (del trabajo)
Fliegen / An die Luft gesetzt werden.
Essere licenziato.

To hit the sack.
Aller au lit.
Irse a acostar / Irse a echar.
Sich langlegen.
Andare a letto.

SACKCLOTH

Sackcloth and ashes.
Faire pénitence / Crier misère.
Llorando miserias / Arrepentido.
In Sack und Asche.
Vestito di sacco e col capo cosparso di cenere / Pentito / Pianger miseria.

SAD

A sad dog.
Une canaille.
Un canalla.
Ein arger Tunichtgut / Ein mieser Hund.
Una canaglia.

SADDLE

To saddle the wrong horse.
Inculper l'innocent.
Culpar a un inocente.
Die Schuld dem Falschen geben (zuschreiben).
Dar la colpa a chi è innocente.

In the saddle.
Au pouvoir.
En el poder.
Fest im Sattel / Im Amt / An der Macht.
Al potere.

SAFE

It's safe to say.
On peut le dire sans avoir peur.
Puede decirse sin peligro de caer en contradicciones.
Man kann mit Sicherheit sagen / Man kann (ruhig) sagen.
Si può dire senza tema di smentita.

Safe bind, safe find. (prov.)
Méfiance est mère de sûreté.
Confiar es bueno, no confiar es mejor.
Erst schauen, dann vertrauen / Schaue, wem Du traust / Vertraue nicht blind.
Fidarsi è bene, non fidarsi è meglio.

They're safe and sound.
Ils sont sains et saufs.
Están sanos y salvos.
Sie sind heil und gesund.
Sono sani e salvi.

SAFETY

There's safety in numbers. (prov.)
L'union fait la force.
La unión hace la fuerza.
Einigkeit macht stark.
L'unione fa la forza.

To play for safety.
Eviter tout risque.
Actuar con las espaldas cubiertas.
Sicher gehen (wollen) / Risiken vermeiden.
Evitare ogni rischio.

SAILING

It's plain sailing.
C'est une tâche très ardue.
Es una taréa muy simple.
Es ist eine leichte Aufgabe.
E' un compito molto facile.

SAILS

To take the wind out of someone's sails.
Rabaisser l'orgueil de quelqu'un / Rabaisser le caquet à quelqu'un.
Quitarle las ínfulas a alguien.
Jemandem den Wind aus den Segeln nehmen.
Sgonfiare l'orgoglio di qualcuno.

SAID

Easier said than done.
Il y a loin de la coupe aux lèvres.
Entre el dicho y el hecho hay mucho trecho.
Leichter gesagt als getan.
Fra il dire ed il fare c'è di mezzo il mare.

No sooner said than done.
Aussitôt dit, aussitôt fait.
En menos que no se diga.
Schneller getan als gesagt / Gesagt, getan.
Detto e fatto.

SAINT (♦)

(♦) It would try the patience of a saint. (p. 497)
Même un saint perdrait patience.
Aún un santo perdería la paciencia.
Da verlöre auch ein Engel die Geduld.
Farebbe perdere la pazienza anche a un santo.

Young saints old sinners. (prov.)
Saints quand ils sont jeunes, pécheurs quand ils sont vieux.
Santos de jóven, pícaros de viejo.
Anfangs Engel, später Bengel / Kleine Engel, grosse Bengel.
Santi da giovani, peccatori da vecchi.

SALAD

In his salad days.
Dans ses vertes années.
En sus años mozos.
In seinen wilden Jugendtagen.
Negli anni della sua giovinezza.

SALT

As salt as brine. (comp.)
Très salé.
Muy salado.
Sehr salzig.
Molto salato.

As salt as a herring. (comp.)
Très salé.
Muy salado.
Salzig wie ein Hering.
Molto salato.

To eat somebody's salt.
Oter le pain de la bouche à quelqu'un.
Quitarle el pan de la boca a una persona.
Jemandes Brot essen.
Mangiare il pane di qualcuno.

You'll have to take that with a pinch of salt.
Tu devras le prendre comme il est.

Tendrás que hacerle buena cara.
Sie sollten das auch schweren Herzens nehmen.
Dovrai prenderlo anche a malincuore.

SANDS

To plough the sands.
Faire un travail inutile.
Arar en el mar.
Den Sand pflügen / Nutzloses tun.
Fare un lavoro inutile.

The sands are running out.
Les choses touchent à leur fin.
Se está acabando / Estamos en las últimas.
Die Tage sind gezählt / Wir sind am Ende.
Siamo agli sgoccioli.

SAUCE

Hunger is the best sauce. (prov.)
La faim est le meilleur assaisonnement.
A buena hambre no hay pan duro, ni falta salsa a ninguno.
Hunger ist der beste Koch.
La fame è il migliore dei condimenti.

What's sauce for the goose is sauce for the gander. (prov.)
Ce qui est bon pour lui l'est aussi pour moi.
Lo que es bueno para el asno es bueno también para el caballo.
Was dem einen recht ist, ist dem anderen billig.
Quello che è buono per lui è buono anche per me.

SAUNTER

To saunter through life.
Prendre la vie comme elle se présente.
Tomar la vida tal y como es.
Durch das Leben schlendern (bummeln) / Das Leben leicht nehmen.
Prendere la vita come viene.

SAVE

To save one's face.
Sauver la face.

Salvar la cara.
Das Gesicht wahren.
Salvare la faccia.

SAVES

A stitch in time saves nine. (prov.)
Ne remets pas à demain ce que tu peux faire aujourd'hui.
Quien tiempo tiene y tiempo atiende, tiempo viene que se arrepiente.
Gleich getan ist viel gespart.
Un punto a tempo ne risparmia cento / Chi ha tempo non aspetti tempo.

SAWDUST

He's just a bag of sawdust!
C'est un ballon gonflé!
¡Es una nulidad!
Er ist aufgeblasen! / Er ist ein hohler Mensch!
E' un pallone gonfiato!

SAY

I say!
Dis un peu!
¡Es a Usted a quien me refiero!
Hör mal! / Sag mal! / Donnerwetter!
Di' un po'!

As much as to say . . .
Comme pour dire . . .
Como diciendo . . .
Als ob er sagen wollte . . .
Come per dire . . .

To have one's say.
Dire la sienne.
Meter baza.
Seine Meinung äussern.
Dire la propria.

Say no more!
N'en parlons plus! / Ça suffit comme ça!

¡No digas más!
Sag nichts mehr! / Genug damit!
Non ne parliamo più! / Basta così!

SCALES

To take away the scales from somebody's eyes.
Ouvrir les yeux à quelqu'un.
Abrirle los ojos a uno.
Jemandem die Augen öffnen.
Aprire gli occhi a qualcuno.

SCAMPER

To scamper away.
Prendre ses jambes à son cou.
Escaparse / Escabullirse.
Sich davonmachen.
Darsela a gambe.

SCARCE

To make oneself scarce.
Se faire désirer / Filer en douce / Jouer la fille de l'air.
Darse a desear / Escabullirse.
Sich rar (dünn) machen.
Farsi desiderare / Svignarsela.

SCATTER-BRAIN

He's a scatter-brain!
C'est un écervelé!
¡Es un aturdido!
Er ist ein Wirrkopf!
E' uno scervellato!

SCENT

He's off the scent.
Il est sur une fausse piste.
Está fuera de pista.

500

Er ist auf der falschen Fährte (Spur) / Er ist von der (richtigen) Spur abgekommen.
E' su una falsa pista (fuori pista).

To get the scent of ...
Avoir vent de quelque chose.
Tener barrunto de alguna cosa.
Eine Nase haben für ... / Einen Spürsinn haben für ...
Aver sentore di ...

SCHOLAR

He's no scholar.
Il a peu d'instruction.
No es muy instruido.
Er ist kein Gelehrter (Studierter) / Er hat wenig Bildung.
Ha poca istruzione.

SCOFF

To scoff at ...
Dérider.
Mofarse de alguien / Escarnecer a alguien.
Spotten über ...
Deridere.

SCOOP

To make a scoop.
Faire un gros coup [journaliste].
Hacer un buen golpe [periodistico].
Einen grossen journalistischen Fang machen.
Fare un colpo grosso [giornalistico].

SCORE

To pay off old scores.
Régler les vieux comptes / Se venger.
Vengarse / Saldar viejas cuentas.
Eine alte Rechnung begleichen.
Regolare dei vecchi conti / Vendicarsi.

SCORN
To laugh to scorn.
Dérider / Se moquer de . . .
Mofarse de . . .
Verlachen.
Deridere / Farsi beffe di . . .

SCOT
To get off scot-free.
Se la couler douce.
Pasarsela bien.
Glatt (frei) davonkommen / Glücklich davonkommen.
Passarla liscia / Farla franca.

SCRAPE (♦)
To scrape through.
S'en tirer de justesse.
Echar adelante a duras penas.
Mit Ach und Krach durchkommen.
Cavarsela per il rotto della cuffia.

To get into a scrape.
Se fourrer dans un guêpier.
Meterse en un lío.
In Verlegenheit geraten / In die Klemme (Patsche) kommen.
Cacciarsi in un guaio.

To get out of a scrape.
Se sortir d'un ennui.
Sacarse afuera de un lío.
Sich aus der Klemme (Patsche) herausbringen / Die Kurve kratzen.
Cavarsi da un guaio.

To scrape together.
Ramasser par ci-par là.
Espigar / Recoger (poco a poco).
Zusammenkratzen.
Raggranellare.

(♦) To scrape a living. (p. 675)
Vivoter / Gagner difficilement sa vie.

Ir tirando / Ir viviendo.
Sich mühsam (durchs Leben) schlagen.
Guadagnarsi da vivere a stento.

SCRATCH

To start from scratch.
Commencer à zéro.
Empezar de la nada / Empezar desde el principio.
Ganz von vorne anfangen / Von Klein anfangen.
Cominciare da zero.

SCREAM

To scream with laughter.
Se tordre de rire / Se bidonner.
Matarse de la risa.
Vor Lachen brüllen.
Sbellicarsi dalle risa.

It's a scream!
C'est une chose très drôle!
¡Es muy chistoso!
Es ist zum Schreien (komisch)!
E' una cosa buffissima!

SCREW (♦)

(♦) To have a screw loose. (p. 350)
Etre cinglé.
Faltarle a uno una tuerca.
Eine Schraube locker haben / Nicht ganz richtig sein.
Essere svitato.

To screw up one's courage.
Se donner du courage.
Darse ánimo / Hacer de tripas corazón.
Mut fassen.
Farsi animo.

His head is screwed on the right way.
Il a la tête sur les épaules.
Tiene las cabeza sobre los hombros.
Er ist in Ordnung.
Ha la testa sulle spalle.

SCYLLA

Between Scylla and Charybdis.
Entre Charybde et Scylla.
Estar entre la espada y la paréd.
Sich in Gefahr begeben.
Tra Scilla e Cariddi.

SEA

To be at sea.
Ne savoir que faire.
No saber que hacer / Estar empantanado.
Schwimmen / Ratlos sein / Im Dunklen tappen.
Non sapere che fare / Essere in alto mare.

Between the devil and the deep blue sea.
Entre l'enclume et le marteau.
Entre la espada y la paréd.
Zwischen zwei Feuern / In auswegloser Lage.
Fra l'incudine e il martello.

SEAL

To seal one's fate.
Signer son arrêt de mort.
Construir la propria ruína.
Sein Schicksal besiegeln.
Firmare la propria condanna.

SEARCH

Search me!
Qui le sait!
¡Quien sabe!
Keine Ahnung!
Chi lo sa!

SECOND

To play second fiddle to somebody.
Rester dans l'ombre de quelqu'un.
Estar bajo la sombra de alguien.
Die zweite Geige spielen / In jemandes Schatten stehen.
Avere una parte di secondaria importanza.

On second thoughts . . .
En y repensant bien . . .
Pensandolo bien . . .
Nach reiflicher Überlegung / Wenn ich es mir recht überlege.
Ripensandoci bene . . .

To come off second best.
Avoir le dessous.
Llevar la peor / Llevar las de perder.
Verlierer sein.
Avere la peggio.

SECRET

Keep it secret!
Motus, bouche cousue!
¡No digas nada!
Halt es geheim! / Behalt es für Dich! / Schweig darüber!
Acqua in bocca!

SEE (♦)

To see into a millstone.
Etre perspicace.
Ser perspicaz.
Das Gras wachsen hören.
Essere perspicace.

(♦) To see through somebody. (p. 506)
Lire dans les pensées de quelqu'un.
Adivinar lo que piensa una persona / Darse cuenta de
las intenciones de una persona.
Jemanden durchschauen.
Scoprire i veri pensieri di qualcuno.

(♦) To see red. (p. 467)
Voir rouge.
Enfurecerse.
Rot sehen.
Veder rosso.

(♦) To see eye to eye wiht . . . (p. 677)
Etre parfaitement d'accord avec . . .

506

Estar completamente de acuerdo con . . .
Übereinstimmen mit . . .
Essere in pieno accordo con . . .

I want to see how the cat jumps.
Je voudrais voir comment s'arrangent les choses.
Quisiera saber adonde irán a parar las cosas.
Ich würde gerne sehen, wie der Hase läuft.
Voglio vedere come si mettono le cose.

I'll see you home.
Je vous accompagnerai à la maison (chez vous).
Les acompañaré a casa.
Ich werde Sie nach Hause begleiten (geleiten / bringen).
Vi accompagnerò a casa.

SEED

To go to seed.
Aller à la ruine / S'abîmer / Se flétrir.
Ir en ruina / Andar desaseado.
In Samen schiessen / Herunterkommen.
Andare in rovina / Sciuparsi.

SEEDY

To feel seedy.
Ne pas ne sentir trop bien.
Sentirse chueco / No sentirse muy bien.
Sich mies (elend) fühlen.
Non sentirsi troppo bene.

SEEP

The news seeped out.
La nouvelle s'est répandue.
Las noticias se han desparramado por doquiér.
Die Neuigkeiten sickerten durch.
La notizia è trapelata.

SEETHE

To seethe with anger.
Bouillir de rage.

Hervir de coraje.
Vor Wut kochen.
Bollire di rabbia.

SEIZED

Panic seized me.
Il fut pris de panique.
Fuí sobrecogido por el pánico.
Mich ergriff Panik.
Fui preso dal panico.

SELF-CENTRED

Self-centred.
Egocentrique.
Egocéntrico / Egoísta.
Ichbezogen / Egozentrisch.
Egocentrico.

SELF-CONTROL

Self-control.
Maîtrise de soi / Self-control.
Dominio de sí mismo.
Selbstbeherrschung.
Autocontrollo.

SELF-CONSCIOUS

Self-conscious.
Timide.
Timido.
Befangen / Gehemmt.
Timido.

SEND

To send coals to Newcastle.
Porter de l'eau à la rivière.
Llevar leña al monte.
Eulen nach Athen tragen.
Portar vasi a Samo.

To send somebody packing.
Envoyer quelqu'un au diable.
Mandar alguien a paseo.
Jemanden zum Teufel schicken.
Mandar qualcuno a farsi benedire.

SEND-OFF

I was given a good send-off.
On fêta mon départ.
Me dieron una buena despedida.
Ich wurde herzlich verabschiedet / Man bereitete mir einen herzlichen Abschied.
Fui festeggiato alla partenza.

SENILE

He's got senile decay.
Il souffre de décrépitude.
Se está volviendo chocho.
Er ist altersschwach geworden / Er leidet an Altersschwäche.
Soffre di decrepitezza.

SENSE

To come to one's senses.
Reprendre ses sens.
Volver en sí.
In sich gehen / Seinen Verstand befragen / Zur Besinnung kommen / Zur Vernunft (zum Verstand) kommen.
Rientrare in sè / Rinvenire.

To talk sense.
Parler de façon sensée.
Hablar con sentido común.
Vernünftig reden.
Parlare assennatamente.

SERIOUS

Are you serious?
Vous parlez sérieusement?
¿Habla Usted en serio?
Ist das Ihr Ernst? / Meinen Sie das im Ernst?
Dite sul serio?

SERIOUSNESS

In all seriousness!
Sérieusement!
¡En serio!
In vollem Ernst! / Mit aller Wichtigkeit!
Sul serio!

SERVANT

Fire is a good servant but a bad master. (prov.)
On ne joue pas avec le feu.
Con el fuego no se juega.
Mit Feuer spielt man nicht.
Col fuoco non si scherza.

SERVES

That serves you right!
C'est bien fait pour toi! / Que ça te serve de leçon!
¡Bien te lo mereces!
Das geschieht dir recht!
Ti sta bene!

SET

To set one's heart on . . .
Avoir une envie folle de . . .
Tener muchas ganas de . . .
Sein Herz hängen an . . .
Avere una gran voglia di . . .

A set of rascals.
Une bande de vauriens (de voyous).
Una pandilla de truhanes.
Ein Kreis von Gaunern / Eine Gruppe von Schurken.
Una banda di furfanti.

To set the Thames on fire.
Faire une chose sensationnelle.
Hacer algo sensacional / Llevar el mar a las montañas.
Das Pulver erfinden / Aussergewöhnliches tun.
Fare una cosa sensazionale.

To set one's teeth.
Serrer les dents.
Apretar los dientes.
Die Zähne zusammenbeissen.
Serrare i denti.

To set the fox to keep the geese.
Faire entrer le loup dans la bergerie.
Meter el lobo en el corrál.
Den Bock zum Gärtner machen.
Mettere il lupo nell'ovile.

To set one's hand to the plough.
Entreprendre un travail.
Emprender un trabajo.
Seine Hand an den Pflug legen.
Intraprendere un lavoro / Mettersi all'opera.

To set a stone rolling.
Réveiller un nid de guêpes.
Meterse en un berenjenal.
Den Stein ins Rollen bringen.
Suscitare un vespaio.

He set things going.
Il a mis les choses en route.
Está echando a andar las cosas.
Er hat die Dinge ins Laufen gebracht / Er hat die Sache in Gang (in Bewegung) gebracht.
Ha messo le cose in moto.

SETTLE

To settle an account.
Régler les comptes.
Liquidar una cuenta.
Eine Rechnung begleichen.
Saldare un conto.

To settle on ...
Se décider pour ...
Fijar algo / Decidirse por algo.
Sich entscheiden für ... / Sich entschliessen zu ... / Sich jemandem oder etwas zuwenden.
Decidersi per ...

SEVENTH

In the seventh heaven.
Au septième ciel.
En el séptimo cielo.
Im siebenten Himmel.
Al settimo cielo.

SHADE

To throw into the shade.
Eclipser / Jeter de l'ombre sur . . .
Eclipsar a los demás.
In den Schatten stellen.
Eclissare / Gettare ombra su .·. .

SHADOW

He's worn to a shadow.
Il n'est plus qu'une ombre.
Se ha vuelto la sombra de sí mismo.
Er ist zum Skelett abgemagert.
E' molto sciupato / E' ridotto un'ombra.

SHADY

A shady character.
Un individu louche.
Una persona sospechosa.
Ein zwielichtiger (fragwürdiger) Charakter / Ein verdächtiger Typ.
Un tipo losco.

SHAGGY

A shaggy-dog story.
Une blague qui finit en queue de poisson.
Un chiste cruél.
Ein surrealistischer Witz.
Una barzelletta con finale paradossale.

SHAKE (♦)

To give somebody the shake off.
Se débarrasser de quelqu'un / Brouiller ses traces.

512

Sacudirse de alguien.
Jemanden abwimmeln.
Sbarazzarsi di qualcuno / Seminare qualcuno / Far perdere le proprie tracce.

(♦) **Shake a leg!** (p. 514)
Dépêche-toi!
¡Apúrate!
Rühr Dich! / Beweg Dich! / Beeil Dich! / Tempo!
Sbrigati!

SHALLOW

Shallow-brained!
Ecervelé!
Tarambana / Uno que tiene la cabeza a pájaros.
Seicht / Hohlköpfig! / Hohlkopf!
Scervellato!

SHAMBLES

What a shambles!
Quel désordre!
¡Que desorden! / ¡Que relájo!
Welch Schlachtfeld! / Welch wüstes Durcheinander!
Che disordine!

SHAME

For shame!
Quelle honte!
¿No te da vergüenza?
Pfui, schäm dich!
Che vergogna!

SHANK

To go on Shank's pony.
Aller à pied.
Ir a pie / Ir a patas.
Auf Schusters Rappen reiten.
Andare a piedi / Andare col cavallo di San Francesco.

514

SHARE

The lion's share.
La part du lion.
La parte del león.
Der Löwenanteil.
La parte del leone.

To take more than one's fair share.
Se servir grassement (copieusement).
Tomar más de lo que a uno le toca.
Mehr nehmen als einem zusteht.
Prendere più di quanto spetta.

Share and share alike.
Partage équitable.
Justa repartición.
Zu gleichen Teilen / Halb und halb.
Equa spartizione.

To share with ...
Partager avec ...
Compartir con ...
Teilen mit ...
Condividere / Dividere con ...

SHARP

As sharp as a needle. (comp.)
Très aigu.
Puntiagudo como un cuchillo.
Spitz wie eine Nadel.
Molto acuto (perspicace).

As sharp as a razor.
Coupant comme une lame de rasoir.
Cortante como una navaja.
Scharf wie ein Messer.
Tagliente come un rasoio.

SHAVE (♦)

(♦) To have a close shave. (p. 517)
L'échapper belle.

Librarse bien / Salvarse por un pelo.
Mit knapper Not davonkommen.
Scamparla bella.

SHED

To shed light on something.
Faire la lumière sur quelque chose.
Sacar a luz una cosa / Poner en evidencia algo.
Etwas ins Licht rücken / Etwas ans Licht holen / Etwas ent-
hüllen / Licht auf eine Sache werfen.
Gettar luce su qualcosa.

SHEEP

The sheep and the goats.
Les bons et les méchants.
Los malos y los buenos.
Die Guten und die Bösen / Die Schafe und die Böcke.
I buoni e i cattivi.

A wolf in sheep's clothing.
Le loup même déguisé en agneau reste toujours loup / Chas-
sez le naturel, il revient au galop.
Un lobo vestido de oveja.
Ein Wolf in Schafskleidern.
Un lupo in veste d'agnello.

A black sheep.
Une brebis galeuse.
Una oveja negra.
Ein schwarzes Schaf.
Una pecora nera.

SHELF (♦)

(♦) To be left on the shelf. (p. 519)
Etre tenu à l'écart.
Ser metido aparte / Hacer de pantalla.
Mauerblümchen sein.
Essere lasciato in disparte / Fare da tappezzeria.

516

SHELL

He's an empty shell.
C'est une tête vide.
Es un cabezahueca.
Er ist ein Dummkopf / Er ist eine hohle Nuss.
Ha la testa vuota.

To go into one's shell.
Se refermer dans sa coquille.
Encerrarse en el ostracismo / Mantenerse en una torre de marfíl.
Sich in sich zurückziehen / Sich verschliessen.
Chiudersi nel proprio guscio.

As easy as shelling peas. (comp.)
Très facile / Simple comme bonjour.
Muy fácil.
Sehr leicht / Kinderleicht.
Molto facile / Facile come bere un bicchier d'acqua.

SHIELD

The other side of the shield.
Le revers de la médaille.
El otro lado de la moneda.
Die Kehrseite (der Sache der Geschichte).
Il rovescio della medaglia.

SHIFT

To shift for oneself.
Faire par soi-même.
Valerse por sí mismo.
Auf sich selbst gestellt sein / Sich selbst helfen.
Fare da sè.

To make shift with something.
Se contenter de quelque chose.
Contentarse de algo.
Sich mit etwas behelfen.
Accontentarsi di qualcosa.

SHINDY

To kick up a shindy.
Faire un boucan du diable.

518

Hacer relájo / Armar bulla.
Einen tollen Lärm (Krach) veranstalten / Radau machen.
Fare un baccano d'inferno.

SHIP

When my ship comes in.
Quand je ferai fortune.
Cuándo seré rico.
Wenn ich mein Glück mache / Wenn ich das grosse Los ziehe.
Quando farò fortuna.

SHIPSHAPE

It's in shipshape order.
C'est tout en ordre.
Todo está en orden.
Es ist in tadelloser Ordnung.
E' tutto in ordine.

SHIRT

Keep your shirt on!
Ne vous mettez pas en colère!
¡No se enoje!
Regen Sie sich nicht auf!
Non adiratevi!

Near is my shirt, but nearer is my skin. (prov.)
Rien ne m'importe plus que moi-même.
No hay otra cosa que me interese más en el mundo que mí mismo.
Die eigene Haut ist einem am nächsten / Nur an die eigene Haut (an sich selbst) denken.
Non mi importa di nulla più che di me stesso.

SHOCKING

What shocking weather!
Quel sale temps!
¡Qué tiempo espantoso!
Welch scheussliches Wetter! / Was für ein Hundewetter!
Che tempaccio!

SHOES (♦)

(♦) I'm glad I'm not in his shoes. (p. 522)
Je suis content de ne pas être dans sa peau / Je suis content de ne pas être à sa place.
Estoy contento de no estar en su lugar.
Ich bin froh, dass ich nicht in seiner Haut stecke.
Sono contento di non essere nei suoi panni.

That's another pair of shoes!
C'est tout autre chose! / C'est une autre paire de manches!
¡Esto es harina de otro costal!
Das sind zwei Paar Stiefel!
E' un altro paio di maniche!

Where the shoe pinches.
Là où le bas blesse.
Donde más duele.
Wo der Schuh drückt.
Dove il dente duole.

SHOP

To talk shop.
Parler affaires.
Hablar de negocios.
Geschäftlich sprechen.
Parlar d'affari.

You're at the wrong shop.
Vous vous êtes trompés d'adresse.
Se han equivocado de dirección.
Sie sind an die falsche Adresse geraten / Sie haben sich in der Adresse geirrt.
Avete sbagliato indirizzo.

SHORT

To cut it short.
Pour couper court.
Para abreviar / En resumida cuentas.
Es kurz machen / Sich kurz (knapp) fassen / Um es kurz zu machen.
Per farla breve.

To make short work of ...
Se débarrasser de ...
Terminar de inmediato / Desembarazarse de ...
Wenig Aufsehen machen von ... / Sich kurzerhand entledigen
von ... / Etwas kurz und bündig machen.
Finirla subito / Sbarazzarsi di ...

SHORTCOMINGS
To have many shortcomings.
Avoir beaucoup de défauts.
Tener muchos defectos / Tener muchos peros.
Viele Unzulänglichkeiten besitzen / Viele Fehler (Mängel) haben.
Avere molti difetti.

SHOT
To take a shot at ...
Faire un essai (une tentative).
Tratar de ...
Versuchen mit ...
Fare un tentativo di ...

To be off like a shot.
Disparaître en un éclair.
Desvanecerse como un relámpago.
Wie der Blitz verschwinden / Sofort weg sein.
Sparire in un lampo.

SHOULDER
To give somebody the cold shoulder.
Tourner le dos à quelqu'un.
Voltearle las espaldas a alguien.
Jemandem die kalte Schulter zeigen.
Voltar le spalle a qualcuno.

To shoulder one's way.
Jouer des coudes.
Hacerse camino.
Sich einen Weg bahnen.
Farsi largo.

SHOVE

Let's shove off!
Allons-nous-en!
¡Vayámonos!
Lasst uns abschieben! / Machen wir uns davon!
Andiamocene!

SHOW (♦)

(♦) To show someone the ropes. (p. 525)
Enseigner les ficelles d'un métier à quelqu'un.
Enseñarle el oficio a alguien.
Jemandem die Kniffe beibringen.
Insegnare a qualcuno un mestiere.

To show one's teeth.
Montrer les dents.
Mostrar las garras.
Die Zähne zeigen.
Mostrare i denti.

To show off.
Se vanter / Se faire voir.
Alardear / Hacer ostentación de ...
Protzen mit ... / Sich grosstun mit ... / Angeben.
Vantarsi / Mettersi in mostra.

To show the door to ...
Mettre à la porte.
Sacar afuera.
Jemandem die Tür weisen.
Mettere alla porta.

To give the show away.
Révéler les tares (les défauts) de quelqu'un.
Revelar lo defectos de alguien.
Den ganzen Schwindel verraten / Den Schleier lüften.
Mostrare le magagne / Rivelare le manchevolezze di qualcuno.

SHRED

To tear to shreds.
Réduire en morceaux.

Hacer pedazos / Hacer trizas.
In Fetzen reissen / Zerfetzen / Etwas zerpflücken (zerreissen).
Fare a pezzi.

SHRIFT

To make short shrift of something.
Traiter de façon expéditive.
Tratar algo de manera expédita.
Kurzen Prozess mit etwas machen.
Trattare qualcosa in modo spiccio.

SHRINK

To shrink into oneself.
Se replier sur soi-même.
Encerrarse en sí mismo.
Sich in sich zurückziehen / Sich verschliessen.
Chiudersi in sè.

SHRUG

To shrug one's shoulders.
Hausser les épaules.
Levantarse de hombros.
Die Achseln zucken.
Alzare le spalle.

SHUT

Shut up!
Tais-toi! / Arrête!
¡Cállate!
Halt den Mund! / Halt's Maul!
Sta' zitto! / Piantala!

SICK

I'm sick and tired of that!
J'en ai plus qu'assez!
¡Estoy cansado de ésto!
Ich habe es satt! / Es hängt mir zum Hals heraus!
Sono arcistufo di quello! / Ne ho fin sopra i capelli!

To be sick at heart.
Avoir la mort dans l'âme.
Tener la muerte en el corazón.
Todunglücklich sein.
Avere la morte nel cuore.

To be sick of ...
En avoir assez de ... / En avoir marre de ...
Estar cansado de ...
Überdrüssig sein / Angewidert sein von ... / Krank sein vor ...
Essere stufo di ... / Averne abbastanza.

SIDE (♦)

To side with ...
Prendre le parti de ...
Ponerse al lado de ... / Ser partidario de ...
Es halten mit ... / Partei ergreifen für ...
Stare dalla parte di ...

To look on the bright side of things.
Voir tout en rose.
Verlo todo color de rosa
Die Dinge nur von der guten Seite betrachten / Alles durch
eine rosarote Brille sehen / Alles rosarot sehen.
Vedere l'aspetto positivo delle cose.

(♦) To get out of bed on the wrong side. (p. 37)
Se lever du pied gauche.
Levantarse de malhumor.
Mit dem linken (falschen) Fuss zuerst aufstehen.
Alzarsi di malumore / Alzarsi col piede sinistro.

SIDEWAYS

He looked at me sideways.
Il m'a regardé de travers.
Me ha mirado de través.
Er betrachtete mich von der Seite / Er schaute mich schief an-
Mi ha guardato di traverso.

SIEVE

To have a memory like a sieve.
Avoir une mémoire comme une passoire.

Tener mala memoria / Tener una cabeza de chorlito.
Ein Gedächtnis wie ein Sieb haben.
Essere smemorato.

SIGHT (♦)

Out of sight out of mind. (prov.)
Loin des yeux, loin du cœur.
Lejos de los ojos, lejos del corazón.
Aus den Augen, aus dem Sinn.
Lontano dagli occhi, lontano dal cuore.

(♦) A sight for sore eyes. (p. 548)
Une chose très agréable à voir.
Una cosa muy agradable de verse / Una vista placentera.
Ein erfreulicher Anblick / Eine Augenweide.
Una cosa molto gradita da vedere.

To look a sight.
S'habiller de façon ridicule.
Verse como un mamarracho.
Komisch (grässlich) aussehen.
Vestirsi in modo da rendersi ridicolo.

SIGHTED

Far-sighted.
Clairvoyant.
Previsor / Sabio.
Weitsichtig.
Lungimirante.

SILENCE

Silence gives consent. (prov.)
Qui ne dit mot consent.
Quien calla consiente.
Wer schweigt, scheint zuzustimmen / Schweigen bedeutet Zustimmung.
Chi tace acconsente.

Silence is golden. (prov.)
Le silence est d'or.

El silencio es oro.
Schweigen ist Gold.
Il silenzio è d'oro.

SILENT

As silent as the dead. (comp.)
Très silencieux / On n'entend pas une mouche voler.
Callado como una tumba.
Totenstill.
Molto silenzioso / Così silenzioso che non si sente volare una mosca.

As silent as the grave. (comp.)
Muet comme une tombe.
Callado como una tumba.
Verschwiegen wie ein Grab.
Muto come una tomba.

SILK

One cannot make a silk purse out of a son's ear. (prov.)
On ne peut tirer de l'huile d'un mur.
No se puede obtener lo que no hay.
Man kann aus einem Kieselstein keinen Diamanten schleifen.
Non si può cavar sangue da una rapa.

SILLY

As silly as a goose. (comp.)
Bête comme une oie.
Tonto.
Albern (blöd) wie eine Gans.
Molto sciocco.

As silly as a sheep. (comp.)
Idiot / Benêt.
Tonto.
Dumm (blöd) wie ein Schaf.
Molto sciocco.

SILVER (♦)

Every cloud has a silver lining.
Chaque chose a du bon.

Todas las cosas tienen su lado bueno.
Jedes Unglück hat auch sein Gutes / Jedes Unglück hat auch eine gute Seite.
Ogni cosa ha il suo lato buono.

(♦) **To be born with a silver spoon in one's mouth.** (p. 66)
Etre né coiffé.
Haber nacido con la camisa puesta.
Ein Glückskind (Sonntagskind) sein.
Essere nato con la camicia.

SINGE

To singe one's feathers.
Se brûler / Y laisser les plumes.
Dejar el pellejo.
Sich verbrennen / Ins Fettnäpfchen treten / Sich die Finger verbrennen.
Scottarsi / Lasciarci le penne.

SINGING

To have a singing in one's ears.
Sentir siffler ses oreilles.
Silbarle los oídos a uno.
Ohrensausen haben / Jemandem klingen die Ohren.
Sentirsi fischiare le orecchie.

SINKER

Hook, line and sinker.
Complètement / Entièrement.
Por completo / Del todo.
Ein Gutgläubiger.
Completamente / Del tutto.

SIT

To sit tight.
Tenir bon.
Mantenerse firme.
Sich eisern behaupten / Sich nicht beirren lassen.
Tener duro.

SIX

To be at sixes and sevens.
Etre bouleversé.
Estar desazonado.
Ganz durcheinander sein / Uneins sein.
Essere sottosopra.

It's six of one and half a dozen of the other.
C'est bonnet blanc et blanc bonnet.
Olivo y aceituno todo es uno.
Das ist gehüpft wie gesprungen.
Se non è zuppa è pan bagnato.

SKATE

He's skating on thin ice.
Il marche sur du verre.
Está navegando en aguas peligrosas.
Er bewegt sich auf dünnem Eis / Er läuft (befindet sich) auf unsicherem Boden.
Cammina su terreno infido.

SKIN

To save one's skin.
Sauver sa peau.
Salvar el pellejo.
Seine Haut retten / Mit heiler Haut davonkommen.
Salvar la pelle.

He's got a thick skin.
Il a la peau dure.
Tiene el cuero curtido.
Er hat eine dicke Haut / Er hat ein dickes Fell.
Ha la pelle dura.

To escape by the skin of one's teeth.
S'en sortir de justesse.
Salvarse por un pelo.
Mit knapper Not davonkommen (entkommen / entweichen; entrinnen).
Uscirne per il rotto della cuffia.

Don't get under my skin!
Ne m'ennuie pas!
¡No me molestes!
Komm mir nicht zu nahe! / Ärger mich nicht!
Non seccarmi!

Beauty is only skin deep. (prov.)
Tout ce qui brille n'est pas or.
No es todo oro lo que brilla.
Schönheit ist äusserlich / Schönheit ist nur oberflächlich /
Es ist nicht alles Gold was glänzt.
Non è tutto oro quel che luccica.

To have a thin skin.
Etre suceptible / Etre hypersensible.
Ser susceptible / Ser delicado.
Zartbesaitet sein / Feinfühlig sein.
Essere suscettibile / Essere ipersensibile.

SKINNED

To keep one's eyes skinned.
Garder les yeux grands-ouverts.
Tener los ojos abiertos.
Seine Augen offen halten.
Tener gli occhi ben aperti.

SKITTLES

Life is not all beer and skittles.
La vie n'est pas toujours rose.
La vida no es todo miel y rosas.
Das Leben besteht nicht nur aus Vergnügen.
La vita non è tutta rose e fiori.

SKY

If the sky falls, we shall catch larks.
A quelque chose malheur est bon.
No hay mal que por bien no venga.
Jedes Unglück hat auch sein Gutes (seine gute Seite).
Tutto il male non viene per nuocere.

SLASH

Prices were slashed at the sale.
Les prix ont subi des rabais considérables à la braderie.
Los precios han sufrido una fuerte rebaja a la venta.
Im Ausverkauf gibt es Schleuderpreise.
I prezzi hanno subito tagli considerevoli alla svendita.

SLATE

He started with a clean slate.
Il a refait sa vie.
Ha comenzado una nueva vida / Ha comenzado otra vida.
Er begann ganz von neuem (von vorne).
Si è rifatto una vita / Ha ricominciato da capo.

SLEEP

To sleep like a log.
Dormir comme un loir.
Dormir como un lirón.
Schlafen wie ein Klotz (Bär / Murmeltier).
Dormire come un ghiro.

Not to have a wink of sleep.
Ne pas pouvoir fermer l'œil.
No cerrar ojo.
Kein Auge zutun.
Non poter chiudere occhio.

To sleep the clock round.
Dormir douze heures de suite.
Dormir la mitad del día / Dormir demasiado.
Einmal um die Uhr schlafen.
Dormire dodici ore filate.

To lose one's night's sleep.
Perdre le sommeil.
Perder el sueño.
Seine Nachtruhe (seinen Schlaf) verlieren.
Perdere il sonno.

SLEEPING

Let sleeping dogs lie. (prov.)
Ne réveillez pas le chat qui dort.

No mover las aguas.
Schlafende Hunde soll man nicht aufwecken / Rühre nicht an alte Geschichten.
Non svegliare il can che dorme.

SLEEVE

He's got something up his sleeve.
Il a la bonne carte.
Tener un ás en la manga.
Er hat etwas auf Lager / Er führt etwas im Schilde.
Ha un asso nella manica.

To laugh up one's sleeve.
Rire sous cape.
Reirse adentro.
Sich ins Fäustchen lachen.
Ridere sotto i baffi.

SLENDER

As slender as a gossamer. (comp.)
Très mince / Elancé.
Delgadito / Flaquito.
Sehr zart und dünn / Sehr schlank.
Molto snello / Molto sottile.

SLICE

I had a slice of bad luck.
J'ai eu un peu de malchance.
He tenido un poco de mala suerte / He tenido mala pata.
Ich hatte eine Portion Pech (ein bisschen Unglück).
Ho avuto un po' di sfortuna.

SLIDE (♦)

(♦) To let things slide. (p. 535)
Négliger les choses.
Dejar pasar algo / No hacer caso de algo / Descuidar las cosas.
Die Dinge laufen lassen.
Trascurare le cose.

535

SLIP (♦)

There's many a slip twixt the cup and the lip. (prov.)
Il y a loin de la coupe aux lèvres.
Del dicho al hecho hay mucho trecho.
Gesagt ist nicht gleich getan / Gesagt ist noch lange nicht getan.
Dal dire al fare c'è di mezzo il mare.

A slip of the tongue.
Dire un mot à la place d'un autre / Un lapsus.
Escaparsele a uno una palabra por otra / Un lapsus.
Sich versprechen / Ein Schnitzer / Ein Lapsus.
Dire una parola per un'altra / Un lapsus.

To give somebody the slip.
Semer quelqu'un en cours de route.
Zafarse de alguien por la calle.
Jemandem entwischen.
Seminare qualcuno per la strada.

(♦) To slip up. (p. 537)
Se tromper.
Equivocarse.
Einen Fehler machen / Stolpern.
Sbagliare.

SLIPPERY (♦)

As slippery as an eel.
Répugnant / Visqueux.
Resbaladizo.
Aalglatt / Gerissen / Schlüpfrig (glitschig) wie ein Aal.
Molto viscido.

(♦) A slippery customer. (p. 538)
Un type louche.
Una persona resbaladiza.
Eine zweifelhafte Person.
Un tipo losco.

SLOW

Slow and sure. (prov.)
Qui veut aller loin ménage sa monture.

Aquel va sano, que anda por el llano.
Langsam, aber sicher / Eile mit Weile.
Chi va piano, va sano.

SLOWCOACH
You're a slow-coach!
Tu es un paresseux! / Tu es lambin!
¡Eres un haragán! / ¡Eres un lento!
Du bist ein Langweiler (Leimsieder)! / Du bist langweilig (wie eine Schnecke)!
Sei un pigrone! / Sei un ritardatario!

SLY
On the sly.
En cachette.
De escondidas.
Insgeheim.
Di nascosto / Alla chetichella.

SMALL (♦)
He made me feel small.
Il m'a humilié.
Me ha hecho sentir una nulidad.
Er hat mich erniedrigt.
Mi ha umiliato.

(♦) Small talk. (p. 540)
Conversation de salon.
Conversación insubstancial / Charladuría.
Oberflächliche Konversation / Geplauder.
Conversazione da salotto.

To sing small.
Parler humblement.
Hablar humildemente.
Kleinlaut werden / Klein beigeben.
Parlare umilmente.

SMART
He's a smart Aleck.
C'est un présomptueux / Un blanc-bec.

Es un engreído.
Er ist ein Neunmalkluger / Er ist ein Klugscheisser.
E' un presuntuoso.

SMELL

To smell a rat.
Flairer un coup.
Sospechar una estafa.
Den Braten (Lunte) riechen.
Fiutare un imbroglio.

SMOKE (♠)

(♠) Put that in your pipe and smoke it! (p. 435)
Tiens, attrape!
A cada quien su conquién / Toma y cóme.
Lass Dir das gesagt sein!
Prendi e porta a casa!

There's no smoke without fire. (prov.)
Il n'y a pas de fumée sans feu.
No hay humo sin fuego.
Irgendetwas ist immer dran / Jedes Gerücht hat ein Fünkchen
Wahrheit / Wo kein Feuer ist, raucht es nicht.
Non c'è fumo senza fuoco.

From smoke into smother.
Tomber de Charybde en Scylla.
De la olla a la sartén.
Vom Regen in die Traufe (kommen).
Dalla padella nella brace.

To smoke like a chimney.
Fumer comme un pompier.
Fumar como turco.
Wie ein Schlot rauchen.
Fumare come un turco; come una ciminiera.

SMOOTH

As smooth as butter. (comp.)
Mou comme du beurre.
Muy liso.

Glatt wie Butter.
Molto liscio.

As smooth as oil. (comp.)
Très lisse.
Muy liso.
Reibungslos / Wie geschmiert.
Liscio come l'olio.

As smooth as glass. (comp.)
Très poli / Très lisse.
Alisado.
Spiegelglatt.
Molto levigato / Molto liscio.

As smooth as velvet. (comp.)
Lisse comme du velours.
Lisa como una rosa.
Weich wie Samt / Samtweich.
Molto liscio.

To take the rough with the smooth.
Prendre le monde comme il vient.
Tomar el mundo como es.
Das Leben nehmen wie es ist.
Prendere il mondo come viene.

SNEEZE

It's not to be sneezed at!
Ce n'est pas à dédaigner!
¡No es despreciable!
Es ist nicht zu verachten!
Non è da disprezzarsi!

SNOOPER

He's a snooper.
C'est un fouinard.
¡Es un entremetido!
Er ist ein Schnüffler.
E' un ficcanaso.

542

SNUG

To be as snug as a bug in a rug. (comp.)
Etre comme un poisson dans l'eau.
Estar muy cómodo.
Wie die Made im Speck leben.
Stare comodissimo.

SOAK

To be soaked to the skin.
Etre trempé jusqu'aux os.
Estar calado hasta los huesos / Estar empapado.
Bis auf die Haus nass (durchnässt) sein / Pundelnass sein.
Essere bagnato fradicio (fino alle ossa).

SOB

He gave me a sob story.
Il m'a raconté une histoire pathétique.
Me ha contado una historía muy triste.
Er erzählte mir eine rührselige Geschichte / Er drückte mir
auf die Tränendrüse.
Mi ha raccontato una storia patetica (strappalacrime).

SOBER

As sober as a judge. (comp.)
Très solennel / Sérieux.
Muy serio / Solemne.
Sehr sachlich / Sehr nüchtern.
Molto solenne / Serio.

SOCKS

Pull up your socks!
Retrousse tes manches! / Travaille!
¡Pónte los pantalones!
Streng dich an! / Spuck dir in die Händel!
Rimboccati le maniche!

SOFT

As soft as butter. (comp.)
Mou comme du beurre.

Muelle / Blando.
Weich wie Butter.
Molto molle.

As soft as down. (comp.)
Doux comme du duvet.
Muy suave.
Weich wie Flaum (Daunen) / Daunenweich.
Molto morbido.

As soft as wax. (comp.)
Très doux.
Muy suave.
Weich (gefügig) wie Wachs.
Molto soffice.

Soft-soap.
Adulation peu sincère.
Falsa adulación.
Jemandem Honig um den Mund schmieren.
Adulazione poco sincera.

SON

He's his father's son!
Il est bien le fils de son père!
¡De tal palo tal astilla!
Wie der Vater, so der Sohn! / Er ist das Ebenbild seines
Vaters / Er gleicht seinem Vater aufs Haar.
E' degno figlio di suo padre!

SONG (♦)

(♦) To sell something for a song. (p. 545)
Vendre quelque chose pour une bouchée de pain.
Vender algo por una nada.
Etwas für ein Butterbrot (einen Apfel und ein Ei) verkaufen.
Vendere qualcosa per un'inezia (per niente).

**(♦) There's no need to make a song and dance
about it.** (p. 546)
Il n'y a pas de quoi en faire un drame!
No veo por qué reñir.
Es ist nicht nötig, deswegen ein Getue zu machen.
Non c'è da farne una questione.

544

SOON

Least said soonest mended. (prov.)
Moins on en parle mieux ça vaut.
Lo mejor será hablar lo menos posible de ésto.
Je weniger geredet wird, desto besser ist es.
Meno se ne parla meglio è.

SORE (♦)

He's like a bear with a sore head.
Il est d'une humeur exécrable! / Il s'est levé du pied gauche.
Está de un humor inaguantable.
Er ist brummig (bärbeissig).
E' di pessimo umore.

(♦) That's a sight for sore eyes. (p. 548)
C'est très agréable à voir.
Aquello es algo que vale la pena de ver.
Das ist ein erfreulicher Anblick / Das ist eine Augenweide.
Ciö è molto piacevole da vedere / Fa bene agli occhi.

SOUL

He had just enough money to keep body and soul together.
Il avait à peine de quoi vivre.
Tenía apenas lo necesario para vivir.
Er hatte eben genug Geld zum Überleben.
Aveva appena di che vivere.

SOUND

As sound as a bell. (comp.)
Etre en parfaite santé.
Sano como un pez.
Kerngesund.
Sano come un pesce.

SOUP

To be in the soup.
Etre frit / Etre frais / Etre cuit.
Estar en el báile / Estar fregado.

In der Tinte sitzen.
Essere bell'e fritto.

A pea-souper.
Temps très brumeux.
Tiempo neblinoso.
Dicker Nebel / Eine Waschküche.
Tempo molto nebbioso.

SOUR

As sour as vinegar. (comp.)
Aigre comme du vinaigre.
Muy ácido.
Sehr bitter / Sehr sauer / Sehr herb.
Molto acido.

SOW

To sow one's wild oats. (prov.)
Mener une vie de bâton de chaise.
Holgazanear.
Sich austoben / Sich die Hörner abstossen.
Correre la cavallina.

As a man sows, so shall he reap. (prov.)
On récolte ce qu'on sème.
Quien siembra vientos recoge tempestades.
Wie ein Mann sät, so wird er ernten / Wie die Saat, so die
Ernte.
Quel che si semina si raccoglie.

He who sows the wind will reap the whirlwind. (prov.)
Qui sème le vent récolte la tempête.
El que siembra vientos, recoje tempestades.
Wer Wind sät, wird Sturm ernten.
Chi semina vento, raccoglie tempesta.

SOW

As drunk as a sow. (comp.)
Soûl comme un Polonais.
Borracho.

Betrunken wie eine Sau (ein Schwein) / Stockhagelbesoffen.
Molto ubriaco / Ubriaco fradicio.

He got the wrong sow by the ear.
Il est arrivé à une conclusion erronée.
Ha llegado a una conclusión equivocada.
Er zog falsche Schlüsse.
E' giunto a una conclusione errata.

SPADE

To call a spade a spade.
Appeler un chat un chat.
Llamarle pan al pan y vino al vino.
Das Kind beim (richtigen) Namen nennen.
Dire pane al pane e vino al vino.

SPANNER (♦)

(♦) To throw a spanner into the works. (p. 551)
Mettre les bâtons dans les roues.
Atascar un proyecto.
Jemandem) Einen Knüppel zwischen die Beine werfen /
Querschiessen.
Mettere un bastone fra le ruote.

SPARE

In one's spare time.
Dans les loisirs.
Tiempo libre / Tiempo disponible.
In der Freizeit / In den Mussestunden.
Nel tempo libero.

I've no time to spare!
Je n'ai pas de temps à perdre!
No tengo tiempo de sobra.
Ich habe keine Zeit (zu verlieren)!
Non ho tempo da perdere!

Spare the rod and spoil the child. (prov.)
La pitié n'est pas toujours le meilleur remède / Il faut savoir
être sévère.

En la vida hay que ser severos.
Wer die Rute spart, verzieht das Kind.
Il medico pietoso fa la piaga cancrenosa.

To spare somebody's feelings.
Essayer de ne pas vexer quelqu'un.
Tratar de no lastimar a nadie (en los sentimientos).
Jemandes Gefühle schonen.
Cercare di non urtare la suscettibilità di qualcuno.

SPARK

A gay-spark.
Faire le joli-cœur.
Petimetre / Gomoso.
Ein flotter Kerl / Ein Galan.
Un bellimbusto.

SPEAKING

Not to be on speaking terms with somebody.
Ne pas être en bons termes avec quelqu'un.
No tener relaciones de amistad con una persona.
Mit jemandem nicht (mehr) sprechen.
Non essere in buoni rapporti con qualcuno.

SPECTACLES

To see everything through rose-coloured spectacles.
Voir tout en rose.
Verlo todo color de rosa.
Alles durch eine rosarote Brille sehen.
Veder tutto rosa.

SPEECH

Speech is silver but silence is gold. (prov.)
La parole est d'argent mais le silence est d'or.
Las palabras son de plata, pero el silencio es de oro.
Reden ist Silber, Schweigen ist Gold.
La parola è d'argento ma il silenzio è d'oro / Chi parla, semina;
chi tace, raccoglie.

SPEED

More haste less speed.
Qui veut aller loin ménage sa monture.
Aquel va sano, que anda por el llano.
Eile mit Weile.
Chi va piano, va sano e va lontano.

SPELL

We had a cold spell in April.
Nous avons eu une vague de froid en avril.
En Abril hemos tenido una ola de frío.
Wir hatten im April eine Kältewelle (eine kalte Periode).
Abbiamo avuto un'ondata di freddo in aprile.

SPEND

To spend a penny.
Aller aux toilettes.
Tener necesidad del interior (del baño).
Auf die Toilette gehen.
Aver bisogno della toilette.

SPICY

A spicy story.
Une histoire piquante.
Una historia picante.
Eine witzige (pikante) Geschichte.
Una storia piccante. '

SPILL (♦)

(♦) It's no use crying over spilt milk. (prov.) (p. 124)
La page est tournée.
No hay que lamentarse por lo que no tiene remedio.
Geschehen ist geschehen, hin ist hin.
Non serve piangere sul latte versato.

SPIN

To go for a spin.
Aller faire un tour en voiture.

Ir a dar una vuelta en coche.
Eine Spritztour machen / Einen Ausflug machen. 7
Andare a fare un giro in macchina.

SPITE

To cut off one's nose to spite one's face.
Faire une méchanceté qui tourne à notre désavantage.
Deshairar aún en contra de los propios intereses.
Sich ins eigene Fleisch schneiden.
Fare un dispetto che torna a proprio danno.

SPLASH (♦)

(♦) To make a splash. (p. 555)
Faire sensation.
Ponerse en vista / Hacer golpe.
Aufsehen erregen / Furore machen.
Fare sensazione.

SPLEEN

To vent one's spleen.
Epancher sa mauvaise humeur.
Desahogar el malhumor.
Seinem Ärger Luft machen / Seine üble Laune auslassen an . . .
Sfogare il proprio malumore.

SPLIT

To split one's sides with laughter.
Se tordre de rire / Se bidonner.
Desternillarse de la risa / Reventar de risa.
Sich kaputt lachen / Sich halbtot lachen / Sich schütteln vor
Lachen / Vor Lachen bersten.
Sbellicarsi dalle risa.

To split hairs.
Regarder par le menu / Couper les cheveux en deux / Chercher la petite bête.
Pararse en pelillos.
Haarspalterei treiben.
Andare per il sottile / Cercare il pelo nell'uovo.

SPOKE

To put a spoke in somebody's wheel.
Mettre le bâton dans les roues à quelqu'un.
Atascar a alguien.
Jemandem einen Knüppel zwischen die Beine werfen.
Metter il bastone fra le ruote a qualcuno.

SPONGE (♦)

(♦) To throw in the sponge. (p. 557)
Se rendre / Jeter l'éponge.
Rendirse / Botar la toalla.
Es aufgeben / Sich geschlagen geben / Das Handtuch werfen.
Arrendersi / Gettare la spugna.

To sponge a meal.
Resquiller un repas.
Gorronear una comida.
Eine Mahlzeit erschnorren / Eine Mahlzeit kostenlos ergattern.
Scroccare un pasto.

SPOON (♦)

(♦) To be born with a silver spoon in one's mouth. (p. 66)
Etre né coiffé.
Haber nacido con la camisa puesta / Ser afortunado.
Ein Glückskind (Sonntagskind) sein.
Essere nato con la camicia.

SPORT

He's a good sport.
C'est un vrai sportif.
Es un buen deportista.
Er ist ein wirklicher Sportler / Er ist kein Spielverderber.
E' un vero sportivo.

SPORTING

She was sporting a mink coat.
Elle arborait un manteau de vison.
Ostentar una piel de visón.

Sie protzte mit einem Nerzmantel.
Sfoggiava una pelliccia di visone.

SPOT

Spot on!
Excellent!
¡Excelente!
Ausgezeichnet! / Vortrefflich!
Eccellente!

On the spot.
Sur place.
Allí mismo / Al punto.
Zur Stelle / An Ort und Stelle / Auf der Stelle / Sofort.
Sul posto.

A spot of gin.
Une goutte (une larme / un doigt) de gin.
Una poca de ginebra.
Einen Schuss (Tropfen / Schluck) Gin.
Una goccia di gin.

SPUR

On the spur of the moment.
Au pied-levé.
Impensadamente, sin la reflexión debida.
Der Eingebung des Augenblicks folgend / Ohne Überlegung /
Spontan.
Così, sui due piedi.

SQUARE (♦)

On the square.
Loyalement.
De buena fé.
Gutgläubig / Ehrlich / Anständig / In Ordnung.
Lealmente / In buona fede.

(♦) To be square. (p. 559)
Etre quites.
Estar en paz / No deber nada / Estar empatados.

558

Anständig (ehrlich) sein / Quitt sein / Quitt sein.
Essere pari.

A square peg in a round hole.
Un poisson hors de l'eau.
Un pez fuera del agua.
Ein Mensch am falschen Platz.
Un pesce fuor d'acqua.

STAKE

His reputation is at stake.
Sa réputation est en jeu.
Su reputación está en juego.
Sein guter Ruf (Name) steht auf dem Spiel.
E' in gioco la sua reputazione.

STALLING

He's stalling for time.
Il essaie de gagner du temps.
Está tratando de ganar tiempo.
Er versucht, Zeit zu gewinnen / Er macht Ausflüchte, um Zeit
zu schinden.
Sta cercando di guadagnare tempo.

STANDS

It stands to reason.
C'est facile à comprendre.
Es razonable.
Es ist leicht zu verstehen.
E' facile da capire.

STARCH

To take the starch out of somebody.
Démonter quelqu'un.
Desanimar a alguien.
Jemandem den Mumm (den Mut / die Courage) nehmen.
Smontare qualcuno.

STARK

He's stark mad!
Il est fou à lier!
¡Está loco de remate!
Er ist total verrückt!
E' matto da legare!

Stark madness!
C'est de la pure folie!
¡Es una locura!
Purer (völliger) Wahnsinn!
Pura follia!

STARRY

Starry-eyed.
Novice.
Ingenuo / Cándido.
Mit strahlenden Augen / Überglücklich / Romantisch / Wirk-
lichkeitsfremd.
Ingenuo.

STEADY

As steady as a rock. (comp.)
Ferme comme un roc.
Firme como una roca.
Felsenfest / Unbeugsam.
Molto saldo / Saldo come una roccia / Stabile.

STEAM

To let off steam.
Se libérer de . . . / Epancher / S'épancher.
Desahogarse.
Dampf ablassen / Seinem Zorn (sich) Luft machen.
Sfogarsi.

STEEL

He's got a heart of steel.
Il a un cœur dur.

Tiene un corazón muy duro.
Er hat ein Herz aus Eisen (Stein).
Ha un cuore di pietra.

STEER

To steer clear of . . .
Eviter.
Evitar.
Vermeiden / Aus dem Wege gehen.
Evitare.

STEP (♦)

(♦) Step on it! (p. 563)
Fais vite!
¡Dáte prisa!
Gib Gas! / Mach schnell!
Fa' presto!

Watch your step!
Attention!
¡Ten cuidado!
Vorsicht! / Gibt acht! / Sieh dich vor! / Pass auf!
Sta' attento!

To keep step with . . .
Aller de pair avec . . .
Marchar al compás con. . . / Ir al paso con . . .
Schritt halten mit . . .
Andare di pari passo con . . .

(♦) To step out of line. (p. 564)
Passer la mesure / Passer les limites.
Pasarse de la raya.
Aus der Reihe tanzen.
Passare la misura.

STEW

To get into a stew.
Se fourrer dans un guêpier.
Meterse en un aprieto / Meterse en un lío.
In Aufregung geraten.
Cacciarsi nei guai.

564

STICK (♦)

(♦) To have the wrong end of the stick. (p. 566)
Commettre une bévue.
Engañarse.
Die Sache falsch verstehen.
Prendere un abbaglio.

To stick up for . . .
Parler en défense de . . .
Hablar en defensa de . . .
Sich für jemanden einsetzen.
Parlare in difesa di . . .

He sticks at nothing.
Il n'a pas de scrupules.
No tiene escrúpulos.
Vor nichts zurückschrecken.
Non ha scrupoli.

To stick together.
Rester unis.
Permanecer unidos.
Zusammenhalten / Zusammenkleben.
Restare uniti.

It sticks out a mile!
C'est évident!
¡Es muy evidente! / ¡Se vé sin necesidad de ojos!
Es sticht aus allem hervor! / Es übertrifft alles! / Es überragt
Si vede lontano un miglio!

To stick through thick and thin.
Tenir bon.
Mantenerse firme / No soltar.
Durch dick und dünn gehen.
Tener duro.

STICKY

To be very sticky about something.
Etre très tatillon (vétilleux).
Ser muy meticuloso en algo.
Sehr pingelig sein in . . .
Essere molto pignolo su qualcosa.

STIFF

As stiff as a poker. (comp.)
Très rigide / Raide.
Muy rígido.
Steif wie ein Stock.
Molto rigido.

As stiff as a post. (comp.)
Raide comme un bâton / Raide comme un piquet.
Tieso como un garrote.
Stocksteif.
Molto rigido / Molto impettito.

To keep a stiff upper lip.
Démontrer une force de caractère / Faire preuve de force de caractère.
Demostrar fuerza de carácter.
Charakter beweisen.
Dimostrare forza di carattere.

STILL

As still as death. (comp.)
Très tranquille.
Quieto / Callado.
Totenstill.
Molto quieto.

As still as the grave. (comp.)
Muet comme une tombe.
Silencioso como una tumba.
Schweigsam wie ein Grab.
Muto come una tomba.

Still waters run deep. (prov.)
Il faut se méfier de l'eau qui dort.
El agua quieta corróe los puentes.
Stille Wasser gründen tief.
Le acque chete rovinano i ponti.

STINK (♦)

(♦) To raise a stink. (p. 568)
Faire une histoire.

Reclamar / Armar jaléo.
Einen Skandal hervorrufen / Einen Krach anzetteln.
Piantare una grana.

STITCH (♦)

A stitch in time saves nine. (prov.)
Un point fait à temps en épargne cent.
Una buena puntada puede salvar las otras cien.
Gleich getan ist viel gespart.
Un punto in tempo ne salva cento.

(♦) To get into stitches. (p. 570)
Se tordre de rire.
Desternillarse de la risa.
Vor Lachen Stiche (Seitenstechen) bekommen / Sich vor Lachen krümmen.
Sbellicarsi dalle risa.

STOCK

To take stock of ...
Evaluer une situation.
Evaluar una situación.
Sich klarwerden über ... / Eine Situation richtig abschätzen.
Valutare una situazione.

To make a laughing stock of oneself.
Se rendre ridicule.
Hacer el ridículo.
Sich zum Gegenstand des Gelächters machen / Sich zur Zielscheibe des Spottes machen / Sich lächerlich machen.
Rendersi ridicolo.

Lock, stock and barrel.
Armes et bagages.
Con todos sus pertrechos.
Mit Stumpf und Stiel / Ganz und gar / Mit Haut und Haar / Mit Sack und Pack.
Armi e bagagli.

STOOL-PIGEON (♦)

(♦) A stool-pigeon. (p. 571)
Un informateur / Un mouchard.

Un soplón.
Ein Lockvogel.
Una persona che fa da esca / Un informatore.

STONE

As hard as a stone. (comp.)
Dur comme pierre.
Duro como piedra.
Hart wie Stein.
Duro come una pietra.

Within a stone's throw.
Très près.
Muy cerca.
Nur ein Katzensprung.
A un tiro di schioppo / Molto vicino.

I'll leave no stone unturned!
Je ne laisserai rien au hasard!
¡No dejaré santo parado! / ¡Lo intentaré todo!
Ich werde nichts unversucht lassen!
Non lascerò nulla d'intentato.

One cannot draw blood from a stone.
On ne peut pas tirer de l'huile d'un mur.
Querer sacar agua de una piedra.
Man kann nicht Unmögliches von jemandem verlangen.
Non si può cavar sangue da una rapa.

STONED

He was stoned.
Il était ivre-mort.
Estaba borracho.
Er war besoffen / Er war völlig besoffen.
Era ubriaco fradicio.

STONES

Those who live in glasshouses should not throw stones. (prov.)
Que celui qui n'a jamais péché jette la première pierre / Jeter
la pierre à quelqu'un.

El que esté libre de pecado que tire la primera piedra.
Wer im Glashaus sitzt, sollte nicht mit Steinen werfen.
Chi è senza peccato scagli la prima pietra / Chi ha tegoli di
vetro, non tiri sassi al vicino.

STONEY

To be stoney-broke.
Etre sur la paille / Etre fauché.
Estar sin un céntimo / Estar pelado.
Pleite sein / Völlig abgebrannt sein.
Essere al verde.

STOREY

He's a little wrong in the upper storey!
Il lui manque un boulon!
¡Le falta una tuerca!
Er hat nicht alle im Kasten! / Er ist nicht ganz richtig im Ober-
stübchen!
Gli manca un venerdì!

STORM

A storm in a tea cup.
Beaucoup de bruit pour rien.
Una tormenta en un vaso de agua.
Ein Sturm im Wasserglas / Viel Lärm um nichts.
Molto chiasso per nulla.

STRADDLE

To straddle an issue.
Ménager la chèvre et le chou / Tempérer les choses.
Contemporizar.
Schwanken / Unschlüssig sein.
Dare un colpo al cerchio e uno alla botte.

STRAIGHT

As straight as an arrow. (comp.)
Droit comme un piquet.
Muy derecho / Muy recto.

Gerade wie ein Pfeil / Pfeilgerad.
Dritto come un fuso.

To get straight.
Se remettre en état.
Reponerse.
Sich wieder aufrichten.
Rimettersi in sesto.

STRAIGHTAWAY

Go straightaway!
Allez-y tout de suite!
¡Vayan en seguida!
Gehen Sie sofort / Gehen Sie auf der Stelle!
Andateci subito!

STRAIN

To strain every nerve.
Faire n'importe quoi / Faire l'impossible.
Hacer todo el esfuerzo posible.
Seine ganze Kraft aufbieten / Jeden Nerv anspannen.
Fare ogni sforzo / Fare l'impossibile.

STRAITENED

In straitened circumstances.
(Se trouver) dans la gêne.
Encontrarse en dificultades.
In beschränkten Verhältnissen.
In ristrettezze (economiche).

STRAW (♦)

To draw straws.
Tirer au sort.
Sortear.
Lose ziehen.
Tirare a sorte.

(♦) It's the last straw that breaks the camel's back. (p. 575)
C'est la dernière goutte qui fait déborder le vase.
Es la última gota la que hace que el vaso se derrame.

Es ist der Tropfen, der das Fass zum Überlaufen brigt.
E' l'ultima goccia che fa traboccare il vaso.

Not to care a straw.
Ne pas s'intéresser le moins du monde . . .
No importarle a uno un comino.
Völlig gleichgültig sein / Sich absolut nicht interessieren.
Non interessarsi minimamente.

STRANDED
She's stranded.
Il a des ennuis.
Está empantanada (en dificultades).
Sie ist gescheitert (gestrandet).
E' nei guai.

STRAYS
Waifs and strays.
Enfants abandonnés / Objets perdus.
Niños abandonados / Objetos extraviados.
Verwährloste Kinder.
Bambini abbandonati / Oggetti smarriti.

STREET
The man in the street.
L'homme de la rue.
El hombre de la calle.
Der Mann auf der Strasse / Der Durchschnittsmensch.
L'uomo comune / L'uomo della strada.

STRENGTH
On the strength of a promise.
Encouragé par une promesse.
Alentado por una promesa.
Auf Grund eines Versprechens / Kraft eines Versprechens /
Auf ein Versprechen hin.
Incoraggiato da una promessa.

STRESS
To lay stress on something.
Donner de l'importance à quelque chose.
Recalcar algo.
Nachdruck (Gewicht / Akzent) auf etwas legen / Etwas betonen (hervorheben).
Dare importanza a qualcosa.

STRETCH
To stretch the truth.
Exagérer / Détourner la question.
Exagerar / Deformar la verdad.
Es mit der Wahrheit nicht allzu genau nehmen / Flunkern.
Esagerare / Deformare la realtà.

STRIDE (♦)
To take something in one's stride.
Faire quelque chose avec facilité.
Hacer una cosa con facilidad / Hacer una cosa como si nada.
Etwas spielend (leicht) schaffen / Etwas mühelos bewältigen.
Fare qualcosa con facilità.

(♦) To make great strides. (p. 578)
Faire des progrès / Faire des pas de géant.
Hacer progresos.
Grosse Fortschritte machen / Aus dem Ärmel schütteln.
Fare grandi progressi / Fare passi da gigante.

STRIKE (♦)
(♦) To strike while the iron is hot. (prov.) (p. 301)
Battre le fer pendant qu'il est encore chaud.
Hay que darle mientras esté caliente.
Das Eisen schmieden, solange es heiss ist.
Battere il ferro finchè è caldo.

To strike home.
Faire mouche.
Dar en el blanco.
Den Nagel auf den Kopf treffen.
Colpire nel segno.

STRING (♦)

To harp on the same old string.
Insister sur le même sujet.
Insistir sobre el mismo argumento.
Immer auf derselben Sache herumreiten.
Insistere sullo stesso tasto.

She's got him on a string.
Elle le tient en main.
Lo tiene en el bolsillo (a una persona).
Sie hat ihn in ihrer Gewalt / Sie hat ihn (fest) am Gängelband.
Lo tiene in pugno.

To pull the strings.
Manipuler quelque chose.
Manipular (las personas o situaciones).
Der Drahtzieher sein.
Manipolare qualcosa.

(♦) To be tied to one's mother's apron strings. (p. 580)
Etre pendu aux jupes de sa mère.
Estar todavía prendido de las enaguas de la madre.
An Mutters Rockzipfel (Schürzenband) hängen.
Essere attaccato alle gonne della mamma.

I've two strings to my bow.
J'ai deux possibilités.
Tengo dos posibilidades / Tengo dos chances.
Ich habe zwei Eisen im Feuer.
Ho due possibilità.

To string along.
Suivre / Adhérer à . . .
Seguir a . . . / Adherir con . . .
Sich jemandem anschliessen.
Seguire . . . / Aderire a . . .

STROKE

Little strokes fell great oaks. (prov.)
La persévérance vient à bout de tout.
Paso a paso se llega a Roma.
Steter Tropfen höhlt den Stein.
La goccia scava la pietra.

He hasn't done a stroke of work in his life.
Il n'a jamais rien fait de sa vie.
No ha nunca hecho nada en su vida.
Er hat in seinem Leben keinen Finger gerührt.
Non ha fatto un briciolo di lavoro in tutta la sua vita.

STROLL

To go for a stroll.
Faire quelques pas.
Ir a pasear / Ir a dar un paseo.
Einen Bummel machen / Spazierengehen.
Fare quattro passi.

STRONG

As strong as a horse. (comp.)
Très fort.
Fuerte como un toro.
Stark wie ein Pferd (Stier).
Forte come un toro.

As strong as a lion. (comp.)
Fort comme un lion.
Fuerte como un león.
Stark wie ein Löwe.
Forte come un leone.

STRUNG (♦)

(♦) To be highly strung. (p. 278)
Etre hypersensible.
Ser muy sensible / Ser como una cuerda de violín.
Überempfindlich sein.
Essere ipersensibile.

STUDDED

Studded with mistakes.
Bourré de fautes.
Plagado de errores.
Mit Fehlern übersät.
Costellato d'errori.

STUDY

To be in a brown study.
Etre pensif.
Estar pensativo.
In Gedanken versunken sein.
Essere soprapensiero.

STUFF

He's got good stuff in him.
Il a de l'étoffe.
Tiene buena estofa.
Er hat in ihm einen guten (tüchtigen) Menschen gefunden /
Er ist aus gutem Zeug (Holz) gemacht (geschnitzt) / Er hat
Talent.
Ha della stoffa / C'è della stoffa in lui.

Stuff and nonsense!
Sottises!
¡Tonteras! / ¡Charadas!
Dummes Zeug!
Sciocchezze!

That's the stuff to give them!
C'est comme ça qu'il faut faire!
¡Este es el pan bueno para sus dientes! / ¡Así se tratan!
So ist's richtig!
Così van trattati!

STUFFED (♦)

(♦) A stuffed shirt. (p. 583)
Un ballon gonflé.
Una nulidad / Un bombeta.
Fatzke / Wichtigtuer / Lackierter Affe.
Un pallone gonfiato.

STUMBLING

A stumbling block.
Des difficultés / Un obstacle.
Un tropiezo.
Der Stein des Anstosses / Ein Hindernis.
Un intoppo / Un ostacolo.

582

STUMPED

I'm stumped!
Je suis perplexe! / Je ne sais sur quel pied danser!
¡Estoy perplejo! / ¡No sé que hacer!
Ich bin verblüfft / Ich bin aufgeschmissen.
Sono perplesso! / Non so che pesci pigliare!

STUPID

As stupid as a donkey. (comp.)
Bête comme ses pieds.
Burro / Tonto.
Dumm wie ein Esel.
Molto stupido / Stupido come un'oca.

STYX

As black as Styx. (comp.)
Noir corbeau / Noir comme le charbon.
Negro como el alquitrán.
Schwarz wie die Hölle.
Nero come l'inferno.

SUBMERGED

The submerged tenth.
Les classes les plus pauvres.
Las clases pobres.
Die ärmste (unterste) Bevölkerungsschicht.
Le classi più povere.

SUCCESS

Nothing succeeds like success. (prov.)
Un succès en appelle un autre.
Triunfo llama triunfo / Dinero llama dinero.
Ein Erfolg zieht den anderen nach sich.
Un successo ne chiama un altro.

SUCH

Such master such servant. (prov.)
Tel maître, tel valet.

De tal amo, tal servidor.
Wie der Herr so der Knecht / Wie der Herr so sein Gescherr.
Tale il padrone tale il servo.

SUCK

To suck up to . . .
Lécher les bottes à . . .
Sobarle la leva a . . .
Jemandem in den Arsch kriechen / Jemandem um den Bart gehen.
Leccare i piedi a . . .

SUFFER

To suffer fools gladly.
Supporter avec patience.
Aguantar con paciencia / Soportar pacientemente a ciertas personas.
Geduldig ertragen (erleiden / erdulden).
Sopportare pazientemente le persone moleste.

SUGAR

A sugar-daddy.
Un vieux dandy.
Un viejo verde.
Geldonkel / Von einer Kokette ausgebeuteter Geldonkel.
Vecchio danaroso che frequenta donne molto più giovani.

SULKS

To have the sulks.
Faire la tête.
Tener murria.
Schlechte Laune haben / Schmollen / Trotzen.
Tenere il broncio.

SUNDAY

A month of Sundays.
Une période très longue.

Una eternidad.
Schrecklich lange / Ewig.
Un periodo lunghissimo / Un'eternità.

One's Sunday best.
Le meilleur habit / L'habit du dimanche.
El mejor vestido / El vestido de fiestas.
Jemandes Sonntagsstaat (Sonntagskleider).
Il proprio vestito migliore / Il vestito della festa.

SUNNY

To look on the sunny side of life.
Regarder le bon côté de la vie.
Ver el lado bueno de la vida.
Die Sonnenseite des Lebens betrachten.
Guardare il lato buono della vita.

SUP

He who sups with the devil needs a long spoon. (prov.)
Il faut être prudent pour traiter avec le diable.
Quien se mete con el diablo es mejor que sea prudente.
Wer sich mit dem Teufel einlässt, muss sehr vorsichtig sein /
Der Teufel ist mit Vorsicht zu geniessen.
Nel trattare col diavolo bisogna andare molto cauti.

SUPPORT

Without means of support.
Sans moyens visibles.
Sin apoyos / Sin medios.
Ohne stützende (unterstützende; fördernde) Mittel / Ohne Rück-
halt / Ohne Unterstützung.
Senza mezzi visibili.

SURE

As sure as death. (comp.)
Bien sûr!
¡Muy cierto!
Totsicher.
Molto certo.

As sure as a gun. (comp.)
Aussi vrai que j'existe.
Verdadero.
Sicher / Unfehlbar.
Molto vero.

He's sure-footed.
Il est sûr de lui.
Seguro de sí mismo.
Er ist sich seiner sicher.
E' sicuro di sè.

SURFACE
On the surface.
Apparemment.
Aparentemente / En apariencia.
Oberflächlich betrachtet / Äusserlich.
In apparenza.

SURLY
As surly as a bear. (comp.)
Bourru comme un ours.
Rudo / Hosco.
Bärbeissig / Grob / Verdriesslich / Mürrisch / Griesgrämig.
Molto burbero / Molto villano.

SWALLOW
He'll swallow anything.
C'est un crédule / C'est un gobeur.
Se lo traga todo / Es un credulón.
Er wird alles für bare Münze nehmen (schlucken).
E' un credulone / Le beve tutte.

One swallow does not make a summer. (prov.)
Une hirondelle ne fait pas le printemps.
Una golondrina no hace verano.
Eine Schwalbe macht noch keinen Sommer.
Una rondine non fa primavera.

SWAMPED

To be swamped with work.
Etre débordé de travail.
Estar agobiado de trabajo.
Mit Arbeit überhäuft sein / Sich nicht mehr von Arbeit retten können.
Essere sommerso dal lavoro.

SWAP

Never swap horses when crossing a stream.
Il ne faut jamais faire de changements dans un moment critique.
No hay que efectuar cambios cuándo se está en un momento difícil.
Nimm keine Veränderungen in einem kritischen Moment vor.
Mai fare mutamenti in un momento critico.

SWARM

A swarm of children.
Une bande d'enfants.
Un enjambre de niños.
Ein Schwarm von Kindern.
Una frotta di bambini.

SWEAR

To swear like a trooper.
Jurer comme un charretier.
Blasfemar como turco.
Wie ein Landsknecht fluchen.
Bestemmiare come un turco.

SWEEP

As black as a sweep. (comp.)
Noir comme un corbeau.
Negro como la noche.
Schwarz wie ein Schornsteinfeger.
Molto nero.

SWEEPINGS

The sweepings of the gutter.
La lie / La racaille / La populace.
El populacho.
Der Abschaum der Gesellschaft / Das Gesindel.
La feccia / La plebaglia.

SWEEPS

A new broom sweeps clean. (prov.)
Tout nouveau tout beau.
El cuchillo nuevo corta mejor.
Neue Besen kehren gut.
Scopa nuova spazza bene.

SWEET

As sweet as honey. (comp.)
Doux comme un agneau / Doux comme le miel.
Dulce como la miel.
Süss wie Honig.
Dolce come il miele.

As sweet as sugar. (comp.)
Très doux / Agréable.
Dulce como la miel.
Zuckersüss / Reizend / Goldig / Angenehm.
Molto dolce / Piacevole.

SWEPT (♦)

(♦) To be swept off one's feet. (p. 590)
Etre transporté par l'enthousiasme.
Dejarse llevar por el entusiasmo.
Hingerissen sein.
Essere trasportato dall'entusiasmo.

SWIFT

As swift as an arrow. (comp.)
Rapide comme une flèche (comme l'éclair).
Velóz como una flecha.

Schnell wie ein Pfeil.
Veloce come un lampo (come una saetta).

As swift as lightning. (comp.)
Rapide comme l'éclair.
Velóz como un relámpago.
Schnell wie der Blitz.
Veloce come il lampo.

As swift as thought. (comp.)
Très vite.
Mùy rápido / Con la velocidad del pensamiento.
Flüchtig wie ein Einfall (Gedanke).
Molto rapido.

As swift as the wind. (comp.)
Très rapide / Rapide comme le vent.
Velóz como el viento.
Schnell wie der Wind.
Veloce come il vento.

SWIMMING

My head was swimming.
La tête me tournait.
Me daba vueltas la cabeza.
Mir war schwindelig / Ich hatte ein Schwindelgefühl.
Mi girava la testa.

SWING (♦)

(♦) There's not room to swing a cat! (p. 88)
On ne peut pas se remuer là-dedans!
No hay lugar ni para moverse.
Da ist kaum Platz zum Umdrehen!
Non c'è nemmeno il posto per girarsi!

In full swing.
En pleine activité.
En su apogeo.
In vollem Gange / In Schwung.
In piena attività.

SWINGING
We had a swinging time.
Nous nous sommes follement amusés.
Nos hemos divertido una barbaridad.
Wir haben uns köstlich amüsiert.
Ci siamo divertiti un mondo.

SWORD
Those who live by the sword shall perish by the sword. (prov.)
Quiconque prendra l'épée, périra par l'épée.
Quien de hierro hiere, de hierro muere.
Wer mit dem Schwert spielt, wird durch das Schwert umkommen.
Chi di spada ferisce, di spada perisce.

SYMPATHETIC
He's very sympathetic.
Il est très compréhensif.
Es muy compasivo / Es muy abierto.
Er ist sehr verständnisvoll.
E' molto comprensivo.

T
It suits me to a T!
Ça me va comme un gant!
¡Me sienta a maravilla!
Das passt mir ausgezeichnet!
Mi va a pennello!

T'S
To cross one's t's and dot one's i's.
Etre tatillon (vétilleux) / Mettre les points sur les i.
Pignúolo / Ser extremadamente cuidadoso.
Peinlich genau sein / Es klar und deutlich sagen.
Essere pignolo / Mettere i puntini sulle i.

TABLES
To turn the tables.
Renverser la situation.

Revolver una situación.
Den Spiess umdrehen.
Rovesciare la situazione.

TACK

To be on the wrong tack.
Etre sur le mauvais chemin.
Estar sobre una falsa pista.
Auf dem richtigen Wege sein.
Essere fuori strada.

To be on the right tack.
Etre sur le bon chemin.
Estar sobre buen camíno.
Auf dem Holzwege sein / Auf dem falschen Weg sein.
Essere sulla pista giusta.

TACKS

Let's get down to brass tacks!
Venons-en au fait!
¡Vayámos a lo nuestro!
Kommen wir zum Kern!
Veniamo al sodo!

TAILOR

The tailor makes the man. (prov.)
L'élégance est de grande importance.
Lo importante es la apariencia / Te veo, te peso.
Kleider machen Leute.
L'eleganza è cosa di gran peso.

TAILS

Head or tails?
Pile ou face?
Cara o crúz.
Kopf oder Schrift?
Testa o croce?

With one's tail between one's legs.
La queue entre les jambes.

Con la cola entre las piernas.
Mit hängenden Ohren / Betreten.
Con la coda fra le gambe.

To twist the lion's tail.
Tirer le diable par la queue.
Tirar el toro por el rabo.
Das Ungluck herausfordern / Den Teufel an die Wand malen.
Tirar la coda al diavolo.

TAKE (♦)

To take for granted.
Présumer.
Dar por descontado.
Als erwiesen annehmen / Als selbstverständlich betrachten.
Dare per scontato.

To take down a peg or two.
Rabaisser le caquet à quelqu'un.
Desairar a alguien / Quitarle los humos a alguien.
Jemanden demütigen.
Sgonfiare qualcuno.

To take to drinking.
S'adonner à la boisson.
Darse a la bebida.
Das Trinken anfangen.
Darsi al bere.

To take a short cut.
Prendre un raccourci.
Tomar un atajo.
Eine Abkürzung nehmen.
Prendere una scorciatoia.

To take a turn for the better.
Améliorer / S'améliorer.
Mejorar.
Eine Wendung zum Guten nehmen.
Migliorare.

To take in someone.
Tromper quelqu'un.
Embaucar a alguien.

Jemanden reinlegen.
Ingannare qualcuno.

To take it easy.
Faire à son aise / Se la couler douce.
Sentirse cómodo / Tranquilizarse.
Es leicht nehmen / Es auf die leichte Schulter nehmen.
Fare con comodo.

(♦) To take things lying down. (p. 596)
Se la couler douce.
Tomar algo a la ligera.
Dinge bequem nehmen.
Prendersela con comodo.

To take after someone.
Ressembler à quelqu'un.
Parecerse a alguien.
Jemandem nachschlagen (nachgeraten) / Jemandem ähneln.
Assomigliare a qualcuno.

(♦) To take the words (right) out of someone's mouth. (p. 597)
Oter les mots de la bouche à quelqu'un.
Quitarle las palabras de la boca a una persona.
Jemandem die Worte aus dem Mund nehmen.
Togliere la parola di bocca a qualcuno.

TALE

An old wives' tale.
Une légende stupide.
¡Cuentos!
Ein Ammenmärchen.
Una sciocca leggenda.

Old wives' tales.
Ragots de bonne femme.
Chismes de mujeres.
Altweiberklatsch / Altweibergeschwätz.
Chiacchiere di donnicciole.

TALK (♦)

He's the talk of the town.
C'est sur les lèvres de tout le monde.

Es el hazmereír de todos.
Er ist Stadtgespräch / Er ist in aller Munde.
E' sulla bocca di tutti.

To talk turkey.
Parler clairement.
Hablar claro.
Deutlich werden.
Parlar chiaro.

Big talk.
Une fanfaronnade.
Fanfarronada.
Aufschneiderei / Hochtrabende Reden.
Spacconata.

(♦) To talk through the back of one's neck. (p. 599)
Parler à tort et à travers.
Hablar a troche y moche / Hablar a topa tolondro.
Ins Blaue hinein schwatzen (reden).
Parlare a vanvera.

TALKING

To give a talking to . . .
Faire une semonce à quelqu'un.
Hacer una reprimenda o un rapapolvo.
Jemandem eine Standpauke halten.
Fare una paternale a . . .

TALL

As tall as a maypole. (comp.)
Haut comme une perche.
Canillón / Muy alto.
Sehr hoch / Sehr gross.
Molto alto.

As tall as a steeple. (comp.)
Très grand.
Muy alto.
Hoch wie ein Kirchturm / Ein hoher Kirchturm.
Molto alto / Alto come il campanile del duomo.

TAME

A tame cat.
Un type serviable.
Una persona servicial.
Eine zahme Katze / Ein unterwürfiger Typ.
Un tipo servizievole.

As tame as a cat. (comp.)
Un endormi.
Un lento.
Friedlich (schläfrig) wie eine Katze.
Molto addormentato.

TANGLE

To be in a tangle.
Etre dans les ennuis.
Estar en un lío.
In einer Verwicklung stecken / In etwas verstrickt sein.
Essere nei pasticci.

TANNED

He tanned his hide!
Il l'a drôlement arrangé!
Le ha zurrado la baldana.
Er gerbte ihm das Fell! / Er verdrosch ihn!
Lo ha conciato per le feste!

TAPE

Red tape.
Bureaucratie.
Burocrácia.
Bürokratismus / Amtschimmel / Papierkrieg.
Burocrazia.

TAR

To have a touch of the tar brush.
Avoir du sang noir dans les veines / Etre métis.
Tener una poca de sangre negra en las venas.

Negerblut (Indianerblut) in den Adern haben / Etwas schwarzes Blut in den Adern haben.
Avere un po' di sangue misto.

TARRED

To be tarred with the same brush.
Avoir les mêmes défauts.
Estar cortados con el mismo molde.
Genauso schlecht sein / Die gleichen Fehler haben.
Avere gli stessi difetti.

TASTE (♦)

(♦) To have a taste of one's own medicine. (p. 602)
Rendre la pareille à quelqu'un.
Pagar con la misma moneda.
Gleiches mit Gleichem vergelten / Wie Du mir, so ich Dir.
Rendere pan per focaccia.

TASTES

There is no accounting for tastes. (prov.)
Les goûts et les couleurs ne se discutent pas.
No hay peros con los gustos / Gustos son gustos.
Geschmack ist Geschmacksache / Jeder hat seinen eigenen Geschmack.
Ognuno ha i suoi gusti.

TEA (♦)

(♦) One's cup of tea. (p. 126)
Le cheval de bataille.
El caballo de batalla de uno.
Nach jemandes Geschmack.
Il cavallo di battaglia.

TEACH

That will teach him to meddle in my affairs!
Je vais lui apprendre à fourrer son nez dans mes affaires!
¡Le enseñaré yo a meterse en mis asuntos!

Das wird ihn lehren, sich nicht in meine Angelegenheiten
zu mischen!
Glielo insegnerò io ad immischiarsi negli affari miei!

TEACUP

A storm in a teacup.
Beaucoup de bruit pour rien.
Una tormenta en un vaso de agua.
Ein Sturm im Wasserglas / Viel Lärm um nichts.
Molto rumore per nulla.

TEARING

He was tearing down the road.
Il courait comme un dératé.
Iba a toda velocidad por la calle.
Er raste die Strasse runter.
Correva a rotta di collo giù per la strada.

TEETH

He escaped by the skin of his teeth.
Il s'en est sorti (tiré) de justesse.
Se ha salvado por un pelo / Ha salido bien librado.
Er entkam mit knapper Not.
Se l'è cavata per il rotto della cuffìa.

To cast something in a person's teeth.
Reprocher quelque chose à quelqu'un.
Reprochar / Tener un reproche con una persona.
Jemandem etwas vorwerfen.
Rimproverare uno di una cosa.

To set one's teeth on edge.
Serrer les dents.
Apretar los dientes.
Die Zähne zusammenbeissen.
Stringere i denti.

To show one's teeth.
Montrer les dents.
Enseñar los dientes.
Die Zähne zeigen.
Mostrare i denti.

In the teeth of opposition.
Malgré toute opposition.
A pesar de las oposiciones.
Trotz des Widerstandes / Entgegen (ungeachtet) der Opposition.
Nonostante ogni opposizione.

TELLING-OFF

He gave me a good telling off.
Il m'a passé un bon savon.
Me ha dado un buen rapapolvo.
Er gab mir ordentlich Bescheid.
Mi ha rimproverato severamente.

TEMPER

God tempers the wind to the shorn lamb. (prov.)
Dieu fait bien les choses.
Dios da el frío conforme la ropa.
Gott schickt dem geschorenen Lamm mildes Wetter.
Dio manda il freddo secondo i panni / Dio misura il vento
all'agnello tosato.

To be in a temper.
Etre hors de soi.
Estar fuera de sí.
Wütend sein. .
Essere fuori di sè.

TENDER

As tender as a chicken. (comp.)
Très tendre / Tendre comme un bourgeon.
Tierno como mantequilla.
Zart wie ein Küken.
Molto tenero.

TENTERHOOKS

To be on tenterhooks.
Etre sur des charbons ardents.
Estar en ascuas.

Auf die Folter gespannt sein / Wie auf glühenden Kohlen sitzen.
Stare sulle spine.

TERMS

To be on good terms with somebody.
Etre en bons termes avec quelqu'un.
Estar en buenas relaciones con alguien.
Mit jemandem auf gutem Fusse stehen.
Essere in buoni rapporti con qualcuno.

To be on bad terms with somebody.
Etre en mauvais termes avec quelqu'un.
Estar en malas relaciones con alguien.
Mit jemandem auf schlechtem Fusse stehen.
Essere in cattivi rapporti con qualcuno.

TETHER

To be at the end of one's tether.
Etre réduit à l'extrême.
Estar agotado.
Am Ende seiner Kräfte (Geduld) sein / Sich nicht mehr zu helfen wissen.
Essere stremato / Essere agli sgoccioli.

THICK

As thick as a cable. (comp.)
Très épais.
Muy espeso.
Dick wie ein Tau (Seil).
Molto spesso.

As thick as hail stones. (comp.)
Très dense.
Muy espeso.
Sehr dicht.
Molto denso.

To be as thick as thieves. (comp.)
Etre très intimes / Etre très amis.
Ser como hermanos / Ser uña y carne.

Dicke Freunde sein.
Essere molto intimi / Essere molto amici.

To lay it on thick.
Etre prodigue en compliments.
Halagar demasiado / Exagerar.
Dick auftragen.
Essere prodigo di complimenti / Esagerare.

We went through thick and thin together.
Nous avons franchi ensemble tous les obstacles.
Las hemos pasadas todas juntos.
Wir gingen zusammen durch dick und dünn.
Abbiamo affrontato insieme ogni difficoltà.

It's a bit thick!
C'en est trop!
¡Esto es el colmo!
Das ist ein bisschen stark!
Questo è troppo!

He's a bit thick!
Il est un peu bête!
¡Es un poco tonto!
Er ist ein bisschen dumm!
E' un po' stupido!

THICK-SKINNED

To be thick-skinned.
Etre solide / Avoir la peau dure.
Ser sólido como una roca / Tener el cuero duro.
Eine dicke Haut (ein dickes Fell) haben.
Avere la pelle dura.

THIEF

Procrastination is the thief of time. (prov.)
Il ne faut pas remettre au lendemain ce que l'on peut faire le jour-même.
No hay que dejar al mañana lo que se puede hacer hoy / El que se duerme se lo lleva el río.
Verschiebe nicht auf morgen, was Du heute kannst besorgen.
Non rimandare a domani quello che potresti fare oggi.

THIN

As thin as a rake. (comp.)
Très maigre.
Flaco como un palillo de dientes.
Dünn wie ein Stecken.
Magro come un grissino.

As thin as a wafer. (comp.)
Très fin / Très mince.
Muy delgado.
Hauchdünn.
Molto sottile.

As thin as a lath. (comp.)
Maigre comme un clou.
Flaco como un clavo.
Spindeldürr.
Magro come un chiodo.

THING

To know a thing or two.
En savoir long.
Ser un lagarto.
Bescheid wissen.
Saperla lunga.

It's not quite the thing.
C'est très incorrect.
No es exactamente lo mismo.
Es ist nicht das Richtige.
E' alquanto scorretto.

The latest thing in ties.
C'est le dernier cri en matière de cravates.
La última moda en corbatas.
Der letzte Schrei (das Neueste) in Krawatten.
L'ultimo grido in fatto di cravatte.

THINGAMABOB

What a strange thingamabob!
Quel drôle de truc!

¡Que extraño artefacto!
Welch komisches Ding da!
Che strano aggeggio!

THINK

To think nothing of ...
Ne fais pas attention à ...
No hacer caso de ... / No dar importancia a ...
Wenig halten von ... / Sich nichts machen aus ... / Sich nichts dabei denken.
Non far caso a ...

To think better of it.
Y réfléchir.
Pensarlo mejor.
Sich eines Besseren besinnen / Es noch einmal überdenken.
Ripensarci.

THISTLE

To grasp the thistle firmly.
Prendre le taureau par les cornes.
Tomar el toro por los cuernos.
Das Übel anpacken / Den Stier bei den Hörnern packen.
Prendere il toro per le corna.

THORN

To be on thorns.
Etre sur des charbons ardents.
Estar en ascuas.
Auf glühenden Kohlen sitzen.
Essere sulle spine.

There's no rose without a thorn. (prov.)
Il n'y a pas de roses sans épines.
No hay rosa sin espinas.
Es gibt keine Rose ohne Dornen.
Non c'è rosa senza spine.

THROW (♦)

(♦) To throw the book at someone. (p. 609)
Taper sur le dos de quelqu'un.

608

609

Agredir a alguien.
Jemanden verhauen (verprügeln) / Mit einem Gegenstand nach jemandem werfen.
Dare addosso a qualcuno.

THUMB

To be under somebody's thumb.
Etre sous la domination de quelqu'un.
Estar en el puño de alguien / Estar bajo el dominio de . . .
In jemandes Gewalt stehen / Unter jemandes Fuchtel stehen.
Essere sotto il dominio di qualcuno.

THUMBS

His fingers are all thumbs!
C'est un brouillon! / Il est maladroit!
¡Es torpe! / ¡Es un chambón!
Er ist ein tappiger Kerl (Tollpatsch).
'E' un pasticcione!

THUNDER

Blood and thunder.
Violent.
Violento.
Gewaltsam / Gewalttätig / Heftig.
Violento.

TICK

On the tick.
Ponctuellement.
Con puntualidad.
Pünktlich / Auf die Sekunde (pünktlich).
Puntualmente.

TICKLED (♦)

(♦) To be tickled to death. (p. 611)
Etre très amusé.
Morirse de gusto / Estar muy contento.

Sich totlachen können.
Essere molto divertito.

To be tickled pink.
Etre très heureux.
Estar muy felíz.
Uberglucklich sein.
Essere felicissimo.

TIGHT

He's in a tight corner.
Il est dans une situation dangereuse.
Está en un callejón sin salida.
Er steckt in der Klemme / Er ist in Verlegenheit.
E' in una situazione pericolosa.

To be tight.
Etre gai.
Estar borracho.
Blau sein / Besoffen sein.
Essere brillo.

Sit tight!
Tiens bon! / Ne cède pas!
¡No te ríndas!
Bleib fest! / Lass Dich nicht beirren! / Rühr Dich nicht!
Non cedere!

To be tight for money.
Ne pas avoir d'argent / Etre sans le sou.
No tener dinero.
Knapp bei Kasse sein.
Non avere soldi.

To be tight with one's money.
Etre avare de son argent.
Ser avariento.
Knickerig (geizig) mit seinem Geld sein.
Essere tirchio coi propri quattrini.

TILT

Full tilt.
A toute vitesse.

A toda velocidad.
Mit voller Wucht (Geschwindigkeit) / In gestrecktem Galopp.
A gran velocità.

TIMBERS

Shiver my timbers!
Au diable!
¡Al diablo!
Rutsch mir den Buckel runter! / Scher Dich zum Teufel!
Al diavolo!

TIME (♦)

(♦) Time flies! (p. 614)
Le temps passe! / Le temps court.
¡El tiempo vuela!
Die Zeit fliegt!
Il tempo vola!

To while away the time.
Tuer le temps.
Matar el tiempo / Pasar el tiempo.
Sich die Zeit vertreiben / Die Zeit totschlagen.
Ammazzare il tempo.

To have the time of one's life.
S'amuser follement.
Pasar un buen rato.
Sich grossartig amüsieren.
Divertirsi un mondo.

There's a time for everything. (prov.)
Chaque chose en son temps.
Todo a su tiempo.
Alles zu seiner Zeit.
Ogni cosa a suo tempo.

TIMID

As timid as a hare (rabbit). (comp.)
Très timide.

614

Tímido como un conejo.
Scheu wie ein Reh.
Timido come un coniglio.

TIP

I had it on the tip of my tongue.
Je l'avais sur le bout de la langue.
Lo tenía sobre la punta de la lengua.
Es lag mir auf der Zunge.
L'avevo sulla punta della lingua.

TIP-OFF

To tip-off.
Conseiller.
Poner sobre aviso a una persona.
Einen Tip geben.
Consigliare.

TIPSY

To be tipsy.
Etre gai.
Estar borracho / Estar bolo.
Beschwipst (angeheitert) sein.
Essere brillo.

TIT

To give tit for tat.
Dent pour dent / Rendre la pareille à quelqu'un.
Pagar con la misma moneda.
Mit gleicher Münze heimzahlen.
Rendere pan per focaccia.

TOE

To toe the line.
Se conformer aux usages.
Respetar las costumbres.
Sich nach den Gewohnheiten richten.
Conformarsi alle usanze.

TOES

To be on one's toes.
Etre en forme / Etre dynamique / Etre plein de vie.
Estar sano y despejado.
Auf Draht sein / In Form sein.
Essere in gamba, in forma, pieno di vita.

To tread on someone's toes.
Ecraser les pieds à quelqu'un / Marcher sur les pieds de quelqu'un.
Pisar los pies a una persona.
Jemandem auf die Hühneraugen treten.
Pestare i calli a qualcuno.

TOM

Tom, Dick and Harry.
Pierre, Paul, Jacques et Martin.
Fulano, zutano y mengano.
Hinz und Kunz.
Tizio, Caio e Sempronio.

TONGS

To do something hammer and tongs.
Faire tout à la va-vite.
Darle con ganas.
Etwas mit aller Kraft (Gewalt) tun.
Darci sotto / Darci dentro.

TONGUE

Hold your tongue!
Tiens ta langue! / Tais-toi!
¡Mantén la boca cerrada!
Halt Deinen Mund! / Halt Deine Zunge im Zaum!
Taci!

To speak with one's tongue in one's cheek.
Parler avec ironie / Mentir.
Hablar sardonicamente / Decir mentiras.
Ironisch sprechen.
Parlare ironicamente / Mentire.

To be tongue-tied.
Ne pas sortir un mot.
Tener trabada la lengua.
Maulfaul (Schweigsam) sein / Sprachlos (stumm) sein (vor).
Non riuscire a spiccicare una parola.

A slip of the tongue.
Un lapsus linguae.
Lapsus cálami / Un deslíz verbal.
Ein Versprecher.
Un lapsus linguae.

TOOTH

To fight tooth and nail.
Se battre toutes griffes dehors.
Pelear con garra / Luchar a brazo partido.
Verbissen (erbittert) kämpfen.
Combattere con le unghie e con i denti.

To have a sweet tooth.
Etre gourmand pour les sucreries.
Ser glotón de dulces.
Gerne Süssigkeiten essen (naschen).
Essere ghiotto di dolciumi.

He's long in the tooth!
Il est vieux!
¡Está viejo!
Er ist alt!
E' vecchio!

TOP

At the top of one's voice.
A gorge déployée.
A voz en cuello.
Aus vollem Halse.
A squarciagola.

He got to the top.
Il a fait carrière.
Ha llegado a la cumbre de su profesión.

Er setzte sich durch / Er machte Karriere.
Ha fatto carriera.

To be on top of the world.
Etre au septième ciel.
Estar en el séptimo cielo / Sentirse la mamá de Tarzán.
Im siebenten Himmel sein.
Essere al settimo cielo.

To sleep like a top.
Dormir comme un loir.
Dormir como un lirón.
Wie ein Murmeltier schlafen.
Dormire come un ghiro.

TORCH

To carry the torch for somebody.
Etre amoureux fou de quelqu'un.
Estar completamente chalado / Estar colgado de alguien.
In jemanden verknallt sein.
Essere cotto di qualcuno.

TOUCH

It's touch and go!
Le risque est grand!
¡Es muy arriesgado!
Es ist riskant!
Il rischio è grande!

To keep in touch with somebody.
Rester en contact avec quelqu'un.
Mantenerse en comunicación con alguien.
Mit jemandem in Verbindung bleiben.
Restare in contatto con qualcuno.

TOUGH

As tough as leather. (comp.)
Très dur / Dur comme la semelle.
Dura como una suela.
Zäh wie Leder.
Duro come il cuoio.

Tough luck!
Quelle malchance!
¡Que mala suerte!
Pech!
Che sfortuna!

TOWEL

To throw in the towel.
Jeter l'éponge.
Botar la toalla.
Sich geschlagen geben / Das Handtuch werfen.
Gettare la spugna.

TOWN (♦)

(♦) To paint the town red. (p. 419)
Faire bombance / Faire la noce.
Ir de juerga.
Die Gegend unsicher machen.
Far baldoria.

TRACES

To kick over the traces.
Secouer le joug / Se rebeller.
Sacudirse del yugo / Rebelarse.
Über die Stränge schlagen.
Scuotere il giogo / Ribellarsi.

TRACK

To be off the beaten track.
Ne pas être dans le coup.
Estar fuera de lugar / Estar extraviado.
Vom gebahnten Weg (vom Thema) abgekommen sein.
Essere fuori strada.

To make tracks.
Couper la corde.
Tomar las de Villadiego.
Abhauen.
Tagliare la corda.

To follow the beaten track.
Prendre les chemins battus.
Ir por buen camíno.
Den einfachen Weg gehen (wählen) / Im ausgefahrenen Gleis bleiben.
Seguire la strada maestra.

TRADE (♦)

(♦) **A dying trade.** (p. 621)
Un métier qui se perd.
Un oficio que está en vias de desaparecer.
Ein aussterbendes Gewerbe / Ein absterbender Berufszweig.
Un mestiere che va scomparendo.

TREE

To be at the top of the tree.
Etre au sommet de sa profession.
Estar en el ápex de la profesión.
Den Gipfel des Erfolgs erreicht haben / In der Spitzenposition (der höchsten Stellung) sein.
Essere all'apice della propria carriera.

TRICKS (♦)

(♦) **To know all the tricks of the trade.** (p. 622)
Connaître toutes les ficelles du métier.
Conocer todas las artimañas del oficio.
Alle Tricks (Schliche) eines Berufes kennen.
Conoscere tutti i trucchi del mestiere.

To know a trick or two.
Etre un sacré fourbe (malin).
Ser un zorro.
Ein ausgekochter Gauner (Schwindler) sein.
Essere un furbo di tre cotte.

That will do the trick!
Voilà ce qu'il faut!
¡Esto es lo que hace falta!
Das ist der Trick!
Ecco ciò che ci vuole!

621

TRICKY

As tricky as a monkey. (comp.)
Très astucieux / Malin comme un renard.
Astuto como un zorro.
Raffiniert (schlau) wie ein Affe.
Molto astuto / Furbo come una volpe.

TRIFLE

To trifle with somebody.
Se moquer de quelqu'un.
Bromear con alguien.
Mit jemandem spielen.
Prendere in giro qualcuno.

TRIGGER

To be quick on the trigger.
Etre rapide.
Ser muy listo.
Schlagfertig sein / Auf Draht sein.
Essere svelto.

TRIVET

To be as right as a trivet. (comp.)
Très bien se porter.
Estar muy bien.
Sich sauwohl fühlen.
Stare benissimo.

TROOPER

To swear like a trooper.
Jurer comme un charretier.
Blasfemar como un turco.
Wie ein Landsknecht fluchen.
Bestemmiare come un turco.

TROUBLED (♦)

(♦) To fish in troubled waters. (p. 624)
Pêcher en eaux troubles.

Pescar en río revuelto.
Im Trüben fischen.
Pescare nel torbido.

TROWEL

To lay it on with a trowel.
Flatter de façon grossière.
Lisonjear.
Zu dick auftragen.
Lusingare in modo grossolano

TRUANT

To play truant.
Faire l'école buissonnière.
Hacer novillos / Capear la escuela.
Die Schule schwänzen / Bummeln.
Marinare la scuola / Bigiare.

TRUE

As true as steel. (comp.)
Très fidèle.
Fiel hasta la muerte.
Treu wie ein Hund.
Molto fedele.

It came true!
Ça s'est avéré!
¡Se ha verificado! / ¡Ha pasado!
Es wurde wahr!
Si è verificato!

TRUMPET (♦)

(♦) To blow one's own trumpet. (p. 59)
Faire ses propres louanges.
Jactarse.
Sein eigenzes Lob singen.
Tessere le proprie lodi.

TRUMPETER

To be one's own trumpeter.
Chanter ses propres louanges.
Decantar las propias virtudes / Alabarse.
Sein eigenes Loblied singen.
Cantare le proprie lodi.

TUCK

To tuck into ...
Faire une ventrée de ...
Darse un hartazgo de ... / Hartarse de ...
Sich vollstopfen mit ... / (Viel Essen) verdrücken.
Fare una scorpacciata di ...

TUCKER

One's best bib and tucker.
L'habit qu'il faut.
El mejor vestido del guardarropa.
Der Sonntagsstaat / Jemandes beste Kleidung.
Il vestito buono.

TUMBLE

To have a nasty tumble.
Faire une mauvaise chute.
Caer malamente.
Einen bösen (schlimmen / gefährlichen) Sturz machen / Bös hinfallen (stürzen).
Fare una brutta caduta.

To tumble to an idea.
Saisir une idée.
Agarrar una idéa al vuelo.
Plötzlich einen Einfall haben / Plötzlich eine Idee kriegen.
Afferrare un'idea.

TUNE

To change one's tune.
Changer de ton.

Cambiar de humor / Cambiar de tono.
Einen anderen Ton anschlagen / Andere Saiten aufziehen.
Cambiare tono (ritornello).

TURKEY

As red as a turkey-cock. (comp.)
Rouge comme un coquelicot.
Rojo como un tomate.
Puterrot.
Rosso come un tacchino (come un peperone).

TURN

To turn on the waterworks.
Se mettre à pleurer.
Ponerse a llorar.
Losheulen.
Mettersi a piangere.

To turn a deaf ear.
Faire la sourde oreille.
Hacer oídos de mercader.
Taub sein gegen . . . / Sich taub stellen.
Fare orecchi da mercante.

To turn the tables.
Changer les cartes.
Alterar las posiciones originarias.
Den Spiess umdrehen.
Cambiar le carte in tavola.

To take a queer turn.
Prendre un mauvais pli.
Tomar un mal caríz.
Eine seltsame Wendung nehmen.
Prendere una strana piega.

To turn down something.
Refuser quelque chose.
Rechazar algo.
Etwas ablehnen / Jemandem einen Korb geben.
Rifiutare qualcosa.

To turn in.
Se coucher.
Acostarse / Recogerse.
Zu Bett gehen.
Coricarsi.

He didn't turn a hair.
Il n'a pas sourcillé.
Se mantuvo sin pestañear siquiera.
Er zuckte nicht mit der Wimper.
Non ha battuto ciglio.

To turn up one's nose.
Froncer le nez / Faire la moue.
Hacer ascos.
Die Nase rümpfen.
Arricciare il naso.

TURTLE

To turn turtle.
Se retourner.
Volcarse / Ponerse al revés.
Umschlagen / Umschwenken.
Capovolgersi.

TWINKLE

In the twinkle of an eye.
En un clin d'oeil.
En un abrir y cerrar de ojos / En menos que no se diga.
Im Nu / Im Handumdrehen.
In un batter d'occhio.

TWIST (♦)

(♦) To twist someone round one's finger. (p. 629)
Faire ce que l'on veut de quelqu'un.
Darle vuelta a una persona / Hacer con una persona lo
que uno quiera.
Jemanden um den Finger wickeln.
Fare di una persona quello che si vuole.

TWO

To put two and two together.
Déduire avec logique.
Deducir con lógica.
Sich etwas zusammenreimen / Seine Schlüsse ziehen.
Dedurre logicamente.

TWOPENNY-HALFPENNY

It's worth twopence-halfpenny.
Ça ne vaut pas quatre sous!
Vale dos céntimos.
Es ist zwei Pfennig wert.
Vale due soldi.

UGLY

As ugly as a scarecrow. (comp.)
Très laid.
Feo como él solo.
Hässlich wie eine Vogelscheuche.
Molto brutto.

As ugly as a toad. (comp.)
Laid comme un pou.
Muy feo / Feote.
Eklig (hässlich) wie eine Kröte.
Bruttissimo.

As ugly as sin. (comp.)
Laid comme les sept péchés capitaux.
Feo como el pecado.
Schmutzig wie die Sünde (ein Sündenpfuhl).
Brutto come il peccato.

An ugly customer.
Un mauvais type.
Un tunante / Un mal bicho.
Ein unangenehmer Kerl / Ein übler Kunde.
Un brutto tomo.

UMBRAGE

To take umbrage.
Se vexer.

Ofenderse / Molestarse.
Anstoss nehmen.
Offendersi / Adombrarsi.

UNAWARES
He was taken unawares.
Il a été pris au dépourvu.
Fue cogido desprevenido.
Er wurde überrascht.
E' stato preso alla sprovvista.

UNCLE
To talk to someone like a Dutch uncle.
Parler sévèrement mais avec bonté.
Hablar con severidad, pero bondadosamente.
Jemanden väterlich ermahnen / Jemandem eine Standpauke halten.
Parlare severamente, ma con bontà.

UNDER (♦)
To be under a cloud.
Ne pas être en état de grâce / Etre en disgrâce.
Estar en desgracia.
In Ungnade (in Verruf) stehen.
Essere in disgrazia.

(♦) To be under the weather. (p. 632)
Ne pas être en forme / Etre à plat.
Estar enfermizo / Estar chueco.
Nicht in Form sein / Einen Katzenjammer haben.
Essere giù di corda / Essere malaticcio.

UNDERHAND
Underhand dealings.
Des affaires louches.
Negocios bajo de agua.
Unsaubere Geschäfte / Geschäfte unter der Hand.
Affari loschi.

UNDONE

What is done, cannot be undone. (prov.)
Ce qui est fait est fait.
Lo que está hecho, hecho está / A lo hecho pecho.
Geschehenes kann nicht ungeschehen (rückgängig) gemacht werden / Geschehen ist geschehen.
Cosa fatta capo ha / Il fatto non si può disfare.

UNION

Union is strength. (prov.)
L'union fait la force.
La unión hace la fuerza.
Einigkeit macht stark.
L'unione fa la forza.

UNSTABLE

As unstable as water. (comp.)
Très instable.
Muy variable / Variable como una veleta.
Labil / Unbeständig.
Molto instabile.

UNSTUCK (♦)

(♦) To come unstuck. (p. 634)
Etre dans les ennuis.
Estar en un aprieto.
In Schwierigkeiten sein.
Essere nei guai.

UNTURNED

To leave no stone unturned.
Faire tous les efforts possibles.
Hacer todo lo posible.
Nichts unversucht lassen.
Fare ogni sforzo possibile.

UNWHIPPED

An unwhipped cub.
Un voyou.

Un hampón / Un calavera.
Ein unerfahrener junger Bursche / Ein Flegel / Ein grüner Junge / Ein ungehobelter (ungeschliffener) Kerl.
Un giovinastro / Un teppista.

UP

The game is up!
Tout est perdu!
¡Todo se ha perdido!
Das Spiel ist aus (verloren)!
Tutto è perduto!

I don't feel up to it!
Je ne me sens pas capable de le faire!
No tengo las fuerzas para hacerlo.
Ich fühle mich nicht stark genug dafür / Ich fühle mich nicht dazu in der Lage.
Non mi sento all'altezza di farlo!

It's up to you!
C'est à vous / C'est votre tour!
¡Queda a su discreción!
Es liegt an Ihnen! / Es hängt von Ihnen ab! / Es ist Ihre Sache!
Spetta a voi! / Tocca a voi!

What have you been up to?
Que diable avez-vous combiné?
¿Que es lo que han hecho?
Was habt Ihr im Schilde geführt (vorgehabt)? / Was zum Teufel habt Ihr angestellt?
Che cosa diavolo avete combinato?

UPON

Upon my word!
Ciel!
¡Por Dios!
Auf mein Wort!
Caspita! / Perbacco!

He took it upon himself.
Il en a pris la responsabilité.

Se ha asumido la responsabilidad.
Er nahm es auf sich / Er übernahm die Verantwortung.
Se n'è assunto la responsabilità.

UPPER

He's the upper storey.
Il est le cerveau.
Él es el cerebro.
Er ist das Haupt (der Anführer / der Boss).
E' il cervello / E' la mente.

To get the upper hand.
Avoir le dessus / L'emporter.
Ejercer dominio o mando / Llevar ventaja.
Die Oberhand gewinnen.
Avere il sopravvento.

He's got something wrong in his upper storey.
Il est un peu fou.
Le falta una tuerca / Es algo chiflado.
Er ist nicht ganz richtig im Oberstübchen.
E' un po' matto / E' un po' tocco.

The upper ten thousand.
L'aristocratie / Le grand monde.
La aristocracia / El gran mundo.
Die oberen Zehntausend.
L'aristocrazia / Il gran mondo.

UPS (♦)

(♦) The ups and downs of everyday life. (p. 637)
Les hauts et les bas de la vie.
Los azares de la vida.
Das Auf und Ab (Die Höhen und Tiefen) des Alltagslebens.
Gli alti e bassi della vita quotidiana.

UPSET

To upset somebody's applecart.
Faire tomber à l'eau.
Romperle los cascos a alguien.
Jemandes Pläne über den Haufen werfen.
Romper le uova nel paniere a qualcuno.

It upset me!
Il m'a chambardé / Il m'a bouleversé!
¡Me ha trastornado!
Es bringt mich aus der Fassung (durcheinander) / Es bestürzt mich.
Mi ha scombussolato!

UPSIDE (♦)

(♦) Upside down. (p. 639)
Sens dessus-dessous.
De abajo para arriba.
Drunter und drüber / Vollkommen durcheinander.
Sottosopra.

UPTAKE

To be slow (quick) on the uptake.
Etre lent (rapide) d'esprit.
Ser lento (rápido) de comprendonio.
Schwer von Begriff sein / Eine lange Leitung haben.
Essere lento (pronto) di comprendonio.

USE (♦)

I have no use for it!
Je ne sais pas quoi en faire!
¡No me sirve!
Ich kann es nicht gebrauchen / Ich kann nichts damit anfangen / Ich hab nichts dafür übrig.
Non so cosa farmene!

(♦) It's no use crying over spilt milk. (p. 124)
La page est tournée.
No sirve llorar por lo irremediable.
Geschehen ist geschehen, hin ist hin.
Non serve piangere sul latte versato.

VACANT

A vacant mind.
Une tête vide.

Una cabeza vacía.
Ein Hohlkopf / Geistlos.
Una mente vuota.

VAIN

As vain as a peacock. (comp.)
Fier comme un paon.
Vanidoso como un pavo real.
Eitel wie ein Pfau / Eingebildet wie ein Affe.
Tronfio come un pavone.

VALUE

To set great value upon . . .
Faire cas de . . . / Attribuer une grande importance à . . .
Dar gran importancia a . . .
Grossen Wert beimessen.
Attribuire grande importanza a . . .

VARIANCE

To be at variance with somebody.
Ne pas être d'accord avec quelqu'un.
No estar de acuerdo con alguien.
Mit jemandem uneinig sein.
Non essere d'accordo con qualcuno.

VELVET

An iron hand in a velvet glove.
Une poigne de fer dans un gant de velours.
Mano de hierro en guante de seda.
Die eiserne Faust unter dem Samthandschuh.
Pugno di ferro in guanto di velluto.

VENT

To give vent to . . .
Epancher.
Desahogarse.
Sich Luft machen.
Dare libero sfogo a . . .

VENTURE

At a venture.
Par hasard.
Por ventura / Acaso.
Aufs Geratewohl / Auf gut Glück.
A caso / A casaccio.

VERY

It's the very thing!
C'est juste ce qu'il faut! / C'est vraiment ce qu'il faut!
¡Es lo que hace falta!
Es ist genau (gerade) das Richtige.
E' proprio quel che ci vuole!

The very idea!
Ça alors!
¡Que ocurrencia!
Das ist die Idee! / Das ist genau die richtige Idee!
Questa poi!

At the very outside.
Tout au plus.
A los más.
Allerhöchstens / Das Alleräusserste.
Tutt'al più.

VICE

As firm as a vice. (comp.)
Très ferme / Très solide.
Firme como una roca.
Fest wie im Schraubstock (in der Zwinge).
Molto saldo.

VIEW

A bird's eye view.
Vue à vol d'oiseau.
A vista de pájaro.
(Ein Blick aus der) Vogelperspektive.
Veduta a volo d'uccello.

With a view to . . .
Dans le but de . . .
Con el objeto de . . . / Con el propósito de . . .
Im Hinblick auf . . . / Mit (In) der Absicht zu / Zu dem Zweck.
Allo scopo di . . .

VINE

To dwell under one's vine and fig-tree.
Vivre en paix sur sa terre.
Vivir en santa paz con las cosas de uno.
In Frieden auf seinem Grund und Boden leben.
Vivere in pace sulla propria terra.

VIRTUE

Virtue is its own reward. (prov.)
La vertu est un prix en elle-même.
El premio de la virtud es la virtud misma.
Tugendhaftigkeit (Rechtschaffenheit) macht sich bezahlt.
La virtù è premio a se stessa.

VISITING

We're on visiting terms.
Nos rapports sont assez cordiaux.
Tenemos relaciones bastante cordiales.
Wir verkehren miteinander.
Abbiamo rapporti abbastanza cordiali.

VOICE

To give voice to . . .
Exprimer / Epancher.
Expresarse / Desahogarse.
In Worte fassen / Ausdruck gehen (verleihen) / Sich äussern.
Esprimere / Sfogare.

With one voice.
A l'unanimité.
Por unanimidad.
Einstimmig.
All'unanimità.

WADE

He waded through a book.
Il a eu toutes les peines du monde à terminer la lecture de
ce livre.
Ha leído aquel libro con cierta dificultad.
Er arbeitete sich mühsam durch ein Buch.
E' arrivato faticosamente in fondo ad un libro.

WAFER

As thin as a wafer. (comp.)
Très fin.
Fino como una hoja de papél.
Hauchdünn.
Sottilissimo.

WAG

To play the wag.
Faire l'école buissonnière / Sécher les cours.
Hacer novillos.
Die Schule schwänzen / Schwänzen.
Marinare la scuola / Bigiare.

WAGGING

To set tongues wagging.
Faire scandale.
Dar escándalo.
Zu einem Gerede Anlass geben / Skandal hervorrufen.
Dare scandalo.

WAGON

To be on the band wagon.
Avoir de l'influence / Etre dans le bain.
Ser influyente / Ser uno de los mandamases.
Einflussreich sein / Seine Hand im Spiel haben / Mit am Steuer
sitzen.
Essere influente / Avere le mani in pasta.

WAIFS

Waifs and strays.
Objets trouvés / Enfants abandonnés.
Objetos extraviados / Niños abandonados.
Verwahrloste Kinder / Herrenloses Gut.
Oggetti smarriti / Bambini abbandonati.

WAIT

To lie in wait.
Rester aux aguets.
Estar en acecho.
Auf der Lauer liegen / Im Hinterhalt liegen.
Stare in agguato.

WAKE

To follow in the wake of . . .
Suivre les traces de . . .
Seguir las huellas de . . .
Jemandem auf dem Fusse folgen / Auf der Spur von . . . / In
den Fusstapfen von . . .
Seguire le orme di . . .

WALK

He walked off.
Il a filé.
Se escabulló.
Er ging davon (fort) / Er verdrückte sich.
Se l'è squagliata.

To walk out on somebody.
Plaquer quelqu'un.
Dejar plantado a alguien.
Jemanden im Stich lassen / Jemanden stehenlassen.
Piantare in asso qualcuno.

A walk-over.
Une victoire facile.
Una victoria fácil.
Mit Leichtigkeit gewinnen.
Una vittoria facile.

People in every walk of life.
Des gens de toute espèce.
Gente de toda clase.
Leute aus allen Schichten (Stellungen / Berufen).
Gente d'ogni ceto.

WALL

To run one's head against a wall.
Tenter l'impossible.
Romperse la cabeza contra de una paréd.
Mit dem Kopf durch die Wand wollen.
Batter la testa contro un muro.

To see through a brick wall.
Etre très perspicace.
Ser muy perspicáz.
Das Gras wachsen hören.
Essere assai perspicace.

To be with one's back to the wall.
Etre dans la gêne / Etre au pied du mur.
Estar entre la espada y la paréd.
In die Enge getrieben sein.
Essere messo alle strette / Essere con le spalle al muro.

The weakest go to the wall.
Les plus faibles ont toujours' le dessous.
Los más debiles no tienen remedio.
Die Schwächsten (Ärmsten) ziehen immer den kürzeren.
I più deboli hanno sempre la peggio.

WALLOWING

To be wallowing in money.
Nager dans l'or.
Nadar en la abundancia.
In Geld schwimmen.
Nuotare nell'oro.

WANDER

To wander about.
Vadrouiller.

Vagar.
Umherwandern (-ziehen / -irren / -schweifen).
Gironzolare.

To wander from the subject.
S'éloigner du sujet / Parler à côté du sujet.
Desviarse de un argumento.
Vom Thema abweichen.
Andare fuori tema.

WANT

Want is a severe but efficient teacher. (prov.)
Le besoin est un maître sévère mais efficace.
La necesidad hace del hombre un lobo.
Not (Armut) ist ein harter aber tüchtiger Lehrer / Not ist der
beste Meister / Not macht erfinderisch.
Il bisogno è il miglior maestro.

WARM

As warm as wool. (comp.)
Très chaud.
Muy caliente.
Warm wie Wolle.
Molto caldo.

WARP

He has a warped mind.
Il a un esprit perverti.
Tiene una mente torcida.
Er ist verschroben.
Ha una mente pervertita.

WART

To paint somebody warts and all.
Peindre quelqu'un sans l'arranger.
Pintar a alguien tal y como es.
Jemanden mit allen Vor- und Nachteilen darstellen / Jeman-
den ohne Verschönerungen schildern.
Dipingere qualcuno senza abbellirlo.

WASH

It was a wash-out!
Ce fut un four!
¡Fué un fracaso!
Es war ein Reinfall!
Fu un fiasco!

I wash my hands of it!
Je m'en lave les mains!
¡Me lavo las manos de ésto!
Ich wasche meine Hande in Unschuld!
Me ne lavo le mani!

WASHED (♦)

He looked washed out.
Il avait l'air chiffoné.
Estaba echado a perder.
Er sah erschöpft aus.
Aveva un aspetto sciupato.

(♦) To be all washed up. (p. 648)
Etre ruinés.
Estar arruinados / Estar jodidos.
Völlig ruiniert sein.
Essere rovinati.

WASTE

Waste not, want not. (prov.)
L'économie est le meilleur gain.
El ahorro es la mejor ganancia.
Spare in der Zeit, so hast Du in der Not.
Il risparmio è il migliore guadagno.

WATCH

Watch your step!
Attention à ce que tu fais!
¡Ten cuidado!
Vorsicht! / Pass auf! / Gib acht!
Attento a quel che fai!

A watched pot never boils. (prov.)
Le temps ne passe pas quand on attend.
Quien espera desespera.
Beim Warten wird die Zeit lang.
I minuti sono lunghi quando si aspetta / Pentola guardata
non bolle mai.

WATCHFUL

As watchful as a hawk. (comp.)
Très vigilant.
Alerta como un halcón.
Wachsam wie ein Indianer.
Molto vigilante.

WATER (♦)

It made my mouth water.
Il m'a mis l'eau à la bouche.
Se me hizo agua la boca.
Es machte mir den Mund wässerig / Mir lief die Spucke im
Mund zusammen.
Mi ha fatto venire l'acquolina in bocca.

(♦) To get into hot water. (p. 287)
Se mettre dans le beaux draps.
Meterse en líos / Meterse en aguas peligrosas.
In des Teufels Küche geraten.
Cacciarsi nei guai.

Written in water.
Vite oublié.
Escrito sobre la arena.
In den Sand geschrieben / Schnell vergessen (verflogen).
Presto dimenticato / Scritto sulla sabbia.

To keep one's head above water.
Se tenir à la surface.
Mantenerse a flote.
Sich über Wasser halten.
Tenersi a galla.

(♦) To be like a fish out of water. (p. 194)
Etre un poisson hors de l'eau.

Ser como un pez fuera del agua.
Am falschen Platze sein / Nicht in seinem Element sein.
Essere come un pesce fuor d'acqua.

(♦) **To tread water.** (p. 651)
Etre en difficulté / Naviguer en eaux troubles.
Hallarse en dificultades.
In Schwierigkeiten schwimmen / In der Patsche (Tinte) sitzen.
Essere in difficoltà / Navigare in cattive acque.

WATERS

Still waters run deep. (prov.)
Il n'est pire eau que l'eau qui dort.
El agua quieta corroe los puentes.
Stille Wasser gründen tief.
L'acqua cheta rovina i ponti.

WAX

To be in a wax.
Etre en colère.
Estar furioso / Estar encachimbado.
In Wut sein.
Essere in collera.

WAY

By the way ...
A propos, ...
De paso ...
Übrigens, ... / Nebenbei bemerkt, ...
A proposito ...

In a way.
Sous certains aspects.
De alguna manera.
In gewisser Hinsicht.
Sotto certi aspetti.

To be in a bad way.
Etre dans de beaux draps!
Hallarse en dificultades.

Auf einem schlechten Wege sein.
Essere in cattive acque.

To pave the way.
Ouvrir la route.
Preparar el camino.
Den Weg bahnen.
Spianare la strada.

Where there's a will there's a way. (prov.)
Vouloir c'est pouvoir.
Donde hay vida, hay esperanza / Querer es poder.
Wo ein Wille ist, da ist ein Weg.
Volere è potere.

To feel one's way.
Aller à tâtons.
Ir a tientas.
Seinen Weg ertasten.
Andare a tastoni.

The farthest way about is the nearest way home.
Il vaut mieux tenir que courir.
Quien deja el camino viejo por el nuevo se lo lleva el arrepentimiento.
Die weitesten Umwege sind selten die kürzesten / Heimwege.
Chi lascia la via vecchia per la nuova mal pentito si ritrova.

To get one's way.
Obtenir ce que l'on veut.
Hacer su capricho / Obtener lo que se desea.
Seinen Willen erhalten.
Ottenere ciò che si vuole.

To be in the way.
Etre une gêne pour quelqu'un.
Obstaculizar / Estar de más.
Im Wege sein.
Essere d'impiccio.

To go out of one's way.
Se déranger.
Incomodarse.
Ein übriges tun / Sich besonders anstrengen.
Scomodarsi.

An out-of-the-way place.
Un endroit qui n'est pas à portée.
Un lugar fuera de mano / Un lugar apartado.
Ein abgelegener (versteckter) Platz.
Un luogo fuori mano.

WEAK

As weak as a baby. (comp.)
Très faible.
Muy débil.
Schwach wie ein Baby / Epfindlich / Schwächlich.
Debolissimo.

As weak as a kitten. (comp.)
Très faible.
Muy débil.
Sehr schwach.
Debolissimo.

As weak as water. (comp.)
Très faible.
Muy débil.
Schwach wie ein Strohhalm.
Debolissimo.

That's his weak side.
Ça c'est son faible / Ça c'est son point faible.
Ése es su punto débil.
Das ist seine schwache Seite (schwacher Punkt).
Quello è il suo punto debole.

WEASEL

To catch a weasel asleep.
Le faire à la barbe d'un sacré malin.
Burlarse de una persona astuta.
Einen Spitzel überlisten.
Farla in barba a un furbo di tre cotte.

WEATHER (♦)

(♦) To be under the weather. (p. 632)
Etre maladif.

Ser enfermizo.
Nicht in Form sein.
Essere malaticcio / Essere giù di corda.

To keep one's weather eye open.
Ouvrir l'œil.
Estar alerta / Estar en guardia.
Gut aufpassen.
Stare in guardia / Stare all'erta.

WEATHERCOCK

As pretty as a weathercock. (comp.)
Très gracieuse.
Es graciosa como una gacela.
Anmutig / Graziös.
Molto graziosa.

He's a weathercock!
C'est une personne très inconstante! / C'est une girouette!
Es como veleta al viento.
Er ist eine wetterwendische Person! / Er richtet seine Nase
nach dem Wind!
E' una persona molto incostante! / E' una banderuola!

WEED

Ill weeds grow apace. (prov.)
La mauvaise herbe repousse très vite.
Hierba mala nunca muere.
Unkraut verdirbt nicht.
L'erba cattiva cresce in fretta.

To weed out.
Eliminer / Epurer.
Eliminar / Entresacar.
Aussondern / Ausmerzen / Säubern.
Eliminare / Epurare.

A weed.
Un faible / Une poule mouillée.
Débil de carácter.

Schwach von Charakter.
Uno debole di carattere / Un rammollito.

WEIGHED (♦)

(♦) To have someone weighed up. (p. 656)
Toiser quelqu'un / Mesurer quelqu'un.
Haber pesado o catagolado a alguien.
Jemanden genau abschätzen.
Inquadrare qualcuno.

WEIGHT

To pull one's weight.
Mettre tout son cœur.
Hacer todo lo posible / Empecinarse.
Alles dransetzen.
Mettercela tutta.

To throw one's weight about.
Se donner trop d'importance / Etre fanfaron.
Darse demasiada importancia.
Sich überschätzen.
Darsi troppa importanza.

WELL

Well begun is half done. (prov.)
A moitié fait qui bien commence.
Quien comienza bien se encuentra a la mitad de lo que tiene
que hacer.
Gut begonnen ist halb getan.
Chi ben comincia è a metà dell'opera.

All's well that ends well. (prov.)
Tout est bien qui finit bien.
Todo es bien lo que termína bien.
Ende gut, alles gut.
Tutto è bene quel che finisce bene.

He's well-off.
Il se trouve dans de bonnes conditions financières.

656

Acomodado / Adinerado / Es una persona acomodada o adi-
nerada.
Er ist wohlhabend / Er ist gut situiert.
E' in buone condizioni finanziarie.

He's very well-meaning.
Il est très bien intentionné.
Está bien intencionado / Es una persona bien intencionada.
Er meint es sehr gut / Er ist sehr wohlmeinend.
E' molto ben intenzionato.

That's a well-worn story.
Ça c'est une histoire rabâchée.
Este es un chiste muy trillado.
Das ist eine abgedroschene Geschichte.
Questa è una storiella trita.

WET

As wet as a drowned rat. (comp.)
Trempé jusqu'aux os.
Mojado como un pollo.
Pudelnass.
Bagnato come un pulcino.

He's a wet blanket.
C'est un trouble-fête.
Es un aguafiestas.
Er ist ein Spielverderber (Störenfried).
E' un guastafeste.

To be wet to the skin.
Trempé jusqu'aux os.
Estar calado hasta los huesos.
Bis auf die Haut nass sein.
Essere bagnato fradicio / Essere bagnato fino alle ossa.

WHACKING

A whacking fib.
Un énorme mensonge.
Una mentira muy grande.

Ein mächtiger (gewaltiger / enormer) Schwindel / Eine faust-
dicke Lüge.
Una bugia madornale.

WHALE

To have a whale of a time.
S'amuser follement.
Divertirse mucho.
Sich wahnsinnig gut amüsieren.
Divertirsi un mondo.

WHAT

What's up?
Qu'est-ce-qu'il arrive?
¿Qué pasa?
Was ist los?
Che succede?

WHEEL

To put one's shoulder to the wheel.
Apporter son aide à une entreprise.
Dar una mano en una tarea / Contribuir a una empresa.
Sich tüchtig ins Zeug legen.
Dare il proprio contributo a un'impresa.

WHET

That morsel whet my appetite.
Ce morceau m'a ouvert l'appétit.
Aquél bocadillo me ha despertado el apetito.
Dieser Happen (Bissen) hat meinen Appetit angeregt.
Quel boccone mi ha stimolato l'appetito.

WHILE

While there is life there is hope. (prov.)
Tant qu'il y a de la vie il y a de l'espoir.
Mientras hay vida hay esperanza.
Solange Leben da ist, gibt es auch Hoffnung.
Finchè c'è vita c'è speranza.

WHIP (♦)

(♦) To have the whip hand on somebody. (p. 660)
Avoir le dessus avec quelqu'un /
Llevar las de ganar respecto a una persona.
Jemanden an der Kandare (in der Gewalt) haben.
Avere la meglio su qualcuno / Avere il coltello dalla
parte del manico.

To whip the cat.
Faire des économies / Serrer la ceinture.
Hacer economías / Economizar.
Den Gürtel enger schnallen / Haushalten / Sparen.
Fare economia / Tirare la cinghia.

WHIRL

My head is in a whirl.
La tête me tourne.
Me da vueltas la cabeza / Estoy mareado.
Mir ist schwindelig / Mir dreht sich der Kopf / Mir dreht sich
alles im Kopf.
Mi gira la testa.

WHIRLWIND

He that sows the wind will reap the whirlwind.
Qui sème le vent récolte la tempête.
Quien siembra vientos cosecha tempestades.
Wer Wind sät, wird Sturm ernten.
Chi semina vento raccoglie tempesta.

WHISTLE

To whistle for something.
Désirer en vain quelque chose.
Desear algo imposible.
Sich vergeblich etwas wünschen.
Desiderare invano qualcosa.

I wet my whistle.
J'ai forcé un peu la dose.
Me he tomado unos tragos.
Ich habe mir die Kehle angefeuchtet / Ich habe einen gehoben.
Ho fatto una bevutina.

WHITE (♦)

As white as a sheet. (comp.)
Très blanc.
Blanco como la leche.
Kreidebleich / Leichenblass.
Bianco come un lenzuolo.

As white as snow. (comp.)
Blanc comme neige.
Blanco como una sabana.
Weiss wie Schnee / Schneeweiss.
Bianco come la neve.

As white as wool. (comp.)
Très blanc.
Muy blanco.
Puderweis.
Molto bianco.

A white lie.
Un mensonge innocent.
Una mentirilla / Una mentira venial.
Eine Notlüge.
Una bugia innocente.

To bleed somebody white.
Saigner à blanc quelqu'un.
Desangrar a una persona / Comportarse como un sanguijuela con una persona.
Jemanden bis zum Weissbluten auspressen.
Dissanguare qualcuno.

To show the white feather.
Se montrer vil.
Demostrar cobardía.
Sich feige zeigen.
Dimostrarsi vile.

(♦) A white elephant. (p. 662)
Un objet inutile.
Un objeto inútil.
Ein lästiger Gegenstand.
Un oggetto inutile.

WILD

A wild goose chase.
Une folle entreprise / Une chose impossible.
Una empresa ardua.
Eine vergebliche Mühe / Ein fruchtloses Unterfangen.
Un'impresa folle / Una cosa impossibile.

To sow one's wild oats.
Mener une vie de bâton de chaise / Jeter sa gourme.
Holgazanear / Hacer novillos.
Sich austoben / Sich die Hörner abstossen.
Correre la cavallina.

WILL

Where there's a will there's a way.
Vouloir c'est pouvoir.
Querer es poder.
Wo ein Wille ist, da ist ein Weg.
Volere è potere.

WIND

There's something in the wind.
Il y a quelque chose dans l'air (une machination).
Hay algo en el áire.
Es liegt etwas in der Luft.
C'è qualcosa nell'aria.

To take the wind out of somebody's sails.
Dégonfler quelqu'un.
Quitarle las ínfulas a una persona.
Jemandem den Wind aus den Segeln nehmen.
Sgonfiare, smontare qualcuno.

To see which way the wind blows.
Voir de quel côté tourne le vent.
Ver por donde van las cosas.
Wissen, woher der Wind weht / Erkennen, aus welcher Richtung der Wind kommt.
Vedere da che parte tira il vento.

663

That'll take the wind out of his sails.
Cela éventera ses plans.
Esto desbaratará sus planes.
Das wird seine Pläne über den Haufen werfen.
Questo sventerà i suoi piani.

WIND

To wind somebody round one's little finger.
Dominer totalement quelqu'un / Mener quelqu'un par le bout
du nez.
Tener en puño a una persona.
Jemanden um den kleinen Finger wickeln.
Dominare completamente qualcuno.

WINDOW (♦)

To have all one's goods in the window.
Etre superficiel.
Ser muy superficial.
Oberflächlich sein.
Essere superficiale.

(♦) Window shopping (p. 665)
Faire du lèche-vitrines.
Curiosear por los escaparates.
Schaufensterbummel.
Il curiosare per le vetrine.

WING

To take somebody under one's wing.
Prendre quelqu'un sous sa protection.
Amparar a alguien / Tomar alguien bajo la propia protección.
Jemanden unter seine Fittiche nehmen / Jemanden unter sei-
nen Schutz stellen.
Prendere qualcuno sotto la propria ala (protezione).

WINGS

To clip someone's wings.
Limiter les mouvements de quelqu'un.

665

Cortarle las alas a alguien.
Jemandem die Flügel stutzen.
Tarpare le ali a qualcuno.

WINK

I did not sleep a wink.
Je n'ai pas fermé l'œil.
No he podido pegar ojo.
Ich habe kein Auge zugetan.
Non ho chiuso occhio.

WINKS

To take forty winks.
Faire un somme.
Hacer una siesta.
Ein Nickerchen machen.
Fare un sonnellino.

WIPE

To wipe the floor with somebody.
Battre quelqu'un de façon humiliante.
Hacer trizas a una persona (aún moralmente).
Jemandem heimleuchten / Mit jemandem Schlitten fahren.
Sconfiggere qualcuno in modo umiliante.

WIRES

To pull the wires.
Manipuler quelque chose.
Mover los hilos (de una situación).
Der Drahtzieher sein / Seine Beziehungen spielen lassen.
Manipolare qualcosa.

WISE

As wise as a serpent. (comp.)
Très prudent.
Sabio como un serpiente / Muy prudente.
Vorsichtig wie eine Schlange.
Molto prudente.

As wise as Solomon. (comp.)
Très sage.
Sabio como Salomón.
Weise wie Salomon.
Saggio come Salomone.

Everyone is wise after the event.
Au retour des plaids on est sage.
Todos saben lo que ya ha pasado / De sabios, poétas y locos
esta lleno el mundo.
Um eine Erfahrung klüger sein / Erfahrung macht klug.
Del senno di poi son piene le fosse.

WISER

I'm none the wiser.
Je n'en sais pas plus qu'au début / Je ne suis pas plus avancé.
Sé lo que sabía.
Nicht klüger sein als zuvor.
Non ne so più di prima / Ne so quanto prima.

WISH

The wish is father to the thought. (prov.)
Il est facile de croire que ce que l'on désire ardemment est
vrai / Il est facile de prendre ses désirs pour des réalités.
Es frecuente tomar por verdad lo que se desea ardientemente.
Der Wunsch ist der Vater des Gedankens.
E' facile credere che sia vero ciò che si desidera ardentemente.

WISHES

If wishes were horses, beggars might ride. (prov.)
Avec un si on pourrait même mettre Paris dans une bouteille.
Si las buenas intenciones fueran pan, no habría más ham-
brientos.
Wenn alle Wünsche wahr würden, müssten auch die Bettler
nicht mehr betteln / Wenn alle Wünsche Wirklichkeit würden,
wären auch die Bettler reich.
I desideri non riempiono il sacco / Se i desideri giovassero,
tutti sarebbero ricchi.

WITHER

To wither somebody with a look.
Foudroyer quelqu'un du regard.
Clavar a alguien con la mirada.
Jemanden mit einem Blick vernichten.
Fulminare qualcuno con lo sguardo.

WITS

To live by one's wits.
Vivre d'expédients.
Vivir de expedientes.
Sich mehr oder weniger ehrlich durchs Leben schlagen.
Vivere di espedienti.

He has his wits about him.
Il est très éveillé.
Es muy listo / Es muy vivo.
Er hat seine fünf Sinne (seinen Verstand) beisammen.
E' molto sveglio.

To be at one's wits' end.
Ne plus savoir à quel saint se vouer.
No saber para donde agarrar.
Mit seiner Weisheit am Ende sein / Sich nicht mehr zu helfen wissen.
Non sapere più a che santo votarsi / Non sapere che pesci pigliare.

WOLF

To keep the wolf from the door.
Retenir sa faim.
Mantener el hambre a distancia.
Sich über Wasser halten.
Tener lontana la fame.

A wolf in sheep's clothing.
Un hypocrite.
Un lobo bajo piel de oveja.
Ein Wolf im Schafspelz.
Un lupo vestito da agnello.

WOMAN (♦)

(♦) To be tied to a woman's apron-strings. (p. 580)
Etre pendu aux jupes d'une femme.
Andar todavía prendido de las enaguas de la madre.
Unter der Fuchtel einer Frau stehen / Am Gängelband einer Frau hängen.
Stare attaccato alle sottane d'una donna.

WONDERS

To work wonders.
Faire des miracles.
Hacer maravillas.
Wunder wirken.
Fare miracoli.

WOOD

Don't halloo till you are out of the wood! (prov.)
Ne crie pas trop vite victoire!
De la mano a la boca se pierde la sopa.
Freue dich nicht zu früh!
Non dir quattro se non l'hai nel sacco!

To be unable to see the wood for the trees.
Se perdre dans les détails.
Ser incapáz de apreciar el todo en aras de los detalles.
Den Wald vor lauter Bäumen nicht sehen.
Perdersi nei particolari.

WOODS

He took to the woods!
Il a pris ses jambes à son cou!
¡Se ha escabullido!
Er nahm die Beine unter die Arme / Er schlug sich in die Büsche.
Se l'è data a gambe.

WOOL

Don't loose your wool!
Ne vous énervez pas!

¡No se enojen! / ¡No se enfaden!
Werden Sie nicht ärgerlich!
Non arrabbiatevi!

To pull the wool over somebody's eyes.
Tromper quelqu'un.
Engañar a una persona / Chanchullar a una persona.
Jemanden hinters Licht führen.
Gettar fumo negli occhi a qualcuno / Ingannare qualcuno.

Much cry and little wool.
Plus de bruit que de besogne.
Mucho ruido y pocas nueces.
Viel Geschrei und wenig Wolle.
Molto fumo e poco arrosto.

WORDS

Good words without deeds are rushes and weeds. (prov.)
Les beaux mots et les mauvaises actions trompent les sages
et les fous.
Las buenas palabras, que no corresponden a los hechos, pue-
den engañar sea a sabios que a locos.
Gute Worte ohne Taten sind wertlos.
Belle parole e cattivi fatti ingannano savi e matti / Detto
senza fatto, ad ognun par misfatto.

WORKED

To be worked up.
Etre surexcité.
Estar sobreexcitado.
Aufgepeitscht sein / Sich in etwas hineingesteigert haben.
Essere sovreccitato.

WORKMAN

A bad workman quarrels with his tools. (prov.)
Un mauvais ouvrier rejette la faute sur ses outils.
Si un trabajo sale mal, la culpa no es de los instrumentos sino
del artesano.
Ein schlechter Arbeiter gibt seinem Werkzeug die Schuld.
Il cattivo operaio se la prende con i suoi strumenti di lavoro.

WORLD

It's the same all over the world (The sun shines everywhere).
C'est pareil dans le monde entier.
Por todas partes cuecen habas.
Es ist überall dasgleiche auf der Welt.
Tutto il mondo è paese.

To feel on top of the world.
Etre comme un roi / Se sentir important.
Sentirse como rey.
Sich wie ein König fühlen.
Sentirsi da papa (da re).

WORM

Even a worm will turn. (prov.)
La patience a des limites.
La paciencia tiene un límite.
Auch der Wurm krümmt sich, wenn er getreten wird.
Anche la pazienza ha un limite.

WORN

I'm worn out.
Je suis crevé!
¡Estoy agotado!
Ich bin völlig erschöpft (todmüde).
Sono stanco morto / Sono esausto.

WORST

If the worst comes to the worst.
Dans la pire des hypothèses.
En la peor de las hipótesis.
Wenn das Schlimmste vom Schlimmen passiert.
Nella peggiore delle ipotesi.

WORTH

A bird in the hand is worth two in the bush. (prov.)
Il vaut mieux tenir que courir.
Vale más un pájaro en mano que cién volando.

Ein Sperling in der Hand ist besser als eine Taube auf dem Dach.
Meglio un uovo oggi che una gallina domani.

It's not worth while.
Ça n'en vaut pas la peine.
No vale la pena.
Es ist nicht der Mühe wert / Es lohnt sich nicht.
Non ne vale la pena.

WRACK

To go to wrack and ruin.
Aller à la ruine.
Arruinarse.
Untergehen.
Andare in malora.

WRECK

He's a nervous wreck.
Il est à bout de nerfs.
Tiene los nervios hechos pedazo.
Er ist ein Nervenbündel.
Ha i nervi a pezzi.

WRONG (♦)

(♦) He's got hold of the wrong end of the stick. (p. 566)
Il a une impression tout à fait erronée.
Tiene una impresión equivocada del asunto.
Er hat es völlig missverstanden / Er hat die Sache in den falschen Hals bekommen.
Ha un'impressione completamente sbagliata.

To have been born on the wrong side of the blanket.
Etre fils illégitime.
Ser hijo ilegítimo.
Unehelich geboren worden sein.
Essere figlio illegittimo.

(♦) He got out of bed on the wrong side. (p. 37)
Il s'est levé du pied gauche.
Se ha levantado con el pie izquierdo.

672

Er ist mit dem linken Bein zuerst aufgestanden.
Si è alzato di cattivo umore.

I'm in the wrong box.
Je suis désavantagé.
Estoy en desventaja.
Ich bin benachteiligt.
Sono svantaggiato.

YARD (♦)

(♦) Give him an inch and he'll take a yard. (p. 297)
Donne-lui un doigt et il te prend tout le bras.
Dar una mano y que le tomen a uno el brazo.
Gibt man ihm den kleinen Finger, so nimmt er die ganze Hand.
Dagli un dito e lui ti prende il braccio!

YARN

Don't spin a yarn!
Ne racontez pas de sornettes!
No cuenten patrañas.
Erzähle keine Lügenmärchen (Abenteuergeschichten).
Non raccontate panzane.

YEARS

It will take donkey's years!
Il faudra un siècle!
¡Será necesario un siglo! / ¡Será necesario un tiempál!
Es wird eine Ewigkeit in Anspruch nehmen!
Ci vorrà un secolo!

YELLOW

As yellow as a guinea. (comp.)
Jaune poussin.
Amarillo como un canario.
Gelb wie Messing / Messinggelb / Metallgelb.
Molto giallo / Giallo come un limone.

YIELDING

As yielding as wax. (comp.)
Très flexible / Maléable.
Muy flexible.
Nachgebend / Nachgiebig / Gefügig / Flexibel.
Molto flessibile / Malleabile.

YOURS

What's yours?
Qu'est-ce-que tu prends?
¿Qué tomas?
Was nimmst Du?
Che cosa prendi?

ZEAL

He's got zip zest and zeal.
Il est très zélé.
Está muy sano y despejado / Es muy arrécho.
Er ist voller Saft und Kraft / Er ist voller Tatendrang / Er ist
voller Schwung und Begeisterung / Er ist auf Zack
E' molto in gamba.

ZOMBI

He's a walking zombi.
C'est un balourd (un nigaud).
Es un bobo.
Er ist ein wandelndes (lebendes) Gespenst.
E' un babbeo.

674

681

Printed in Italy

Stampa OFSA - Casarile (Milano)